THE
BIG BROTHER GAME

SCOTT R. FRENCH

Edited by Margaret McFadden French

PRODUCED BY:

GNU PUBLISHING, INC.
P.O. Box 6820
San Francisco, California 94101

PUBLISHED BY:

LYLE STUART, INC.
120 Enterprise Avenue
Secaucus, New Jersey 07094

WITH SPECIAL THANKS TO:

Hal Lipset	Private detective/surveillance expert
Ben Jamil	Communications Control Corporation
John Wilson	Private detective/surveillance expert
Paul McWilliams	Electronics Engineer/Sound Security
Ted Scharless	Surveillance expert
Ted Cannon	Surveillance expert
Mr. Jones	Fargo Police Equipment
Mark Howard	"Ex" a lot of things. . .

And several people who would rather not have their names mentioned. . .

PRODUCTION:

Alfred Klosterman	Art
Dana Middleton	Typesetting

I would like to borrow a quote from Hal Lipset to best sum up this book: "It's too bad when the prosecution can, and does utilize these techniques all the time, but the defense is not permitted the same liberties."

I would also like to borrow a quote from George Orwell, but I am going to resist temptation...............

Sixth printing

Copyright© 1975 by Scott French. All rights reserved, including the right to reproduce this book or any portions thereof in any form. Queries regarding rights and permissions should be addressed to: Lyle Stuart, Inc., 120 Enterprise Ave., Secaucus, N. J. 07094. Published simultaneously in Canada by George J. McLeod Limited, Toronto, Ontario. Manufactured in the United States of America.

ISBN 0-8184-0240-7 —*hardcover*
ISBN 0-8184-0241-5 —*paperbound*

TABLE OF CONTENTS

Other books by Scott R French include: The New Earth Catalog, The People's Yellow Pages of America, The Catalog of Challenge and Adventure, The Complete Guide to the Street Drug Game..

A WORD

This is a word from your author. Now, this is not a foreward, nor afterward, and most certainly is not THE word. It is just a word.

Everyone who reads this book will formulate a different opinion of its true purpose, or at the very least, my moral and political beliefs. The point being, that this book was not written to convey any esoteric messages that are going to tear down/save the world. Nor is it presented as a radical do-it-in-the-streets handbook. In fact, I have done my level-headed best to resist temptation and keep my political/apathetical beliefs from darkening these pages. For that matter, it should not concern you, any particular book reviewer, or English teacher just exactly what I believe in or fail to believe in (it seems to rarely concern my own mother, God knows she's too polite to ever come right out and say so, but she seems to be nodding her head more and more absent mindedly during my dissertations these days).

You see, this information exists, it is a finite quality in an infinite world. Many people already have this information; some are using it within the for-the-people, by-the-people law bit, some are not. Some are very definitely using it against you and me, (by this point, probably more the latter than the former . . . . .)

Now, by God, we've all got it. I don't know if that is good, looking at what a mess that people generally make of things when given the opportunity, but it's true. Which is possibly more important. Should you choose to go into the industrial spy business, start snooping around on your spouse, use this information for personal gain, use it to prevent others from abusing your rights, or simply just read it for the love of curiosity's sake, the responsibility is yours. I don't really give a damn . . . . . .

Well, that's just about the extent of my word. I would like to point out that this society, and most likely the whole world, is a bit on the corrupt side and these ideas and techniques (and other similar ones) are being employed all the time for one neferious purpose or another, and whether the people in power sanction it or not, it usually winds up in some vaguely immoral or illegal plot. Paranoid? Uh, well, maybe a little bit. Some days I tend to view the whole government, FBI, CIA, police included, as no better than a huge block to keep the people in power IN POWER, and on other days I feel like rushing to help any of the above villains shoot some son-of-a-bitch that has ripped me off .... so, I guess it's generally a matter of viewpoint. After all, a good agent bends with the proverbial wind; and God knows, does his best to establish a bank of good karma.

Some of my best friends have turned Republician after inheriting money. If enough of you would-be radicals, spies, and snoops buy this book, I may even pull a chameleon and start lobbying to protect those tax loopholes . . . . . so keep your chin up, knickers buckled above the knee, walk softly and don't believe what you read in the newspapers.

ELECTRONIC SURVEILLANCE

Some time in 1970, an ultra-sophisticated LASER bug was placed in the Oval Office of the White House. This device sent all room conversations over a considerable distance, and could differentiate between speakers.

The device was installed by one of the US intelligence agencies and may have very well operated without President Nixon's knowledge.

ELECTRONIC SURVEILLANCE

Over the last few years, the average American citizen, Mr. Doe, so to speak, has been exposed to an ever continuing barrage of information and misinformation about the wonders of electronic surveillance, or bugging.

The information filtered down to the media - attuned public is just the tip of the proverbial iceberg. While we have come to accept the fact that the FBI and assorted other legal agencies employ electronic snoopers, and of course, politicians give in to the base desire on occasion, few of us realize just how serious the situation really is.

A very popular book on electronic surveillance came out in 1967 and listed some of the buyers of bugging equipment. Those who read the book were quite surprised to find Avis Rent A Car, various hotel chains, Coca Cola, various life insurance companies, and the like, were spending millions for specialized bugging devices, but to find that Walt Disney was a major customer of such things, really pushed some of us over the edge.

During the sixties and early seventies AT LEAST 50 to 75 companies were eeking out a full-time living selling nothing but specialized surveillance and counter-surveillance instruments and information. The majority of these companies would sell to anyone with the necessary credentials, i.e. the money required . . . . .

Admittedly, some would only deal with law or detective buyers, but these were few and far between, besides being generally overpriced. Most would happily supply you with a "telephone conference transmitter" capable of utilizing the telephone company's own power to put both sides of a telephone conversation over the other for a distance of "several city blocks" for $69.95, or a "miniature pocket transmitter" capable of "picking up a whisper at 20 feet and rebroadcasting it for ½ mile", for a mere $39.95.

No one knows for sure how many of these units were sold or to whom, nor can an even semi-passable guess be hazarded as to the number of home-built units that were assembled by backyard electronic hobbyists for the same purpose as their professional counterparts.

Bugs have been found in embassies, men's bathroom's of major corporations, cars, telephone booths, political headquarters, and in at least one case which was brought to court, in every hotel room of a California hotel because the owner felt she "had a right to know if customers were defrauding her by bringing in more guests after the room had been rented". It is unknown if she graduated into the blackmailing business after she left the hotel field . . . .

Bugs are generally used to discover facts which would be a help to an uninvolved party. This, of course, conjures up all sorts of notions of international espionage and such, but it is amazing to see just how many bugs were designed to fit into objects which would fit into the decor of a bedroom.

Now in the wake of Watergate, and God knows what else, the laws have become quite stringent about the illegality of possessing, buying or selling, devices which are used to put someone under electronic surveillance, except to authorized law enforcement agencies. (Not private detectives.)

This has caused the majority of the bugging companies to close up shop, a few to switch to soliciting police departments, and some to go into the manufacture of "wireless babysitters" which can be set near the dear thing's crib and which will "pick up a whisper at 20 feet and rebroadcast it. . ."

Needless to say, these "electronic babysitters" more than slightly resemble the bygone bugging transmitters.

While this approach is fine for some applications, primarily small transmitters, it is hard to call a spike mic, or a laser window-vibration reader, or even a phone tap, as an electronic babysitter (Well your honor, the kid uses the phone a lot . . . .) so they have pretty much closed up shop, above the counter, that is.

There are still a vivacious number of individuals and "companies" selling these devices under the counter, although the price has risen with the illegal status a bit, separating the men from the boys.

It must also be realized anybody who can wield a soldering gun can whip together his own goodies and any TV repairman can mostly assuredly put said goodies together from plans and parts purchased at your friendly neighborhood electronic hobby shop. So the practice of electronic surveillance is far from over, it has just shifted to more professionals, more expense, and more police departments.

BRASS TACKS

Irregardless of the paraphernalia involved, all successful bugging operations follow one simple rule of play: get a good microphone as near as possible to the mouth of the person you want to bug. Period. Lasers and infinity transmitters are exotic, impress the hell out of your casual dates, and prospective clients, but really never work quite as well as one might expect for the investment.

MICROPHONES

A good agent should have some idea of what is going on with respect to microphones. There are several types available for surveillance work: Dynamic, magnetic, crystal, condenser and carbon are all employed in surveillance work. Each has certain characteristics which benefit certain jobs (carbon are extremely sensitive, but react badly to loud noises, heat, jarring etc. - crystal will not take great variations in temperature, etc.) but the main things to bear in mind are thus (ly):
The dynamic and crystal mics both generate a small electrical current when brutally struck by sound waves: this current is amplified by one's trusty amplifier or transmitted to a nearby radio. They require no current . . . .

Condenser mics, on the other hand, require a current supplied by no other than yourself and they simply act upon the current causing variations equal to the sound approaching them. This situation of changing rather than producing gives condensers the ability to be more sensitive to a wide variety of sounds than its producing cousins.

All microphones can have their pick-up patterns altered to some degree although this feature is most noticable in the dynamic variety. These particular microphones can be purchased to pick up sound in a general pattern, i.e. equally from all directions (omni-directional) or in a front-weighted heart shaped pattern (cardio) etc. The right choice of pickup pattern will do much to eliminate unwanted background noise. Condenser mics are not as selective and tend to pickup sound equally from most directions.

4

BUGGING: THE LAWS AND THE WAYS AROUND THEM........

The laws against public bugging are quite explicit; it is illegal to own, sell, use or transport devices designed for elect-ronic surveillance within the US. We have already seen how the loopholes in this law permit devices that could be for legitimate purposes, i.e. wireless babysitters, telephone burglar alarms, legal phone recording, etc, etc.

How about the laws having to do with the law enforcement bodies? How explicit they are, and how are they followed?

Nobody really knows just how widespread government surveillance is, virtually every government agency of any size including the FBI, CIA, DEA, Defense Agency, Secret Service, IRS, Department of Justice, and so on, have extensive bugging capabilities. Recent news articles have brought to light some of the surveillance activities going on, or at least, that have gone on, including the spying of one department or another on radicals, politicians, sports figures (my personal favorite is the diligence with which the late J. Edgar Hoover reportedly pried into Joe Namath's love life. I mean we, you and me, paid for that, we should at least get a look at what went on, don't you think?) and "enemies" of the party in power.

Thanks to the outpourings of money from the LEAA, any police department of any size at all also has the knowledge and equipment to conduct bugging operations.

To top it off, as this is written, there is no law stopping the Telephone companies from monitoring calls to "check on the quality of service and stop fraudulent use of the phone system". In fact, between 1965 and 1970, by their own admission, the phone company made just under 2 MILLION such unannounced taps, recording many of them.

At any rate, right now a law enforcement agency must get a federal order for a tap or bug. This means they must convince a judge there is probable cause to believe a crime is being committed and that electronic surveillance is the only way to solve it. Many judges are now reluctant to grant such an order unless he knows where the bug is to be planted and what the chances of innocent persons being heard along with the guilty party.

If it is a Federal agency requesting the tap, the approval of the Attorney General is also necessary before going to court. If such approval is given the bug can be left in place for 90 days before it must be removed and the person told he/she was under surveillance. Of course, if it is productive, the person would be arrested, so such notification would not be necessary....

Even here there is a loophole; if national security is threatened, no court order is required, just the approval of the Attorney General and there is no pressing need to show why it is required, or to inform the subject of the bug's presence if it fails to produce......

In 1973 there were a total of 864 applications for electronic surveillance devices NOT COUNTING THE NATIONAL SECURITY BUGS...of which the government does not make public.....

The other problem is the very fact that there is all this equipment and knowledge floating around, even if it is fairly hard to get a court order to use it. This leads to a situation known as "wildcatting", wherein a police or Federal agent places an unreported tap. This means it, and the information gotten through it, cannot be used in court, BUT any information the agent/cop hears that can lead to an arrest on some other grounds....well nobody really has to know about the bug....

One police officer we talked with freely admitted this went on all the time, "hell, if we waited for a court order on most of these guys, we'd never get anything. This way it's quick and clean....."

One narcotics officer was quoted as saying an illegal wiretap was the best informer you could have.....it just kept turning up raw data all the time....

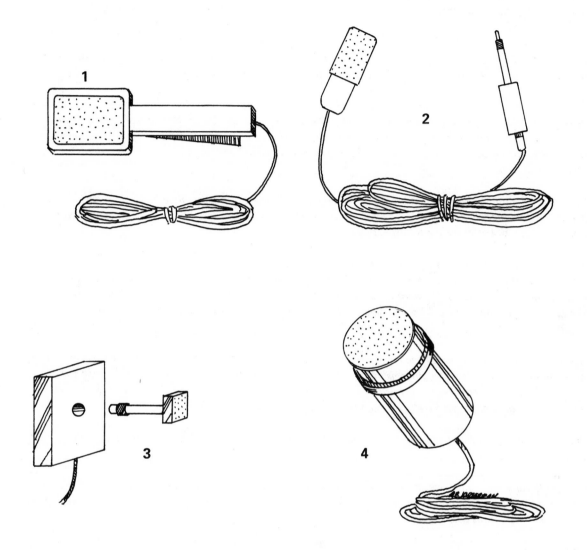

Several types of specialized microphones of interest to the surveillance expert:

1. A tie clasp mic; available in either dynamic or condenser versions. Dynamic begins at under $5.00 from radio suppliers like McGee and Lafayette.

2. Electret Condenser lavalier mic. Can be hung from neck, hidden in clothes or clipped on tie. Battery power supply often in plug. Starts at $30 from McGee Radio, $25-$60 from Olson Electronics. Quite sensitive.

3. Broadcast quality tie tack Electret mic available from Electrovoice, Sony. Mic head is very small and plug pokes through tie into amplifier section. Very nice quality. Figure about $150. . .

4. "Salt shaker" type of condenser mic. Requires outside battery supply. Starts at $18 from Toolco, also from Sony, etc., in the $40 range.

If you're not into fantasy, or paranoia, maybe I can help....Many "arts", including that of surveillance, are being pushed along so fast by old mother technology that one can only hope to get an idea of what's PROBABLY going on.

The invent of the IC (integrated circuit) which contains a number of components such as transistors, resistors, and the like in a small block of plastic the size of one transistor, has shrunk electronics into the almost unreal stage.

The first example of this was the infamous "martini olive" bug of the late sixties. This entire unit was the shape and size of a real olive; the toothpick was the antenna. The unit did not operate in the "conventional" fashion but, instead, the unit was built to very exacting sizes and acted as a small micro-wave transmitter. The range was limited to a very small area, but could not actually be soaked in a martini and work in any sort of credible fashion, much like the rest of us.

So-called sugar cube mics appeared next on the scene, and in fact these units can still be built or bought in the right places. Several models are available, at least one of which actually does resemble a sugar cube enough to be stirred into a cup of coffee by the unsuspecting victim.

The final, and one can only hope, final for some time, stage of idiocy, involves the use of bugs modified from bio-medical applications and incorporated into surveillance devices. One such device is built into a pill, yes a real pill, designed to be swallowed by the victim. So far, this device just radiates a series of beeps, sort of a modified "bumper beeper", but they are working on using the bones of the body to actually resonate and transmit voice transmissions....

One can only speculate on the use of such a strange device; so let's.....speculate, that is; suppose a diplomat, or let's say a newspaper publisher's daughter, is kidnapped. Now the conditions for his/her release include the re-lease from jail of some other parties. Just prior to the culmination of said deal one of the about to be released prisoners suddenly develops a chemically induced headache. He is given a pill to "cure" it. . .

After his release the authorities need only follow the radiated signal from a safe distance with their receiving system.....

It is also deeply rumored, among those who would have good reason to substantiate such rumors, that "bugs" are being designed to be surgically implanted under an agents skin and draw its power from his nervous system. . .Giving a constant "readout" of his position and dealings.

You are what you eat.

On da udder hand, do such things seem like a truly unnatural extension of a technology that has devices which can make a person feel bad, lose his memory and eventually die, from some distance, without the person actually being aware of the device being used? Or a country that uses, one must presume, thousands, maybe millions of dollars on super high altitude planes and even satellites which are in turn used to track down a person whose philosophy disagrees with theirs by flying over a deeply wooded countryside until their infrared cameras locate the glow from his cooking stove (not even an open fire, mind you) thousands of feet below and then dispatch a group of Green Berets to kill him with machine gun fire? (This really happened, you know.....not that I was for nor against Che', but still, the absurdity of the whole thing....)

For that matter did you know that our government has a series of "ears" stretching across the entire ocean floor which can hear just about everything that goes on down there? Not that this would rival Ed Sullivan mind you, but we also have a computer that knows the noise "fingerprint", of virtually every ship in the world and keeps constant tabs on each said ship's whereabouts?

Well, I digress a bit much now and then, George Orwell where are you when we need you?

Microphones used for bugging are generally very small (known as sub-miniature) and quite sensitive. These mics can still be purchased from radio suppliers and installed in or behind some covering object. When the great bugging rush was still above board, these small mics could be purchased already installed in various objects such as buttons, wrist watches, pen and pencil sets, cufflinks, roses, sugar cubes, wives, and so on. These are still available though the, wouldn't-you-know-it, law enforcement agencies and occasionally through electronic suppliers.

The simplest type of bug is simply to hide one or more microphones in the area to be bugged and then run wires to some point where you can attach an amplifier and earphones (or speaker), or tape recorder. Of course, the wires should be hidden or concealed in some clever fashion, or you may find you have unexpected company at your little listening party.

One popular method is to utilize the telephone cord for your wires, or even burglar alarm wires.

INSTALLATION

If a tube, contact, or spike mic is to be used through a wall, a different sort of care must be observed. Tube mics which are poked through small holes into the target room must be carefully installed. Holes must be drilled with small bits and light pressure or large pieces of the opposite wall may choose this moment to fall into the other room giving rise to suspicion. Small hand pressure drills are often used with great success. If at all possible, try to perform this little bit of connivery when the target area is deserted, or better yet, when you have access to the target room and can make sure any holes are well hidden. Any mouldings that have finishing nail holes in them are ideal targets.

In the use of flexible tube mics for through the wall, or under-door, into-keyhole use, it is a good idea to paint the end of the tube a different, (dark) color, then the rest of the tube. This painting should occupy about ½" of the end of the tube; in this fashion, it is possible to judge the penetration depth to a more accurate degree.

Larger diameter, stiff plastic tube mics are used in cheapie-rooms, such as motel rooms where a common hole is drilled for electrical outlets into two adjoining rooms. The cover may then be removed and the tube mic poked through to the inside surface of the opposite outlet, providing a good opportunity for eavesdropping. It must be remembered those wires in there are HOT. Although the plastic tube will not conduct, your fingers will . . . . a most unpleasant, sterile experience . . . .

Pay attention to impedances. All microphones have an output impedance and all amplifiers and transmitters have an input impedance. THESE TWO MUST NEARLY MATCH FOR PEAK PERFORMANCE. If a high impedance mic is used and a low impedance amplifier (or vice versa) a matching device must be used. This can be a small transformer designed for this job, or a pre-amplifier which will match and also boost the signal a bit. High impedances cannot be run over about 15 feet (crystal mics, including contact and spike types, are high impedance) without extreme signal loss. A preamp must be used in this situation, or the microphone must be lowered to low-impedance and then passed along the cable (and, if necessary, be made high again at the other end).

If possible, always use shielded microphone cable between a mic and an amplifier, short runs of twisted together, thin wire may be used to go into the cable for ease of concealment. If the mic cable is run near AC lines, hum will be introduced into the amplifier, or a strong local radio signal may be injected (nothing like getting a heavy dose of rock and roll while trying to monitor a conversation). This can usually be remedied by grounding both ends of the shielded portion of the cable, a 001 uf capicitor may be hooked up between the mic lead and the shield.

Microphones may be installed almost anywhere in a room. A good guide to the "proper" installation of a hidden mic is simply to read the anti-surveillance, handy-dandy, new and improved room search guide, backwards . . .

However, like any other successful venture in life, (I'm really sorry about this style of writing, but my mom washed floors to get me through college and that damn philosophy degree is going to do some good . . .) a truly classy mic hiding job requires some attention to detail. If a mic is to be hidden in something, i.e. floorboarding, wall sockets, telephones, etc., great care must be utilized as to cover ALL marks of the agents' passing. This includes a brush or battery operated vacuum to suck up any little particles produced by drilling or cutting, soap and cloth and perhaps a number of stains and paints, even if only of the watercolor variety, will help disguise any installation.

If wires are to be run, it is wise to choose very thin wiring, (in the proverbial pinch, a transformer may be unwound for thin wire access) and run it to the nearest covering; floor moulding is a typical example. The moulding is removed, wires hidden, and then the moulding is re-installed with the same nails, or at least same nail holes if possible.

A really nice trick, especially if the wiring must cross a visible area, is to buy some conducting paint sold at Radio Shack and the like, used to repair printed circuit boards, and "paint" wires across the worry area. As soon as the thin paint dries (a couple of minutes) the surface may be repainted or sprayed over with some finishing material, and poof! no wiring is visible . . . the conductive "paint" can be taken off with real wiring in a safe area by using little connectors designed for this same application in burglar alarm set-ups.

SPECIALIZED MICS

There are available (again to those with the power) certain specialized mics which can make the job of bugging much easier than with conventional mics.

Electronic Stethoscopes: By mounting a sensitive mic in a stethoscope and running the output into a good amp, it is possible to hear through thin walls and doors.

Keyhole and tube mics - Certain suppliers make mics with long hollow tubes, either flexible or stiff, which can be run through cracks and keyholes or mounted deep in (or on the other side of walls) walls with only a small pin hole in the wall itself. However, these mics DO require air conductance and MUST have a small hole to operate.

CONTACT AND SPIKE MICS

A contact mic is a device which does not respond to air vibrations as a conventional mic does, but rather translates actual vibrations into sound. This type of mic requires a sounding board of some type to operate. This sounding board may be a wall, window, electrical or mechanical device, (such as a motor), or a steel spike.

Contact mics are utilized, by conventional society types, to listen to motor or other mechanical vibrations, or to amplify the vibrations of musical instruments which are not designed for electrical use.

SPECIALIZED MICROPHONES

Tube mics have long been a favorite toy of buggers. The devices are still seen in law enforcement sources, on the black and sometimes gray market, but you, mein freund, can make one with just a bit of skill and even fewer parts, which will easily equal the most exotic law enforcement special.

The mic can be constructed either of two ways (or both, for that matter); by using a long, flexible piece of very thin (1/8 or 1/16 inch inside diameter) plastic tubing. This tube should be at least 14 inches long and is known as a key-hole mic, for rather obvious, if not mundane, reasons; it is used by sticking into keyholes, cracks, or under doors. The second approach is to use a piece of stiff, larger (inside diameter of 1/4 inch) plastic tube of about one foot in length. This variety is used most often in apartment houses or hotels where the adjoining rooms share electric socket mountings-one simply unscrews one's own side and pokes the tubing through the hollow wall to reach the other socket where the room noises will be picked up and transmitted down the tube into your greedy little ears.

First take a GOOD quality dynamic (or even condenser, if you leave another set of wires for external power) miniature mic element and set it on a layer of cork in the bottom of a 35 mm film can. The tube is now glued to the mic element where it covers the hole in the element, and extended out the top of the can (usually by drilling a hole in the can top to provide support). Run the wires from the mic element out a small hole you have drilled in the side of the can.

Now fill the entire can with fiberglass resin (hobby stores), and leave it to harden. Sound can now enter only through the tubing, where it resonates to some degree before reaching the microphone. This set-up also stops all other, unwanted sounds from reaching the mic.

Now simply hook the whole microphone up to your Super Deluxe Spy Amplifier and you're in business.

A contact and/or spike mic is another handy tool in your repertoire. There are again, grasshopper, several ways to approach this problem. The easiest and possibly the best, is to purchase a commercial contact microphone. This device "hears" vibrations, rather than sound and is utilized in various commercial practices.

If this is not practical, or you are the weird type, you can also try another angle or two; one is to get a crystal phono cartridge (used in cheap or old phonographs) and solder a metal plate (or spike as discussed later) to the needle. Now you simply play walls, rather than records....

Musical instrument pick-up mics available from radio/hobby shops can also be used. The best (Frapp, for instance checking in at around $100) work quite well, the cheaper, do work. BE SURE THEY ARE OF THE CONTACT TYPE AND NOT CONDENSER OR DYNAMIC substitutes.

Any of these contact mics can be held against a thin wall, window, etc., by hand or by tape or even rubber glue to listen through the material. They can also be attached to a spike, made from steel stock and ground to a point on one end as shown. This spike is pushed through a drilled hole onto the exact surface to be monitored (as described in the text) and the contact unit rubber-banded or soldered on.

Once again, your handy-dandy, Super Deluxe Spy Amplifier will serve as the pickup unit. When using ANY mic and your amp, you can, of course, connect the output to a tape recorder (watching impedances) and listen-in on the monitor feature of the recorder.

Oh yes, many contact mics, especially if they are of the crystal variety, are high impedance and should be connected through your matching transformer. It is a good practice to always try the opposite (high/low) impedance jack on any microphone when the output seems lower than normally expected.

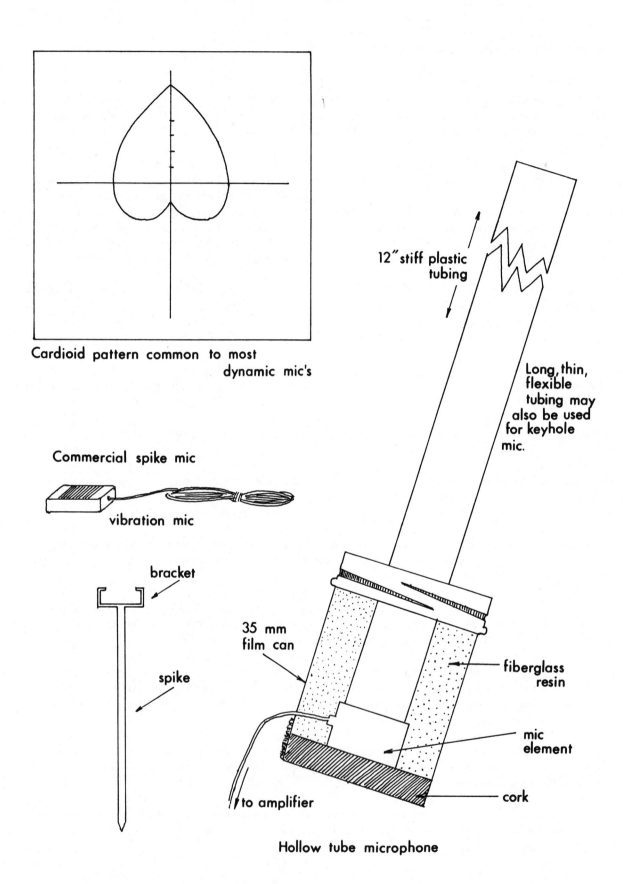

Cardioid pattern common to most
dynamic mic's

Commercial spike mic

vibration mic

bracket

spike

12″ stiff plastic
tubing

Long, thin,
flexible
tubing may
also be used
for keyhole
mic.

35 mm
film can

fiberglass
resin

mic
element

cork

to amplifier

Hollow tube microphone

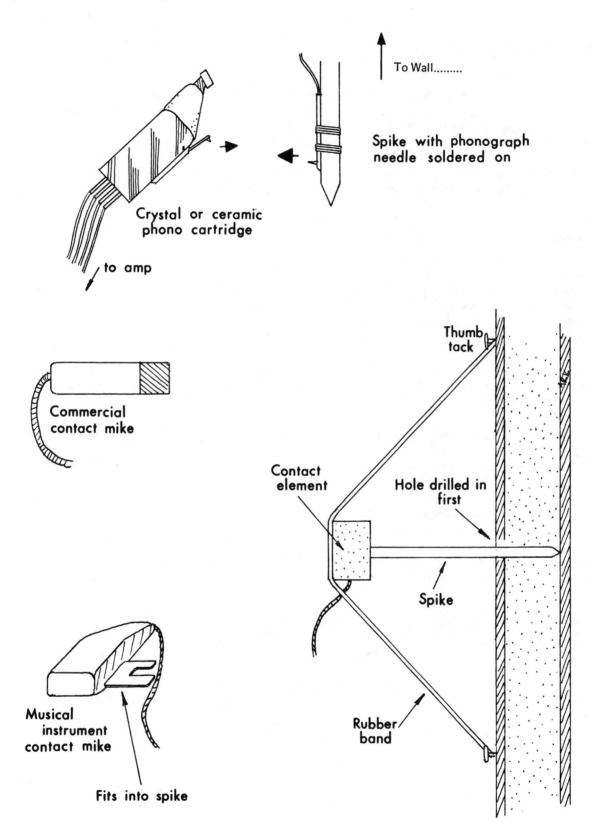

To Wall........

Spike with phonograph needle soldered on

Crystal or ceramic phono cartridge

to amp

Commercial contact mike

Musical instrument contact mike

Fits into spike

Thumb tack

Contact element

Hole drilled in first

Spike

Rubber band

RIFLE MICROPHONE

This is a most unusual project; we are going to mount a sensitive microphone behind a series of acoustic wave guides and hope for the best....Actually our wave guides are aluminum tubes cut to resonate at frequencies near the human voice range. This arrangement also serves to make the unit highly directional as sound other than that arriving at the mouth of the tubes arrives at the mic in an out-of-phase condition and cancels itself out.

With this easily constructed device it is possible (under ideal conditions) to pick up conversations several HUNDRED feet away, in fact, reports of recording conversations up to 30 yards away THROUGH A CLOSED WINDOW have been made.....

The device is quite easy to construct: First get together the following materials:

56' of 3/8" outside diameter aluminum tubing (hardware suppliers)
1 sensitive amplifier with operating paraphernalia (our Super Deluxe Spy Amp works quite nicely, thank you).
1 sensitive microphone element-use either a good condenser or a crystal, as their outputs tend to be a bit higher than their dynamic counterparts.
1 funnel
Assorted small hardware

Cut the tubing into 37 pieces ranging in length from 1" through 36" in one inch divisions. Now bundle them together symmetrically with one end flush (as shown). As you assemble them glue them together in several places to assure they remain in the state you have put them in (were it only so easy with people...).

Take the funnel and fit it around the flush end of the tube bundle. Being astute enough to buy this book, I am sure you will notice the tubes do not exactly fit into the funnel. At this realization, take a small hammer and beat the funnel to fit a nearly as possible. Now fill the remaining spaces with a good rubber based caulking compound.

The microphone element is placed in the neck of the funnel (with a rubber grommet if it is small enough to fit up into the neck-otherwise set it into the other end of the neck before caulking the tubing in place.) Glue the mic into place and caulk any air space around it.

Run the microphone wires out the neck of the funnel, glue in place, and also caulk to give a closed, fairly air invincible seal around the entire unit. If you really feel up to it, fiberglass resin can be used instead of caulking compound.

Run the output wires to your amplifier and place the entire unit on some sort of support, a camera tripod being ideal. (Need I remind you to check matching impedances?). The unit should be aimed at the subject and then panned about for maximum volume (sound does not travel in a straight line, but may vary with wind, etc).

If wind noise overrides your target noise you can place a piece of cheesecloth across the end of the unit. If a particularly difficult noise interferes with your pick-up you can often plug up the tube (s) carrying this noise with a cork.

Good hunting, avoid paranoid people who may feel your rifle mic more than resembles the real thing......

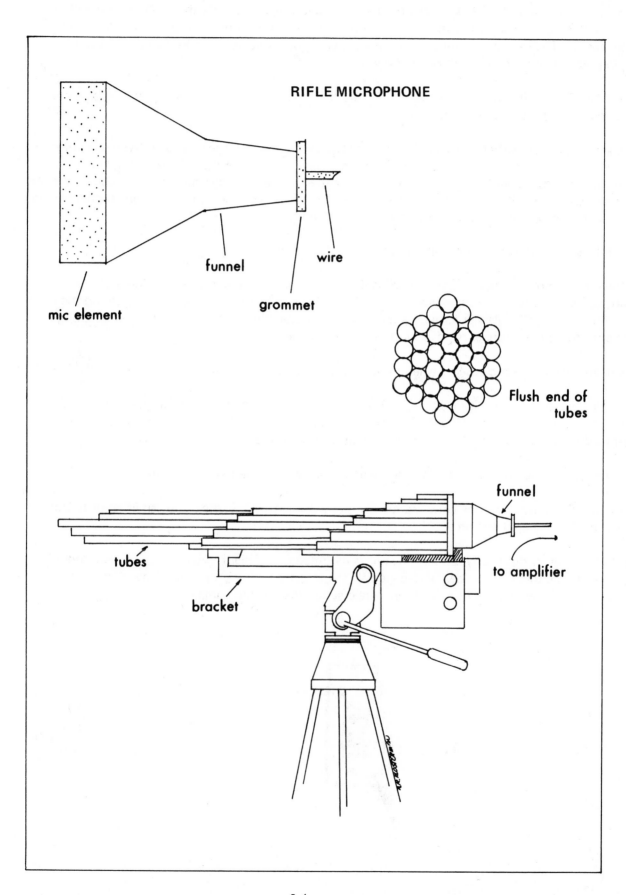

RIFLE MICROPHONE

mic element

funnel

grommet

wire

Flush end of tubes

tubes

bracket

funnel

to amplifier

A contact mic can be hooked to a sensitive amplifier and placed against a thin wall, or especially a window (including a phone booth) and will reproduce the minute vibrations of the wall/window with clarity. The mic can be glued to the window with rubber cement, or, in the case of a wall, securely taped with fiberglass, masking, or gaffer's tape.

In the case of a wall which is constructed of more than one panel (as most walls are) it is far better to employ a spike mic to reproduce the vibrations.

The spike mic is constructed (usually) in at least two separate units: the spike and the mic-amplifier unit(s). To use the mic one drills a small (although larger in diameter than the spike) hole in the wall adjoining the room to be bugged. The spike is then pushed through the hole until contacting the opposite wall where it is carefully driven into the wall a short distance. Of course, one should first tap the wall to locate, and avoid, the wall studs before drilling . . . .

The mic is then attached to the spike and the amplifier turned on.

If the mic is a professional unit, it will probably screw onto the spike; if it is a bit more of the home built, garden variety, the contact area of the mic will have to be placed against the spike and then tape (once again, fiberglass or gaffer's is the best) is run over the mic and on to the wall, securing the mic onto the spike. Rubber bands and thumb tacks can be utilized also.

There are several rules to observe when utilizing a contact or a spike mic:

Always make sure the mic is in full contact with the spike or sounding board surface. If using a spike mic, insure the spike DOES NOT come in contact with the sides of the hole drilled into the agent's side of the wall, as this will absorb a great portion of the minute vibrations.

BE QUIET! Noises in your side of the sounding board will also be fed into the mic.

If extraneous noises mask the conversation (music, TV, street noises, etc.) one can attempt to run the output of the amp into an equalizer.

Lastly, but surely not leastly, be sure the mic is mounted out of sight; if using a spike, care should be taken to see that the tip does NOT penetrate the target wall and project into the room, or the unwary agent may discover he hears more conversation than he has bargained for . . . . .

Spike mics are no longer available to the honest, man-in-the-street, but can be constructed by the clever/wary.

Directional mics - There are two types of directional mics. Parabolic and shotgun (or rifle). The parabolic has been reduced to the status of a child's toy with the plastic, "$9.95 wonders" on the market. They consist of a large plastic "dish" which focuses sound waves on the center-mounted mic and small transistor amplifier. These devices work quite well for the small investment, and will collect normal voices from a range of a couple of hundred feet, even through a partially opened window. The only minor disadvantage to the whole set-up is explaining why you are aiming this three-foot plastic dish at certain people . . . .

The shotgun mic is a device long employed from show business, where it is used to pick up voices across a crowded hall or from a cross-field football huddle with remarkable clarity.

It is a large, unwieldy instrument, which costs several thousand dollars, but does a remarkable job. It is possible to make a low-priced counterpart as detailed in later pages. If used properly, this device will often pick up voice transmission, even through closed windows. However, due to its operating principle of like-reasonance, it will also amplify an unwanted noise to a great degree and should always be used with a frequency equalizer to help shut out covering noises.

AMPLIFIER

It is always advisable to have a good little pocket amplifier with which to hook-up microphones and assorted paraphernalia.

Mics can either be low or high impedance, and some can be switched from one to the other. It is possible to use an amp with both high/low inputs to cover all bases.

If you are not up to a construction job, it is possible to buy any one of the little $5 - $10 breadboard transistor amps from Radio Shack or the like, and substitute them with good results.

For direct amplification of spike mics and vibration jobs, a super high gain, direct coupled amp should be employed. Some of these small, little amps can produce a gain of up to 100,000 times.

FREQUENCY EQUALIZERS

During the last couple of years, a number of cheap (around $100 sort-of-cheap, that is) frequency equalizers have appeared on the market. These little miracles are designed to allow you to control sounds by cutting out certain frequencies at will. They are employed professionally in recording studios and are oriented towards consumer use in PA systems and hifi systems.

These equalizers can be hooked up to any mic, amp or tape recorder and will allow you to reduce certain frequencies while "boosting" the effects of others. This means you can shut out the noise of an electric fan, water running, machine noise, wind, static, etc., while retaining the conversation. They are a must for the serious bugger.

The next piece of necessary equipment is the tape recorder. Almost any unit can be utilized, provided the necessary conditions for power and space are adequately provided. Most buggers prefer to use the small battery powered, Japanese-influenced jobs. These fall in the price range of $24.95

SUPER DELUXE SPY AMPLIFIER

The first device any practical bugger, de-bugger, or general nut needs is a good all-around audio amplifier. We have come up with a little gem which we call our Super Deluxe Spy Amplifier, in the best Madison Ave traditions. It is: cheap, quite good, and needs little construction, just like in the good old days.

To start, order a "5 transistor miniature push-pull audio amplifier, number 99-90375" from Lafayette Electronics (see the suppliers page). Now you will also need a couple of other parts, most of which can also be gotten from Lafayette: a small matching transformer for attatching the amp to a high impedance device such as a crystal mic, Lafayette's 99 E 60345 will do nicely. Get a 10K volume control with a built in switch (how about Lafayette's 32 E 22528 ?) and a pair of LOW (around 8 ohm) earphones (the diagram shows a speaker, which will work, but phones are better).

Mount the amp in a small metal or plastic box (also sold by various radio suppliers) with jacks to get access to both a high and low impedance input, the output, and connect your battery and volume control and you're ready to roll at a cash outlay of about $12.00. This will out perform many of the "law enforcement" amplifiers sold for well over $100. If you need more power add an external pre-amp, or go the whole hog and order F.G. Mason's $175 super sensitive amp that will lift the minute audio from a pair of phone lines after shorting out the cradle......

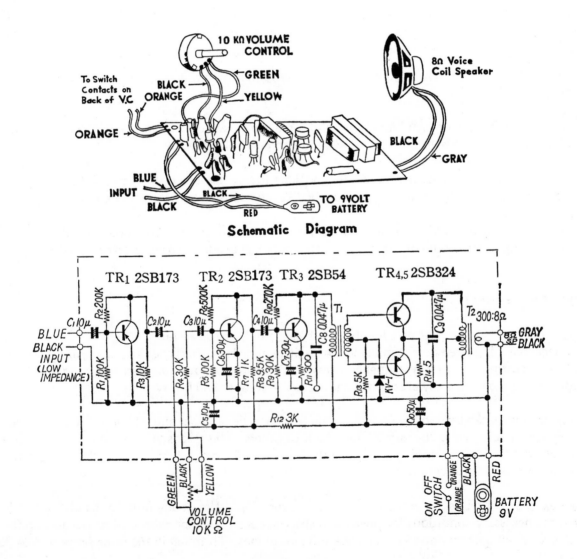

Schematic Diagram

to $200.

If operating time is the primary concern, a reel-to-reel should be the only choice. If size is the first priority, a cassette should be employed. The small cassette units put out by Craig, Panasonic, Sony, etc., are ideal for most applications, BUT you should not plan on using over a 90-minute cassette (that is 45 minutes per side) on these little units, as the longer cassettes necessitate extremely thin tape which tends to jam the small recorders at an alarming rate.

If you are planning on a cassette, make sure you get the following "built-ins"; condenser mic, with remote mic jacks, automatic level control, auto-shut off, monitor jack, AC adapter. Any compromise will make one operation or another difficult.

A good, cheap choice is the little Panasonic, which sells for under $100 at the time of this writing. Sony makes several in the $90 to $160 price range with varying features. I have heard the top model is an excellent performer. Of course, if you're serious (and rich) the $1500 Nagra reel-to-reel is really tops. These recorders will provide you with a wide choice of applications. They can be worn on the body (usually in a "shoulder harness" set-up, to record your conversations. They can be hooked up to a phone (see that section) for 24-hour monitoring of all calls, they can be coupled with an FM radio to record wireless bugs, or the recorder itself can be used as a bug in a variety of ways; the whole unit can simply be turned on and stuck with gaffer's tape to the underside of beds, chairs, etc., where it will do a good job of picking up all room sounds with its sensitive condenser mic. The further back, or under something it is mounted, the more "hollow" noise it will pick up. This comes out as a hum, which can often be lifted out with the frequency equalizer.

A clever ploy which has been used more than once is to secrete the recorder in a briefcase with a disguised mic, or a small series of holes leading to the inside mic. The whole briefcase, is then forgotten in an office after a crucial interview. The owner "remembers" it sometime later and returns to pick up a complete record of the previous conversation. Most people would not poke around in another man's briefcase, but it is always a good idea to lock it securely.

A most useful addition to the mini-recorder, is a voice-operated-relay, or VOX. Occasionally, it is possible to purchase a recorder already equipped with the same, but for all practical purposes, you should figure on making your own, or buying it separately.

The VOX hooks into the remote jack of the recorder and allows it to remain in an "off" position until the VOX's own microphone senses a sound in the room. At this point, a relay is closed and the recorder starts running. The relay is set with a time-delay to prevent the recorder from shutting off between words or sentences.

The proper use of the VOX will condense days of listening time into an hour's worth of tape, saving both power and valuable tape time.

A VOX can also be adjusted to listen on a dead spot of the FM band, starting the tape recorder only when a hidden transmitter broadcasts some sound over the air. With this set-up, a room (or phone) but can be installed and the recorder-radio-VOX can be left in a nearby car for days at a time, recording the good stuff with no human help.

It should be noted here that the new laws require BOTH parties (or all as the case may be) of a conversation to agree to recording the conversation before it may legally progress (the old laws only required the agreement of one party).

A couple of disadvantages crop up with VOX equipped recorders. The VOX, and probably the recorder's amplifier, are ON whether the recorder is running or not, and battery drain, while reduced, is still present. This necessitates placement of the recorder soon before you expect the conversation to take place.

The VOX may not be as sensitive as the recorder, and may not start up if the speaker is too far away to register properly. By the same token, if it is too sensitive, background noise may activate it and waste the tape.

REMOTE CONTROL

There is one other solution to the problem of starting and stopping the recorder, or bug. Most hobby shops will sell you a remote control transmitter/receiver combination, designed to operate model airplanes, for $100 or so. This combination can start/stop a recorder, or bug from a distance of ½ - 1 mile away. This allows placement of the recorder when access is available, and then a simple binocular-assisted stakeout should tell you when to start the machine . . . . .

WIRELESS SURVEILLANCE

The next step up the ladder of sophistication is the use of wireless mics, or miniature transmitters, to gather sound and pass it along. These miniature transmitters operate on the same principles as your friendly neighborhood radio station, but on a bit less pretentious level.

The simplest wireless room-bug is simply a walkie-talkie, with the transmit button taped in on the "on" position. This quick set-up can be hidden behind drapes, on bodies, etc., and will do a passable job of passing along data, although they are a bit bulky and limited in sensitivity.

The next simplest bug is a commercial wireless mic. These mics are used to transmit the voice of a tour leader, actor, MC, etc., to a nearby FM radio, without the hassle of mic cables strung about the premises. They are fairly compact in size, a pack of cigarettes is about the average mass, and quite inexpensive, averaging around $40 (although Radio Shack has a $17.95 special out . .). The wireless mic does a fair job of sound pick-up and will transmit a distance of 50 to 150 feet, depending on antenna size, walls, etc. They are tunable over the entire FM band.

The commercial wireless bug is usually smaller in size, has more sensitivity, and will broadcast over a longer distance. The average bug runs off its own batteries, (which may last from 15 hours to a week or so, depending on battery capacity and transmitter strength) and will transmit a distance of 200 feet up to ½ mile. The range is directly dependent on transmitter strength, thickness of walls, sensitivity of receiver and to a small extent, the weather.

Wireless bugs were/are manufactured in a variety of sizes, shapes and prices. They are available from the size of a sugar cube (or olive) up to the average half-a-pack of cigarette size.

It should be noted that the gimmicky postage stamp and martini-olive type transmitters are: a. expensive. b. fairly useless. and c. have a normal range of about 40 feet.

The total size of a transmitter must also take into consideration the type of power used. Most are run off of their own, self-contained batteries, but some use an external pack, which can more than

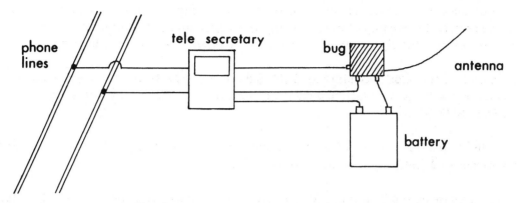

A drop-out relay or commercial Tele-Secretary can be installed across the phone lines and then into a phone-bug by running the audio channel wires directly into the bug and then the on/off wires into a break in one side of the bug's battery supply. In this fashion the bug will remain off until the phone is lifted from its cradle, whereupon it will begin transmitting. With this sort of set up one set of batteries can last for weeks, or even months.

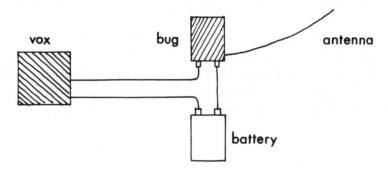

In the same fashion it is possible to hook a VOX up to a room bug so that it also cuts off one side of the bug's power supply until it senses room noise, whereupon it switches the bug on.

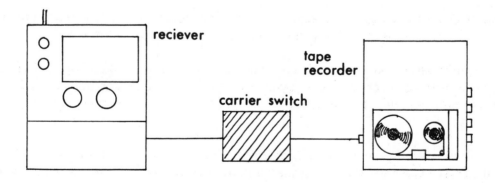

Now the next logical step is to take a carrier switch and hook it between your receiver and tape recorder (via the remote start feature) so the recorder will only start when it picks up the bug's signal. This works especially well with the telephone bug set-up mentioned above. In a pinch, a VOX can be attuned to the radio's speaker so it turns the recorder on with any sound, but a carrier switch works much better.......

double the size of the whole set-up. There is one type of room bug that uses the wall current and actually broadcasts over the existing power lines (through capacitors). This unit will allow anyone equipped for it, to recover the signal anywhere short of the power company's transformer.

It is possible to construct a good room bug for $15 - $25 worth of parts, or buy one (if you are, or have close association with, or are blackmailing a cop) for $65 to $400, or buy one under the counter for $75 to $500.

The ideal bug will be small, sensitive, not draw too much power, have a fairly short antenna (anywhere from 4 inches to 3 feet), a good range, and be stable.

It is possible to purchase exotic bugs built into picture frames, bouquets of flowers, fountain pens, heels of shoes, ad infinitum. It is even possible to find automatic bugs which, using the aforementioned VOX principle, shut themselves off when no sound is present to conserve their batteries.

Another simple alternative is to buy a wireless mic "module" from one of the hobby electronic places, attach a small, microphone, a set of batteries, and Voila! You're in business.

Any wireless mic can be made a bit more sensitive and less directional by substituting a mini-condenser mic in place of its own dynamic or crystal, AS LONG AS THE IMPEDANCES ARE STILL MATCHED. Most condensers are low impedance. It should also be noted that condenser mics must have a power source to operate, this is circumvented by purchasing one with its own power supply, such as the mini-Sony ECM-16 - or other similar types.

TRANSMITTERS

Two types of transmitters are commonly used for surveillance operations, the first is a one-three transistor, non-crystal controlled circuit, wherein the final one or two transistors constitute an oscillator circuit and the first, if used, is generally an audio amp. This type is cheap, small, easy to construct, and gets a fairly long battery life.

The problems with this sort are: short range, signal drifting, which usually requires returning of the receiver, and frequency shifting if a body (alive, that is) is moved close to the antenna.

The other, common variety bug is a crystal controlled 5-10 transistor goodie. This type gives much longer range at a sacrifice in battery life, and will not drift off frequency for any reason short of a nuclear attack in the near vicinity. It cannot be changed from its one operating frequency, without changing the crystal.

The non-crystal type sells in the region of $65 - $300, while the crystal varieties go for $350 - $500. The bit is, the crystal types are usually just the transmitter sections of commercial walkie-talkies . . . one simply picks a one-two watt, crystal controlled walkie-talkie ($80), removes the transmitter section, removes the final RF amp, couples the output of the RF driver (this will give one about 250 milliwatts of output ......) to the antenna. Now you have a fairly powerful, fairly reasonable battery life, "bug". One other possibility is to install a good mic instead of the cheapie, or, God forbid, speaker used in the walkie-talkie (being careful to match impedance, of course).

An even simpler method is to buy from someone like Motorola, an already-apart (strip) transmitter-receiver section(s). Now you have a crystal controlled transmitter and "matching" receiver just like

DO-IT-YOURSELF-ALMOST-RIGHT-OFF-OF-THE-SHELF, BUG........

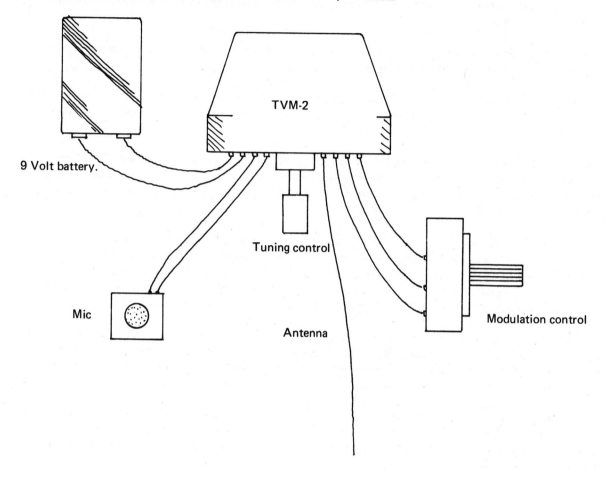

9 Volt battery.

TVM-2

Tuning control

Mic

Antenna

Modulation control

Probably the best deal in the cheapie module-type bugs is the Cordover TVM-2, TV Wireless Microphone Transmitter. This little black box checks in at $5.00, can be tuned for operation on several TV channels, as well as outside the TV band (s) and into the public service bands for reception on your trusty Sony-type receiver.

This unit is hooked up to a transistor radio battery, a low impedance mic (the TVM-1 is for high impedance), a 100,000 ohm potentiometer, and a wire antenna of, hopefully, about 30 inches. The device is then tuned for the approximate spot on the tuning dial and placed in place.

Once so placed the potentiometer is adjusted for maximum signal strength.

This device has a remarkable range for such things, under ideal conditions it may get over two to three blocks, long battery life (about six days on one battery), and can be made quite sensitive by the addition of a condenser mic.

The total price for this set-up would be about $8 or $9 with a miniature dynamic mic, and maybe $25 with a sub-miniature, sensitive, condenser mic element.

Not too bad of a deal, say what?

Is paranoia really paranoia when it's justified? Think nobody is really into illegal surveillance? Take the strange case of one Antonio Randaccio......

Antonio is an Italian gentleman who has two features that are of particular interest to this little anecdote: 1. He enjoys a challenge. 2. He has always been interested in radio.

Antonio was a ham radio operator since childhood, and, due to an unusual family situation wherein he was not forced to spend 90% of his waking hours trying to pay off his credit card bills like the rest of us, had some spare time kicking around.

With this love of challenge and excess of time, he decided to help his government clear up the huge number of illegal citizen band (private-walkie-talkie kind of thing) radio operators doing their thing in Italy. He set to work and designed special antennas and receiving equipment and fished out many, many such clandestine operations. Suddenly, no more challenge....

Then, one fine fall day, Antonio noticed the huge selection of bugging devices available on the local market and began to wonder actually how many such devices were in use. He sectioned off the Rome area into two mile square blocks, put together little-short-of-amazing antennas (with a 20 dB gain, for you sticklers out there), reworked his receivers to cover the entire radio spectrum and set out to find the highest vantage point within each section. Once so situated, he began tuning the whole RF bandwidth, identifying each signal as to contents and type.

Now here you must realize there are literally thousands and thousands of such signals across the radio band, each of which is operating with some sort of fairly large amount of power output designed to propel it across great distances. The signals Antonio was searching for were scattered about the band, not always active, and designed to go a distance of 50-1000 feet, never more.....Such a brazen feat had never before been attempted.

Antonio kept up his search for a period of several months; during this time he averaged two bugs in every three days of searching. When he found the devices he would notify the owners of the premises or the local authorities that such a device was in operation. They could then, using conventional equipment ferret out the device and put it out of whack, or feed it false information.

The devices were discovered in bedrooms, factories, meeting rooms, and even in the Malta embassy. At one point Antonio had his equipment smashed into small bits and pieces by someone obviously not overly pleased with his operations.

In several instances the owners of the devices were apprehended when they returned to see why their toys had quit functioning.

Antonio's next project borders on the fantastic; he is designing equipment now, even as I sit here writing this and you sit here (or there) contemplating some strange act, not only to find the bug, but, by focusing in on the oscillator section of the receiver tuned to that frequency (receivers produce minute RF fields of their own), track down the person listening to the bug. This sort of thing may not bring tears to the eyes of you, Mr. Average Reader, but it will bring full grown electronic engineers down to their knees............

TRANSMITTERS: GENERAL RULES.......

There are several basic factors to bear in mind when placing a transmitter; any transmitter, whether a homemade special, or a $500 crystal controlled babysitter.....

Firstly, these devices are a bit on the sensitive side, due to their very nature. They have no moving parts and should last several years if treated with tender loving care, and a bit of common sense (well borrow some then.....).

Do not carry the units where they will receive a dosage of rough use, i.e., in pockets with keys, glove compartments where they roam about freely, etc. Never yank a battery or antenna loose from its clip. Do not expose to heat of over 125° nor place in the direct sun (as on an automobile dashboard) where transistors can come to resemble Betty Crocker's Transistor souffle......

When testing a transmitter NEVER yell or blow directly into a sensitive microphone. This very act of sacrilege will ruin the microphone. Be sure and conduct your tuning/testing by setting your receiver some distance away (hopefully in another room) and having someone count in a normal tone of voice 5 or 6 feet from the transmitter. If necessary turn on a commercial radio and allow your friendly local radio station to serve as your tuning source by placing the unit several feet from the radio and then retreating into your tuning room.

It is important to bear in mind that all FM transmitters; from the local 50,000 watt rock and roller, to your 15 milliwatt babysitter special, operate on a line-of-sight basis. This means, in layman's terms, the signal will go in a straight line until it is diffused by the local flora and fauna, or just fades into radio heaven. If the unit is placed high above ground, this line-of-sight will be quite a bit greater than if the unit is placed at ground zero.

Other factors also come into play when we discuss such factors as range. If the unit has to push its tiny signal through several large buildings to reach your receiver, the signal will be sorely diminished (steel sucks up radio waves like a woman does money). On the same side of the coin (of the realm?), if you can place your receiver on the same side of the building as the transmitter, the results will be vastly improved.

Antenna placement is also of prime import; normally you always try to place the antenna in a vertical arrangement, COMPLETELY UNFOLDED. Now the signals radiate from the antenna in a circle VERTICALLY. This means your receiver antenna should also be aligned VERTICALLY. The exception to this rule is if you plant the bug in a large building and plan to monitor directly above or below the unit. In this case you would place both your antennas in a horizontal position.

If this "generally vertical" rule cannot be adhered to because of lack of space (say you are mounting the little bugger [no pun intended] on the back of a bookshelf or some such) place the antenna (with tape if necessary) in the shape of a W. Never, never curl your antenna up if you expect any range at all. . .

If you are observant, or just believe me, you will discover the higher frequency you operate at, the shorter both the receiver and transmitter antenna should be. With this factor in mind always rotate your receiver antenna around and vary the length of it for best indication on the signal strength meter (or best volume if your unit lacks this basic feature).

NEVER place the transmitter near large bodies of metal (i.e., filing cabinets, metal desks, or chair seats with metal springs, etc) as this will absorb much of the radiated signal right at the start of things. If you are mounting in a picture, or otherwise on a wall, try to avoid wall beams.....

Always observe correct battery polarity and voltage. Always check batteries, even new ones, before depending on them in a crucial job. If you wish to increase the "on" time of a unit, find a larger battery of the same voltage, or connect a series of like batteries IN PARALLEL. Each additional battery will double your operating life.

If the transmitter is able to be tuned (by varying the coil slug, or a trimmer cap, or some such device) always do it on location with a plastic "diddle stick" (no, I didn't make that one up), available at your local radio supply house. Tune with a cheap field strength meter for maximum RF output.

One final note, if installing a phone bug, dial the weather to test it, or for a nice touch, if you're into that sort of thing, use Dial-A-Prayer........and tune by that.......

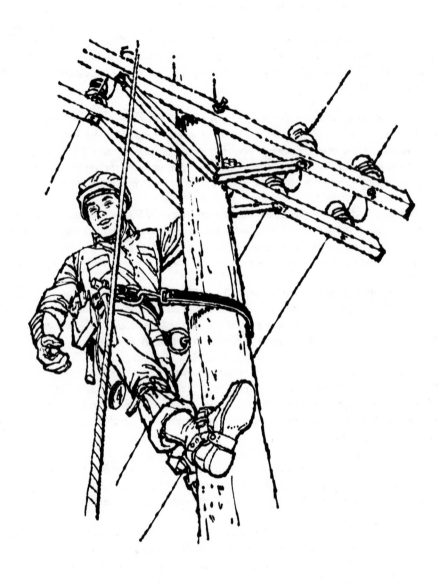

the $700 model for a hundred or so . . . . If you want more power (with greatly reduced battery life) simply put the final RF amp back in place . . . .

These units come in various bands, it is wise to avoid the CB bands and get a business (low-band, 40-80 Mhz) or public service band where your little subterfuge is not so likely to attract the attention of everyone in the area with a comparable receiver.

RECEIVERS

It should be remembered that most wireless mics operate on the commercial FM band. The mic is simply tuned to an unused spot on the dial and a conventional FM receiver is used to monitor the signal. It must be held in mind that not just you, but ANYONE with an FM receiver within the bug's range can also pick up the signal if they happen to tune in the wrong (or right, depending on your viewpoint) spot.

This has happened more than once: a jealous boyfriend bugged his girlfriend's apartment which happened to be located in one of those "swinging singles" complexes on the West Coast. All went according to plan until someone happened to turn their radio on and recognized the "disc jockey's" voice. In a matter of hours, the entire wing of the complex was listening in on an unusual radio program, sort of an X-rated soap opera. This unmerciless listening went unchecked for some time until a kind soul tipped the victim off. Needless to say, the relationship between her and her boyfriend took a turn for the worse.

Because of this unwanted feature, many professional buggers employ bugs which operate either above or below the commercial band and purchase special receivers, or modify commercial receivers to operate in these ranges.

If you are selecting a receiver with the eventual thought of maybe, just maybe, someday doing a bit of amateur espionage, you should endeavor to find the most sensitive FM receiver you can afford, and be certain it is equipped with defeatable automatic frequency control (AFC) to prevent needless drift. Automatic level control (as you would probably suspect by this time - ALC) is a good thing on occasion, but the minor level of power put out by bugs will not set off the ALC and can actually defeat the whole shabang. It is always convenient to be able to hook-up a tape recorder directly into the receiver.

PASSIVE

The dream of every bugger, voyeur and general pervert is a passive surveillance system, (i.e. one which does not require any transmitter to operate, just a receiver). The only real passive systems are the long distance microphones already described, and they do have their disadvantages, as to size, conspicuousness, etc.

The answer to this dream has always felt to be in the realm of lasers. To visualize this concept, it is necessary to understand a bit of high school physics; any light or other energy, including sound waves, if directed at a reflective surface, will be slightly modified in, by the movements of that surface. The movements can be caused by the reaction of the surface to stimuli such as noise. The directed energy will produce patterns in a direct relationship with the stimulus. This is sort of the principle all microphones work under.

Now it has been felt that a beam of light could be directed at such a surface, say a window pane, for example, and be modulated by the movements of the pane and then the reflections picked up by a photo cell and connected to an amplifier to produce reproductions of the sounds.

The problems of this idea include the fact that light rays reflect in all directions from the source, thereby scattering the reflected rays over a wide area in a short distance. Well, as any amateur scientist knows, a laser produces light rays which all travel in the same direction and stay "tuned" for extremely long distances (they have been bounced off of the moon with the resulting beam spread over a distance of ½ mile or less).

So, it is only natural to assume a coherent, tuned beam of light could be used to be focused upon the target "sounding board" and received in the modulated condition with far less problem than its uncoherent cousin.

In theory, this sounds all well and good, but, as with many things in life, it does not come out quite that easily. One famous (and good) electronic surveillance book stated that the problems in this sort of system would not make it available during this century, or at best the CIA "might have something workable by 1988 - 1990". And as I write this very paragraph, I see in the paper a columnist denying these devices . . . .

Well, button your knickers above the knee, my friends. Devices like this DO exist. Workable models have been produced that will allow one to make a legible recording through a closed window at a range of several miles.

The existing models are by no means perfect, but man, they do exist. One still-to-be-ironed-out bug is the fact that outside noises also modulate the window, meaning such things as automobiles, jack hammers, etc., get amplified right along with the good stuff. The use of a frequency equalizer on the amplifier will limit this somewhat. One other problem with the early models, is the fact that a glowing, red laser-dot is placed on the victim's window, which may not exactly tip one's hand, but is sure to produce some consternation in the average person.

I am including plans for a laser device, which can be constructed by someone with a fair knowledge of electronics. This device has the advantage of using infrared laser beams to avoid the red dot problem, and is claimed to give up to 1 MILE RANGE under ideal conditions with a top-of-the-line telescope.

Photo courtesy of Communications Control Corp

Several firms offer seminars in surveillance, usually from a counter standpoint. Communications Control Corp (the young lady above is pointing out their seminar phone board) offers a de-bugging seminar which lasts one day and costs $150. They offer about one such seminar a week in New York City, and will travel anywhere and give a seminar for $150 plus all travel expenses.

Mason offers an anti-seminar to purchasers of their equipment free at their plant, or on a sliding scale in most major cities (from $33 elsewhere in Connecticut to $585 in California).

Fargo Police Equipment offers a several day seminar in San Francisco for just under $500 which includes both de-bugging and a touch of the other side of the story.......Both Fargo and CCC (before they were called CCC) used to offer real break-and-enter-plant-bugs-pick-locks, etc, etc, seminars........

IGS

The private spy game has reached such world wide proportions that one can even join a "club" for private spies, or as their brochure so etiquettely states it; "special agents".

This organization goes under the unauspicious title of the INTERNATIONAL GADGET SERVICE, and is located at B.P., 361.02, Paris, France. For a mere 30 Francs one can gain "particuliers" or for the grand sum of 100 Francs one can actually become a "Affaires commerciales". This final honor gains one various mailers and brochures, the best being the IGS catalog itself.

This catalog lists just about every state-of-the-art spy device in existence in the world today along with price, particulars, and ordering info. The catalog is actually reproductions of the best sections of actual manufacturer's advertising catalogs in France, Germany, the US, Italy, etc. It helps to be at least bilingual to grasp all the minor intricacies (although IGS thoughtfully offers a quick tourist translation list in the back of the brochure: transmitter-ou "bug", punaise-transmetteur ou microemetteur, locator ou "de-bugger"-localisateur de micros et de microemetteurs dissimules, without-sans, [example; sans batteries] , etc, etc.) The main thing is of course, to read the price correctly... IGS members receive some discounts on certain "materiels speciaux".

The IGS catalog is quite comprehensive, one can purchase just about any sort of transmitter from fountain pen jobs that begin sending when the cap is removed and placed on the opposite end of the beast, shotgun and rifle mics, spike mics, telephone drop-ins, all types of tape and wire recorders, scramblers, jammers, detectors, and some nice passive night vision devices. They even mention the laser mic, although confess not to know exactly where to get one......

Their prices are good to average, and they offer just about everything the modern businessman could possibly need to go about minding his own business. There is only one minor hitch (always is, right?), they can no longer legally export into the USA.

In fact, it is theoretically impossible to even get the IGS literature in the US. Our copy was rumored to have entered these friendly shores in the back of a diplomatic pouch............

L'I.G.S. est une sorte de Club — fondé en 1967 — et tout spécialement créé pour apporter à ses Adhérents des informations sur des sujets sortant de l'ordinaire, et leur rendre aussi éventuellement divers services.

Ces informations concernent non seulement les gadgets et autres nouveautés originales, curieuses, insolites, pratiques, amusantes ou « spéciales », etc., mais encore les inventions et découvertes réalisées dans le monde entier.

Par ailleurs, diverses idées exploitables, services originaux, innovations sont aussi signalés, de même que les projets, recherches ou travaux en cours et brevets émanant des Membres adhérents.

Toutes ces informations et bien d'autres encore figurent dans le Bulletin de Liaison de l'I.G.S. paraissant tous les deux mois.

Ce Bulletin — hors commerce — a pour devise :

« Savoir ce qui se fait afin d'en dégager un enseignement prospectif, source d'émulation et de progrès »,

est adressé gratuitement aux Adhérents qui peuvent y faire passer des « petites annonces » gratuites de leur choix : offres, demandes, échanges, propositions diverses, etc.

BUG DETECTION

There are several approaches to debugging any area; the first, and often most successful is a thorough visual inspection. Attacking the problem one room at a time, bearing in mind EVERY SQUARE INCH MUST BE COVERED. This includes the floor, walls, ceiling, inside and outside of windows and all room furniture fixtures and friends.

WHAT TO LOOK FOR

Start your search by checking over any recent additions to the local decor. Have pictures been recently hung? New or different desk blotters, pen sets, chairs? New secretaries with strange little bodily lumps? (Caution: don't get TOO thorough here. . .)

Remember, most bugs are big enough to be recognized, and will probably have a small wire antenna, and may have an external battery. Examine all picture frames, lamp bases, undersides of desks and drawers, behind drapes, in books and bookends and other commonplace objects. Unscrew wall sockets and examine the inner workings, VERY CAREFULLY, it might be added.

Now approach the walls, ceilings and floors. Look for mismatched paint which could indicate recent disturbances, small cracks or flaking paint which could indicate a spike mic on the other side of the wall, watch for fine wires running along floor boards and examine every inch of the available surface area for fine holes which could easily lead to a pinhole mic planted in the wall or panelling.

If suspicious wires are located, one can either follow them to find the source (both ways) or hook a small commercial debugging device known as a screamer (or use an AF generator) to the wires. This device causes the hidden microphones to let loose a prodigious howl, to aid in locating.

If small holes show themselves where one would not expect small holes to be, a long thin nail, or stiff wire can be pounded inward to get at the root of the thing, and smash it into oblivion.

Don't forget to check out the wastebaskets . . . .

If you suspect bugging, but have a wide choice of possible areas, mentally regurgitate the last few weeks and re-consider any visits from repairmen, termite or "county" inspectors, telephone company people, meter readers, and other naturally suspicious types. Many buggers would rather risk this sort of fraud than pull a breaking and entering to plant a bug.

If anyone comes to mind, start with all the areas he/she/it would have had access to and search, search, search.

ELECTRONIC SEARCH

Coupled with a good visual inspection is the more technical electronic search. There are a variety of gadgets available for commercial bug hunting, but the important ones can be built or at least bought (usually with a substantial saving) from your friendly radio supplier.

Checkpoints for surveillance devices in an office/home:

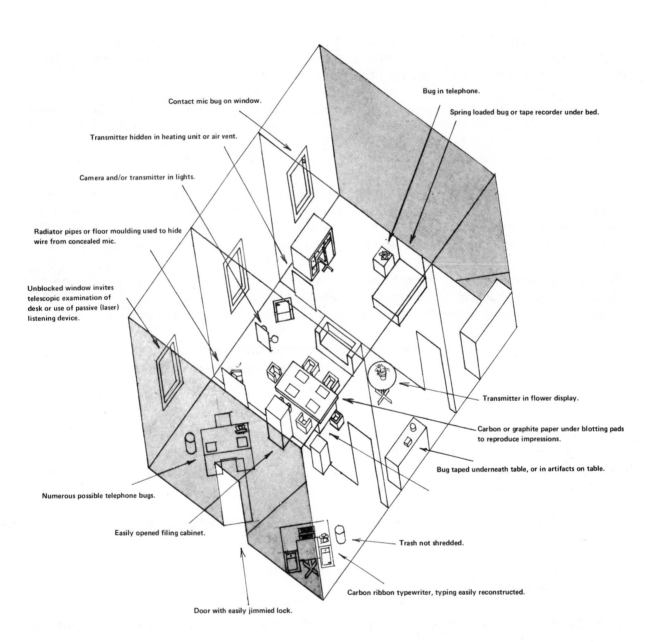

Contact mic bug on window.

Bug in telephone.

Spring loaded bug or tape recorder under bed.

Transmitter hidden in heating unit or air vent.

Camera and/or transmitter in lights.

Radiator pipes or floor moulding used to hide wire from concealed mic.

Unblocked window invites telescopic examination of desk or use of passive (laser) listening device.

Transmitter in flower display.

Carbon or graphite paper under blotting pads to reproduce impressions.

Bug taped underneath table, or in artifacts on table.

Numerous possible telephone bugs.

Easily opened filing cabinet.

Trash not shredded.

Carbon ribbon typewriter, typing easily reconstructed.

Door with easily jimmied lock.

PROFESSIONAL SWEEPING

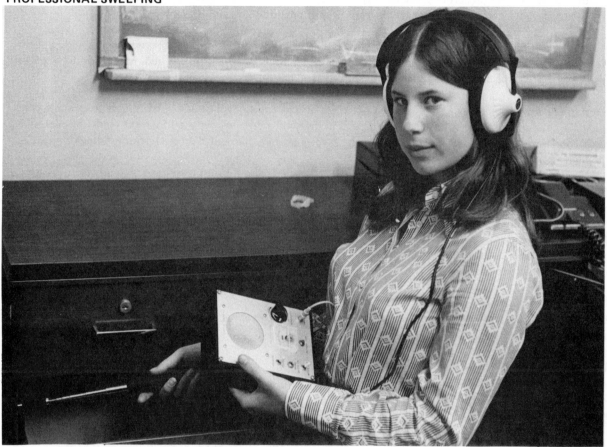

Photo courtesy of Communications Control Corp

A good professional sweep is really the only way to be 100% certain an office, or other area for that matter, is free of area or room bugs. With the proper equipment and techniques presented herein you can sweep your own areas, but it is often easier, and cheaper in the long run to have a pro do it for you.

There are a number of companies specializing in de-bugging; many were operating on the other side of the fence when bugging was more legal. Besides these large outfits, a number of private detectives and other individuals offer de-bugging services. Unfortunately many of this latter crowd do not have the proper equipment or knowledge to do a good job.

Remember, a good surveillance expert will often plant several bugs; the first one or two will be considered expendable and will be fairly easy to locate. The next ones will be the best units, and the hardest to find. Often the amateur or semi-pro will come up with the first bug and everyone (including the eavesdropper) will be happy.......

A good de-bugger should at least have a good telephone analyzer (Mason, CCC, Dektor, etc), a good RF detector or full spectrum receiver/analyzer (in fact, if he uses a RF detector, he should have some means of verification such as a broadband receiver), a number of small tools and back-up items including a metal detector, several screwdrivers and/or probes, possibly a high gain amplifier, etc.

The person doing the search should have a good knowledge of electronics, along with a state-of-the-art knowledge of bugging techniques and countermeasures. He should spend more time in a physical search of the premises than an automated electronic search. Be wary of anyone who comes in and pokes a wand around for a couple of hours and announces everything is quite in order.....

Who utilizes the services of a professional de-bugger? We talked with Mr. Jamil of Communications Control Corporation, a company which has been in the de-bugging business since 1948 about his clients.

"We have swept just about every type of business and individual. I would say the largest group of victims are people like attorneys, ad agencies, importers, political figures, etc. We have found bugs in just about every sort of business imaginable, if someone doesn't need our services in July, they need them in January.I

In one of our strangest cases, we were asked to sweep the office of the mayor of one of the largest cities in the US; he felt the chief of police might be bugging him. Within the same month we got a call from the chief of police asking for the same service—he felt the mayor's office might be bugging him. We ended up selling both of them protective equipment......

Most bugs we find are common, about 99% we have seen before and can just about tell where they came from. The most exotic sort of bug we find with any regularity is the infinity transmitter."

Mr. Jamil's observations seem to hold true with most of the professionals. Not every call finds a bug, and many times only the evidence of one can be located because people are geared to think of electronic surveillance lastly when considering a leak of information.

The other problem with a sweep is clean today does not mean clean tomorrow—a good de-bugger should be able to recommend security precautions as well as suggest countermeasure equipment IF SUCH A MEASURE IS JUSTIFIED, as part of his normal search procedure.

RECOMMENDED COMPANIES:

Communications Control Corporation-441 Lexington Ave, New York, New York 10017, 212-682-4637. CCC has been in the business for nearly 20 years (under a different name) and employs about 20 search teams in the NY area. They have teams in other areas of the country and will travel anywhere for expenses. CCC makes quite a bit of anti-tap equipment that is sold by other companies. Average search runs about $200 for a normal office, $300 for a large office, plus $60 for telephones and $80 for call directors.

Sound Security, Box 867, San Francisco, California 94101, 415-626-7742. SS consists of several federally licensed electronic engineers who operate anywhere in California (for travel expenses, of course). They use top equipment and charge about $200 for an office including a RF/Physical and telephone search. Phone searches without any premise search run $40 for a normal phone, $50 for a call director. Large offices, unusual areas by consultation. Search also includes a written report with suggestions for improving security and they will recommend or sell protective equipment. SS helped research and design several items for this book......

Mason Engineering-1700 Post Road, Fairfield, Connecticut 06430, 203-255-3461. Mason is a well respected firm which designs and sells anti-bugging equipment and conducts searches anywhere in the country through their numerous field offices. They work at a rate of $40 per man hour.

Dektor Counterintelligence and Security, Inc.-5508 Port Royal Road, Springfield, Va. 22151, 703-569-2900. Once again, Dektor designs and markets top countermeasure equipment as well as conducting searches. Price is by consultation.....

Western Electronic Control-Box 1562, Riverside, Ca. 92502. WEC handles CCC's protective equipment and also conducts searches. They average $300 for an office, with large offices running up to $500. Telephones are $75 per instrument, higher for the more complex models. Minimum fee is $800.

This list is by no means complete, if you decide to go elsewhere, use the guidelines presented herein to at least see you get your money's worth.......

WHERE'S JOHN MITCHELL WHEN WE NEED HIM?

Okay, let's say you're not all that electronically oriented, no Reddy Kilowatt, so to speak. . .How hard is it for you to get a professional to do a bugging job for you?

Three University of California students; Tima Farmy, John Schwada and Albert Thompson, decided to find out. First they approached those who would possibly have the most contact with professional surveillance; private detectives.

The students interviewed a number of Bay Area private eyes and surveillance engineers who are known to have participated in electronic surveillance when it was still legal. From these talks, and from their own sources, the students put together a video tape on the subject of bugging.

Several facts quickly emerged from the interviewing; all the former "buggers" were now into "counter-surveillance", i.e. finding the bugs they once planted. None of them admitted they still had anything to do with illegal surveillance. (Although a couple hedged a bit pretty visibly, and one Freudian slipped when discussing a foray and said, "on our last bugging, er, ah, de-bugging mission.....").

All of the de-buggers stressed the fact that they qualified prospective customers in an attempt to weed out the obvious paranoids, and only accepted those jobs which might bear fruit. The number of clean sweeps against the number of finds appeared to run about 6 to 1. . .

So there actually were some bugs being planted. Who then were the guilty parties now that all the private eyes, who had previously done these things were, by their own admission, not doing so anymore?

The students went to the head the private detective license bureau in the Golden State and posed this paradox to him.

Admittedly, this was an area that concerned him, however, he did not feel any California private eyes were still into illegal surveillance.

Dammit all, who was placing all these mysterious bugs? In order to throw some light on the subject, one of the students created a hypothetical situation; he suddenly became a vice president of a small consulting firm. The firm was bothered by a problem - they had been losing bids to a competitor at an alarming rate, often at very narrow margins. So narrow as to give rise to the possibility that information might be leaking out. Now, the hypothetical competitor was about to have a conference with a government official and the "vice-president" wished to know what went on during said conference, and the resulting bid, if any. How to go about it?

Well, the student simply opened the let-your-fingers-do-the-walking-Yellow Pages and began dialing private detectives at random explaining the situation, but never hinting at any possible solutions.

After 6 such random calls in San Francisco and 6 in Oakland, a private detective, in both cases, over the phone to a person he had never even met, offered to commit a felony and bug the room and furnish the student with a complete transcript of the meeting........

FIELD STRENGTH METERS

One of the stock-in-trade items for the pest controller is the field strength meter. This is simply a crystal radio set (ah, brings back memories, eh - what?) connected to a meter. It "listens" for any radio signals and registers them on the meter.

Field strength meters are an easily purchased commercial item as they are used to check ham and CB radios. For our use, it is necessary to cover all surfaces in the area to be checked from a distance of a foot or so, watching for the tell-tale meter swing. Indications can be followed to the source of the signal.

Couple of problems crop up with the FS meters: They pick up ALL signals, including commercial stations, nearby transmitters, etc., without differentiating. Now, you can figure our little bug is not going to show up well in competition with the local 50,000-watt teeny-bop radio station.

This problem can somewhat be eliminated by the use of a tunable FS meter. In this fashion, each particular band of frequencies can be checked out and spurious ones avoided.

If you are planning this approach, be sure and get an FS meter with at least one stage of amplification for those weak signals.

RECEIVER

Another method is to take a sensitive radio receiver that covers ALL POSSIBLE BANDS from 30 up through 120, including commercial FM bands of 88-108. Now one can perform a feedback-squeal search.

First turn the volume of the receiver up HIGH. Now walk around the room slowly and begin tuning the receiver up through all the bands. At the same time you must have a source of noise in the room. One of the better approaches is known as the "singing investigator" approach. For those of us who are a bit more on the mundane side, counting also suffices.

If there is a bug operating in the near vicinity, a loud howl will emanate mysteriously from your receiver as you hit its frequency. The howl is simply the feedback loop between the receiver and the bug manifesting itself. You can then follow the howl to the source by noting the volume increases as you walk around.

If you do not have a good all-band FM receiver, you can still get a pretty effective search by using harmonics. Every transmitter puts out a primary signal on one frequency, say, in our case, 46 mcs. At the same time, smaller signals are put out on double,(92) triple, (128) etc., frequencies. The harmonics decrease in power as you go up, but will still suffice for a close search into the second, and often third levels.

As you can see, a bug operating below the commercial band will often have a secondary or third harmonic level within these bands, so a careful search pattern with a sensitive commercial FM receiver will often uncover the culprit, even if it lies out of range of the receiver's circuits.

THREE COMMON BUG DETECTORS

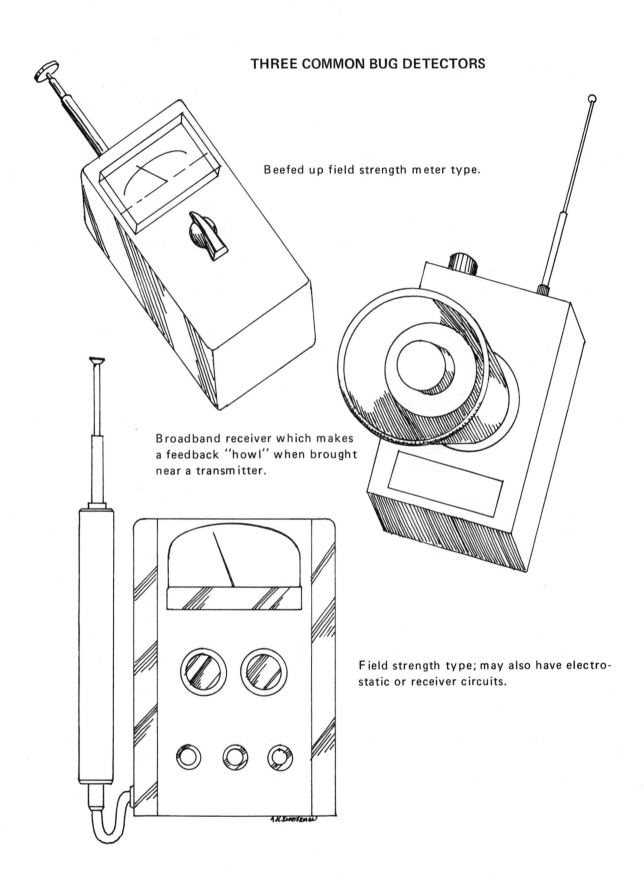

Beefed up field strength meter type.

Broadband receiver which makes
a feedback "howl" when brought
near a transmitter.

Field strength type; may also have electro-
static or receiver circuits.

A wider range can be gotten by turning your TV set (which has an FM audio section) to Channel 2, turning the volume down and then sweeping the fine tuning from one side to the other while maintaining your room noise component.

If you do run across a bug, your room noise will show up as a jagged line across the picture tube. Verify it by yelling and watch the line jump with your sudden noise.

Be sure and use only your inside antenna when doing this sort of thing. If the set is not so equipped, put a pair of rabbit-ears onto the antenna jacks.

All US TV bands are 6 mz in width. If one starts at Channel 2 and goes to 6, one will hit 54 to 88 mz. At 7, it jumps to 174 mz, so if you continue up to 13, you get 174 to 216 covered. If you have UHF, you can get 470 to 890 by careful tuning. While this does not hit each and every one, it does a good job of getting most of the bands and/or harmonic possibilities.

A final device is a metal detector, such as those used to find "buried treasure" and advertised in the classified sections of most hobby magazines. They can be swept over walls and will indicate if metal is present therein. Now, they won't tell you exactly what kind of metal, mind you, nor will they tell between a large nail and a small microphone, but they can be valuable for spike mics and deeply buried bugs. Metal detectors can be rented at various rental agencies.

FINDING THE CULPRIT

If you do find a bug, you may wish to know who put it there. If it is a wired bug, simply follow wires and stake out the recording point.

If a wireless little devil is uncovered, you must decide where the receiver is located. Remember - most bugs have a very limited range of a few hundred feet, and this can be dropped down considerably by concrete walls, steel reinforcing rods, etc. A wise bugger will locate his receiver as near as possible to the actual bug to insure best reception.

With this in mind, make a check out of the surrounding area. Many times a receiver-recorder-VOX combination will be left under a newspaper or coat, inside a locked, parked car directly outside of the bugged area.

Unfortunately, there is no practical method for electronically finding the receiver at this time.

The other alternative is to stake out the bug until the SOB returns to replace the battery or pick up his bug. Of course, there is not guarantee he is going to do that.

Another problem is the fact that the bugger may hear you searching for his device and may vacate the premises before you arrive on the scene. This is one reason the singing technique is preferred over the counting technique . . . . . .

COUNTERMEASURES

There are a few counter measures which you can employ if you suspect you are the probable victim of a bug. If you can judge the most likely direction for the bug, you can direct a stream of covering noise towards it. A loud radio aimed at a possible hidden mic, or spike mic will often completely drown out any other noise in the room by sheer volume.

If you are unsure of the most probable direction, a covering noise will often help mess up conversation. The normal tricks are electric fans, running water, record players, etc. A microphone will not discriminate between noises, it simply records the loudest noise loudest, and so on. However, as we know, if both the conversation and a cover noise are audible on the tape, the good bugger may be able to filter out the covering noise. For this reason, it may be preferable to utilize a noise in the same frequency range as the human voice, say radio or TV talk show would be an ideal choice.

It is also possible to jam radio bugs by employing a hash transmitter. This is simply a wide band radio transmitter that puts out a large amount of white noise, or simply static. This will effectively overpower and render useless any low-powered transmitters in the vicinity. It may also cause extreme interference in your neighbor's TV or radio and is strictly illegal.

There is one other possibility. I have included plans for a jamming device that will make almost anything with a microphone box inoperative for some distance around the user. This device creates a set of two, high-frequency, noises that cause microphones to vibrate rapidly at a differential frequency. Proper use of this device should knock out tape recorders and all other mics by producing a loud squeal in the receiver or amplifier. This device will also mess up telephone microphones and hearing aids to the same degree, so it becomes useless over the phone (more than useless, it will jar the hell out of the guy on the other end) or when talking to hearing-aided persons.

It is a fairly good way to jam most other devices, however, and can easily be constructed small enough to mount on one's person.

The most effective countermeasure, bar none, is, of course, to not discuss important things. Second to carrying a note paper around with you at all times, must come simply watching where you say what.

To counter the use of spike mics, hollow tube mics, laser mics, and shotgun or parabolic concentrators it is only necessary to affix a noise generator to the "sounding board". The easiest way to accomplish this is to tape a transistor radio directly to the window, or wall and turn the volume UP.

A more sophisticated approach is to attach a buzzer or vibrator, directly to the glass (or wall). This will vibrate the surface and effectively block all response from other noise.

TELEPHONE CARTRIDGE (DROP-IN)
STAKEOUT TRANSMITTER

This transmitter was designed for pay telephones and for quick installation. It can be used on any telephone and can be installed in 10 seconds. It requires no battery as its power is taken from the telephone. It looks like an ordinary telephone cartridge. It is the same basic transmitter and can be used as a replacement on our Unit No. 121-581 which is illustrated on page 121 of this catalog.

Cat. No. 127-597 . . . .$189.00

"ROOM-BUG" MINIATURE TRANSMITTER

This all new palm size miniature transmitter was designed exclusively for "Room-Bugging". Unit comes complete with battery and antenna. It is the same basic transmitter and can be used as a replacement on our Unit No. 120-579 which is illustrated on page 120 of this catalog.

Cat. No. 127-595 . . . .$138.00

TELEPHONE STAKEOUT IN-LINE TRANSMITTER

This miniature high powered unit was designed for "phone-tapping" without batteries. It is powered by the telephone line and therefore will transmit indefinitely. It is the same basic transmitter and can be used as a replacement on our Unit No. 121-580 which is illustrated on page 121 of this catalog.

Cat. No. 127-596 . . . .$169.00

Some fine examples of your average, run-of-the-mill commercial bugs.....................................

This tiny "chip" is connected up to any pair of wires, such as an unused phone pair (or used, for that matter) where it will pick up all conversation within a 50 foot radius, encode it to where if an amplifier or anaylzer is connected to the wires in an audio search it will hear nothing but some random sounding "white noise", and send it up to 25 miles. At this point a small "black box" decodes the noise and produces audio. The power source is supplied from the receiving unit.

This unit was developed by a company called Fox, reportedly under the auspices of a government contract. Fox is no longer active due to the death of a partner, but was also reportedly working on laser bugs for one or more government agencies. The above de-activated unit is owned by Communications Control Corporation.

THE BEST?

BERTSCHE ELECTRONICS LABORATORY, 1475 Bush St., San Francisco, Ca. 94109. Mr. Bertsche operates from this innocuous looking little building where he designs (ed?) some of the finest surveillance gear in the world. Mr. Bertsche reportedly worked for many of the big names in the surveillance business including the likes of Hal Lipset, other private eyes, a police supplier or two and possibly a government agency or two. He has designed some fantastic equipment and was one of the pioneers in the field with such items as the infinity transmitter. Reportedly he still does custom design work on devices which could have a legal application, and works as a counter sweeper for several private eyes. He will not mail a catalog, and does not like to talk to writers..................

MASTER ELECTRONIC INTELLIGENCE INVESTIGATION OUTFIT

Eavesdropping!　　**Wire Tapping!**　　**Room-Bugging!**

Espionage!　　　　　　　　　　　**Counter Espionage!**

Surveillance!　　　**De-Bugging!**　　**Telephone Stakeout!**

Secret Recordings!　　　　　　　**Undercover Intelligence!**

Crystal Controlled

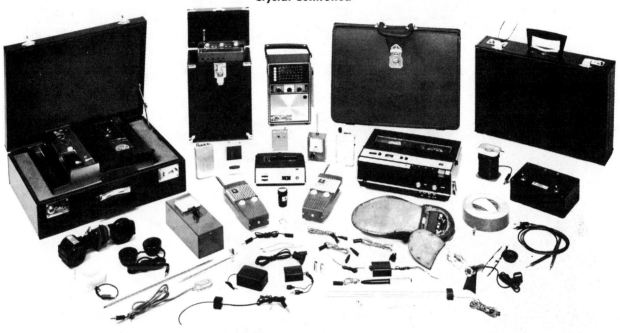

COMPLETE UNIT CONSISTS OF

Accessory carrying case

Leather briefcase

Pocket size amplifier with volume control & recording output

Batteries, for all portable equipment

Undercover earphones, hearing aid type

Direct recording cable for amplifier

Telephone eavesdropper unit

1 high power long range transmitter

1 A.C. transmitter power supply

1 Telephone stakeout attachment

1 medium range room-bug transmitter

1 medium range telephone-tap transmitter

Crystal controlled transmitter

Crystal controlled receiver

Telephone "Drop-In" transmitter

1 pocket size battery operated receiver

1 high power battery operated receiver

Tape recorder, long play voice-actuated battery operated

Secret attache case with built-in hidden microphone & switch

Complete set of accessories for battery operated tape recorder

Complete set of installation tools, including coils of wire, tape, etc.

Hand held crystal recording microphones

In-line telephone stakeout transmitter

Broom transmitter, w/broom

Telephone terminal test lamp kit

Undercover police pocket, long play 5-hour recorder, w/microphone

Complete set of accessories for undercover pocket recorder

Minox undercover camera, complete

Butinsky telephone unit

Wall spike contact eavesdropping unit w/spikes & bracket

The ferret transmitter locator

The squealer microphone locator

2 deluxe long range walkie-talkie units, complete

Group listening loudspeaker for all portable equipment

Pocket volt meter

Recording tape eraser

Two-way adhesive tape

Transmitter testing meter

Recording tapes for all recorders

Standard headphones

Conference microphone

Hollow tube microphone

Keyhole microphone

Windowpane microphone

Postage stamp microphone

Fingernail microphone

Fountain pen microphone

Shoe heel transmitter, w/shoes

Cat. No. 142-633 ....**$3,995.00**

What do you do if you're a police department with $4,000 and no surveillance equipment? Waste all that time pouring through catalogs? Make lists and lists? Hell no, you just order CRP's Master Electronic Intelligence Investigation Outfit.......

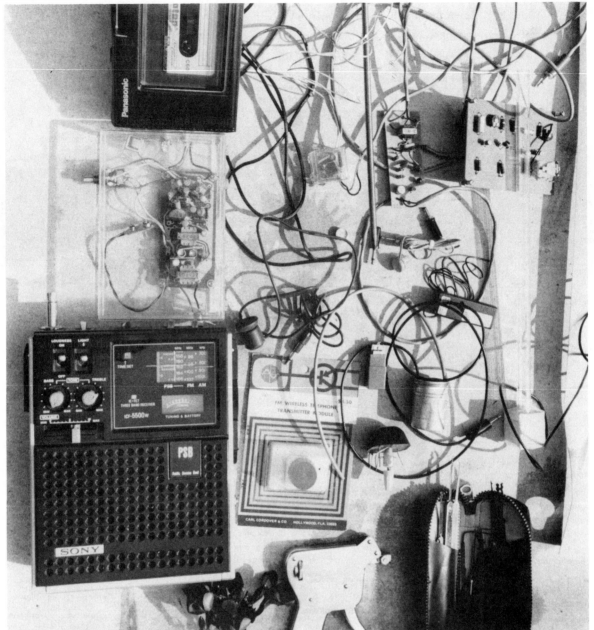

HOBOY! In the best Madison Avenue tradition, we are proud to present, complete with a cast of thousands, the new and improved BIG BROTHER GAME CHEAPO SPY KIT. Just think, for under $500, and with no electronic skills beyond simple connect wire A to tab B, you can stick your nose where it doesn't belong with the best of them....

Contents: Panasonic cassette recorder, phone line matching tap, auto start device (Tele-Secretary), VOX, handy-dandy mini-amplifier, contact mic and spike, thin and thick tube mics, AMC Sales mini-transmitter, Cordover phone conference broadcaster module, Cordover TV module, micro-switch for "weight start" of recorder, several mini-mics, sensitive hi/low and FM receiver, assorted wire, patch cords and matching plugs.

To help in your placement of above items we are also including; lock pick set, Lock-Aid gun, and a car shim tool or two. Good luck, don't mention this book if you're busted, I don't even want to KNOW about it...........

*Also small bunch of flowers

DUE IN PART, to the overwhelming response we got on our BIG BROTHER GAME CHEAPO SPY KIT, we are hereby including a BIG BROTHER GAME NOT SO CHEAP SPY KIT. Now you're in the big leagues kid, these devices DO require some construction, but the circuits come right out of our own circuit section. If you do not have the necessary knowwhat to put them together, any friendly or bribable electronics student, or good TV type repairman can do it for you.

This kit is too be used in conjunction with our first kit and includes: long range rifle mic, phone transmitter, drop-in phone transmitter, Minox C camera, binoculars, infinity transmitter, condenser mic, mini-transmitter, 5 watt pulsed transmitter, carrier switch, rigged briefcase, Minox-to-binocular attattchment, induction coil with amplifier that can be hooked to transmitter, wall socket transmitter (can also be in extension plug outlet), etc.

Besides these you should have the necessary paraphernalia for installing (double sided tape [Scotchgaurd is best], field strength meter, tuning wands, screwdriver, and so on). This whole set-up will cost maybe $700-$1,000 as opposed to at least $5,000 or more if purchased from a law enforcement supplier........
(*rifle mic wouldn't fit...one editor using binoculars to look at girl down block; substituted flowers...)

TELEPHONE SURVEILLANCE

"Margruder says he and Mitchell nixed Liddy's plans to shanghai radicals and bugged-call-girls plans, but they did indulge in most of his other inspirations.........White House aides Egil Krogh and Gordon Strachen reportedly did their best to smooth Liddy's plans. Nixon's special counsel, Colson, who reportedly organized a Homosexuals for McGovern campaign, called to say the White House wanted a tap installed on Democratic National Chairman Larry O'Brien's phone because he was causing trouble about the ITT mess..."

WIRETAPPING

The telephone is always a favorite target for the potential spy as it provides access to a capsule summary of many important decisions and transactions. It also offers a number of easy tap-in points which may not even necessitate premise trespass, and are generally harder to discover.

Numerous devices have been marketed by professional bugging suppliers to tap the telephone, and in some cases, even utilize the telephone as a room bug when not transmitting phone conversations.

Literally thousands of these devices which could be installed by almost anyone, were sold prior to the great surveillance scare laws. Access to commercial devices of this type is now pretty much limited to law enforcement bodies, although there is un undeniable blackmarket for "radio repairmen specials".

Common "conference line broadcasters" sold for as little as $30 from the schlock "private eye" suppliers in the late 60's, while a top law enforcement counterpart brings a couple of hundred bills from the more viably financed police and investigative departments.

The state of the art is such in wiretapping that it is possible to buy (or build, as a point of reference we have included plans for just such a device ......) such exotic taps as the microphone which drops into the handset in as long of a time as it takes to unscrew the cap, looks identical to the regular microphone, and broadcasts both sides of the conversation (using the phone's own electrical power) to a nearby FM radio.

Another popular exotic is the famed "infinity transmitter"; a small, cube-shaped device which hooks into the phone and just lies there, hibernating, one might say, until the phone is dialed 'from an outside line (anywhere in the world - as long as it is direct dialing) and a small whistle blown into the mouthpiece of the dialing phone.

Upon "hearing" this sound the infinity transmitter stops the parent phone from ringing, and turns on the phone's own carbon microphone or uses its own to broadcast the room's sounds over the phone line to the listening whistle-blower.

This device was a popular (for those of us who had $400 to blow on such things) gimmick for traveling businessmen who had an extension phone in the bedroom where their wife slept . . . . A quick call from any port would let the listener know exactly what was transpiring in his absence.

In phone tapping, much as in most forms of surveillance, the key is the same: keep it simple and direct. The less complicated a system, the better the chance of success.

DIRECT TAPS

Phone tapping falls into two general categories; direct, meaning an actual electrical contact from the phone or line, to the listening post, or wireless, this latter being a combination of a phone tap and a mini-transmitter.

Direct taps are the easiest, and often the best. The quickest method of tapping into a phone is simply to locate a good point along the phone line, strip away the insulating cable to expose the four enclosed wires, disregard the ground wire (see the counter-wiretapping section for explicit

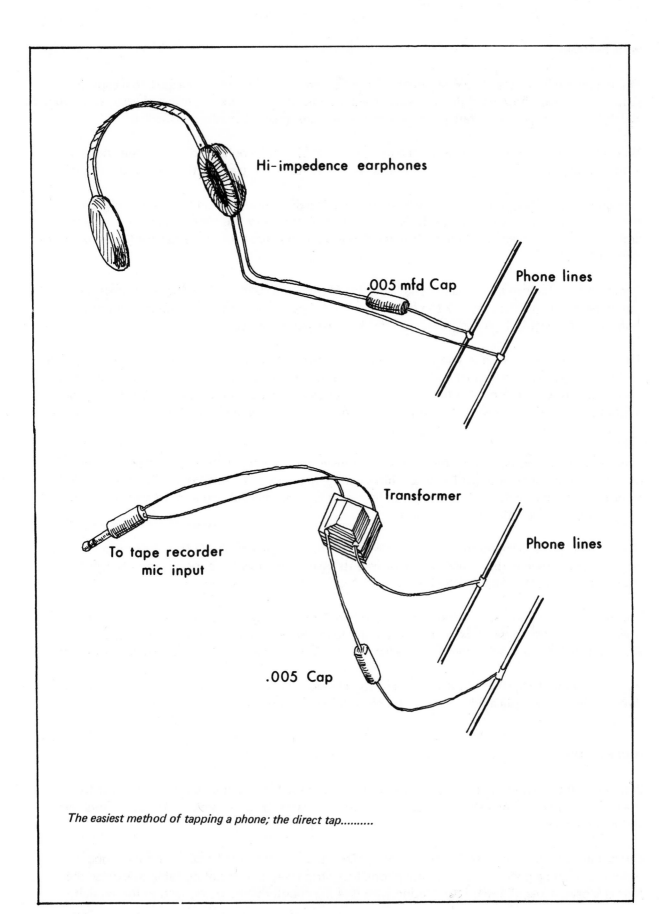

Hi-impedence earphones

.005 mfd Cap

Phone lines

Transformer

To tape recorder
mic input

Phone lines

.005 Cap

The easiest method of tapping a phone; the direct tap..........

instructions on this procedure) strip away a small piece of insulation on the two hot (red and green) wires WITHOUT CUTTING THE WIRES, and attach a set of high impedance headphones. One side of the phones is directed through a small .005 mfd capacitor to keep out the 48 volt phone power.

With this simple set-up, the bugger simply has to go listen on the headphones whenever a call is made on the instrument in question. The disadvantages to this system include spending most of one's spare time waiting for the phone to be used and then rushing to the garage every time it happens . . . it is often difficult to explain one's presence when discovered in such situations.

The next logical step up the ladder of progressive involvement is to add a small inter-stage transformer along with the capacitor as shown. The primary of the transformer should be at least 10,000 ohms (but not more than 20,000) to match the phone lines' high impedance, the secondary should be of a near value to the equipment it is going into (about 200 ohms for most mini-tape recorders).

This set up provides a clear passageway for the audio (conversation) to pass through, while not loading the phone line. This "not-loading" is a real factor to consider, as a draw of over 20 mills or so might trip the central exchanges relay (trips around 40 milliamps) and send a phone repairman scurrying to the scene of the crime.

This output can now be fed directly into a tape recorder, eliminating the crouching-at-the-phone syndrome. However, one must still endeavor to turn the recorder on and off at the proper moments, a task sometimes easier said than done.

To eliminate this final problem, one adds a tiny bit of sophistication; the drop-out relay. This is a small device that senses the condition of the phone line in question, and, through the remote start feature found on most modern tape recorders, turns the recorder on when the phone is lifted off of it's cradle. This, of course, limits the waste of tape, and needs attention only when it is necessary to turn over or install more tape.

Another, more esoteric value of this set-up is the fact that it is most probably the kind of thing used to tape record all the calls made out of the White House. Now, this in no way reflects on the quality of the recordings obtained, with a bit of care one would not find any unexplained gaps in the tape . . . .

There are several types of drop-out relays, we have shown two of the most popular; one cheap and simple, which can be lost without too much pain (but may require a bit more work to get operating perfectly) and one more sophisticated, transistorized sensing relay.

It is possible to employ any of these methods at any point along the "pair", either as it leaves the phone, before the surge protector, on the drop cable running to the telephone pole, or at the terminal or junction boxes located on the pole or in the building garage or basement.

NEAR DIRECT

There is one other form of almost direct tap - the induction pick-up. These can be commercially purchased in electronics shops for a couple of bucks and are designed to be fed into a home tape recorder. They have a few important limitations: they must be physically attached to the phone, usually on the base near the sidetone coil, to work properly, and also the volume level is not the best, and they are subject to AC hum from nearby electric devices.

A bug, whether a transmitter or a direct connection, may be installed almost anywhere from the telephone instrument itself, along the line, or at the junction or terminal box.

Certain procedures must be followed. If it is installed at a terminal box, such as one in the basement of an apartment building or office, the correct pair of jacks must be located. There exists a couple of ways to go about finding this pair. If you know, or suspect the subscriber is using his telephone at the time of installation, you can take an earphone, or telephone handset, isolate it with the usual capacitor/transformer as described herein, terminate it with a pair of alligator clips. Now place one clip of one side of the pair of jacks, wet your finger with "lineman's helper" (spit) and place your finger on the opposite jack. Now place your other clip on the wet part of your finger towards the jack. The conversation will gradually become audible somewhere along the line. If you wish to install the clip, keep sliding slowly until the clip is attached. This will eliminate all clicking noises in the subscriber's phone.

If you do not feel he/she/it is home, and have to make a decision as to which jacks, or wires, are his/her/its; have a fellow conspirator dial the number and let it ring; now you can do several things, depending on your bravery, skill and bankroll. The easiest method is to wet both fingers and run them down the jacks, lo and behold, you will "notice" the ringing voltage when you run across it. A half dollar run down until sparks are seen will do the same thing with less "notice". A real classy approach is to connect a 100K resistor in series with a neon bulb. Actually, for real class, a whole set of these little gems can be wired together. Now one side is attached to one jack, the other to the other jack. When a ringing voltage is applied, the jack receiving it will cause the lamp to light and stay lit.

In most parts of the country, it is possible to dial a special number (San Francisco is 640, Colorado 1-200-555-1212, 958 or 311 in the NY area, etc.) a friendly phone co-employee can let you in on your area's little secret. Then one simply connects on hand-dandy line set, or even purloined phone (with the bell disconnected) to the jack, dials the test number, and gets the phone number read off of a computer back to one.

Some transmitters (or even simple taps) are capacitively-coupled by wrapping the leads of the devices around the phone pair, one side at a time, until several inches are covered with one's coil. A high gain amp or pre-amped transmitter will sometimes lift the voice right out of the wire . . . . .

Another effort that requires a bit more sophistication is simply to flood the phone with a rf (radio frequency) signal by sending a large dose of it down the one pair of phone lines. Theoretically, some rf will leak through, be modulated by room noise, leak back into the microphone and travel down the outgoing pair where it can be picked up by a suitable receiver and translated back into speech.

This process has worked under test conditioning and may be in service on a limited basis, but it is by no means fool proof.

The telephone instrument itself can be used as a microphone by any number of simple alterations (the addition of the infinity transmitter being the most common). Any of these alterations will allow the bugger to listen to room conversation when the phone is on the hook, but will NOT pass on phone conversations. To use any of these methods, the bugger simply connects a sensitive amplifier anywhere on the phone line.

A. The most common is to place a resistor ACROSS the hook switch (this is the switch activated by the placing of the phone on the cradle). This resistor must be fairly low as not to throw the trip relay in the central station. This set-up allows a bit of current to trickle through the microphone and activate it, sending the conversation down the line much as an ordinary phone call will do, albeit at a lower level.

B. A capacitor can be installed across one side of the hookswitch allowing a bit of audio to pass on by, but keeping the DC current where it belongs.

C. A SCR (silicon controlled rectifier) can be placed across the hook switch; a high voltage (say, around 100 volts) will now short out the hook switch, however, it may also burn up some of the phone equipment. A suitable sized diode can also be used for this application.

D. A tone activated latching relay can be used to short it out upon command.

In ALL of the above applications, ONE side of the double pole hook switch must be shorted out, leaving the open side to accept your short-upon-command device.

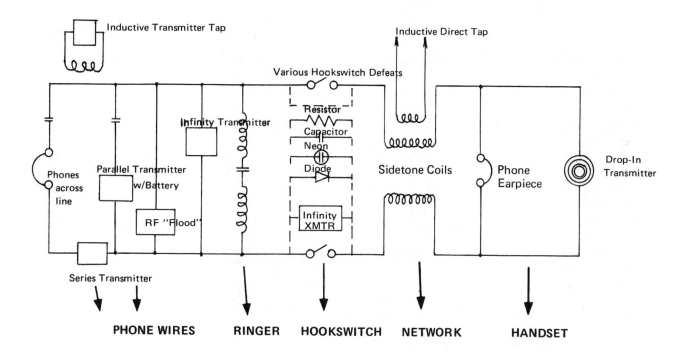

Terminal box showing exposed pair terminals. Usually located at the rear of an office or basement of an apartment building. This is a favorite spot for wiretaps of all types.

51

COAST TO COAST "ROOM-BUG" TRANSMITTER

"TRANSISTORIZED"

"FIRST TIME OFFERED"

The Coast to Coast Transmitter is a combination microphone amplifier, switching device and transmitter, housed in one case, that is capable of picking up conversations within a 30 foot radius of its' placement and transmitting this information directly over telephone lines for unlimited distances. This is done without disturbing the actual use of the telephone.

- One of the greatest advances in miniaturized electronics
- All solid-state for the utmost in reliability and dependable performance
- Installs in less than 90 sec. inside the phone or away from the phone
- No radio transmission . . . it is practically-powered . . . no batteries required
- Phone-to-Phone between any 2 points in any one country
- Does not interfere with normal phone operation

The Coast to Coast Transmitter is connected anywhere on the phone line, inside or outside of the premises under surveillance. With an extension microphone connected, the unit can be concealed anywhere as only the microphone need be on the premises.

In use, the Coast to Coast Transmitter is connected to the phone of the suspect's apartment, home, or place of business. The operator can then go to any telephone, pay booth, or otherwise, dial the phone number in question, and with his remote activator, activate the phone under surveillance so that it answers itself AUTOMATICALLY, WITHOUT RINGING. When this is done, the operator can now listen in on the conversation taking place in the suspect's premises. The Coast to Coast Transmitter, unlike any other transmitter, can actually be used for Coast to Coast Surveillance.

The Coast to Coast Transmitter has all the features you can expect. Trouble free reliability, excellent performance and high sensitivity.

Size of unit is 2" x 1½" x ¾". Weight is 1½ Ounces.

NOTE: THIS **IS NOT** A TELEPHONE TAP UNIT. IT SIMPLY USES THE TELEPHONE LINE TO CARRY THE ROOM CONVERSATION FROM WHERE IT IS PLANTED TO THE LISTENING POST WHICH IS ANYWHERE IN THE COUNTRY FROM WHICH THE OPERATOR MADE THE UNIT ACTIVATE.

COAST TO COAST TRANSMITTER COMES COMPLETE WITH ACTIVATOR & INSTRUCTIONS

Cat. No. 125-585 . . . .$595.00

Here it is, the infamous "infinity transmitter", as sold by Criminal Research Products. Notice how much it acts like the various "phone burglar alarms" on the market today........

A way around some of these limitations is to hide the induction coil in some little object (desk blotter, pen set, etc.) that may be placed near the phone, and then employ a small, direct coupled amplifier to beef-up the weak signals. In this manner, the induction pick-up becomes a bit more practical as it and the amplifier (and in some cases, tape recorder) can be concealed in a drawer under the phone, or in a nearby artifact.

Commercial hidden induction units are sold by the usual law enforcement suppliers cleverly secreted in such things as fake flowers (which only reinforces my natural dislike for plastic flowers) desk blotters, picture frames, etc.

The unit we have shown will function in this manner and will also work if placed near the side tone coil of an extension phone, even though the extension phone is still lying peacefully in its cradle.

It is also possible to use a powerful induction tap near the phone line, but a real beefy amp must be employed and this sort of thing never works out quite like the spy movies would have us believe: be practical, stick to direct routes when possible.

WIRELESS

The other approach to the problem of not knowing what is said over your neighbor's phone is to secrete a small transmitter in the phone, or along the line, which broadcasts the conversation to a nearby receiver/tape recorder as covered in the wireless surveillance section.

TELEPHONE TAP DETECTION

Only the most amateurish wire tapper would betray his (or her) presence by producing spurious noises, i.e., "clicks" on a telephone line while in use. Most line noise is a naturally occurring phenomenon which does not indicate the presence of a third party on the conversation.

Therefore, bug fighting requires more than a mere surface understanding of the game. To begin the process, one should have more than a passing grasp of the dear old telephone company itself . . . . .

Telephone exchanges use a 48-volt DC power to operate their equipment. The phone is rung by inserting an AC ringing voltage of about 20 cycles. The central telco office contains a series of frames wherein each subscribers wires are attached to a set of contacts and a system of relays.

Your instrument is basically a microphone/earphone combination, a bell, a large coil (near the base of the phone) known as a sidetone coil, and a relay.

When the phone is on the hook, this relay is open. When you lift the receiver up from its cradle, the relay contacts are closed (in effect you are just closing a switch). When you dial, this relay is opened and closed a number of times. The central relay reads this series of openings and closings and then connects you to the proper set of contacts to reach the number you are dialing.

When your wire leaves the main office, it is in a cable containing many similar wires, or "pairs" (it takes two wires for every phone). This cable comes to your pole where it goes into junction box, and then to your house or apartment. When the pair reaches your residence, it comes to a device known as a surge protector. At this surge protector a third wire is added. This third wire is in the middle of the other two and is the ground wire. For most de-bugging applications we are not concerned with this middle wire.

From the surge protector the three wires run into your telephone. A number of bugging devices can be utilized in just about any of the aforementioned areas to record and/or transmit your phone conversations, and sometimes even room conversations.

TYPES OF BUGS

One of the most common types of bugs for the teley is the line powered parallel bug. This type of bug draws its power directly from the line and radiates a constant signal, whether the phone is in use or not. Its major advantage is lack of batteries (it can conceivably run for years). Its major disadvantages are: the constant signal makes it easier to detect, and the current it draws can often be measured.

This unit can be installed anywhere on the phone line (even on the pole) or in the phone itself. Although the in-the-phone-mounting is considerably harder to effect due to limited access, it has the advantage of only operating when the phone is in use.

This type of bug can also be battery powered. This means a better range, and less chance of detection, but a much shorter life, or battery replacement at selected intervals.

A series bug is even more common. This unit requires the installer to actually cut the phone wire (rather than just attaching as the parallel bug) and install the unit, but it only works when the telephone is in use, and does not load the phone line at all when the phone is not in use, meaning the chances of the phone company detecting it are considerably smaller.

By utilizing a phone induction pick-up (purchased at tape recorder stores for a couple of bucks) a bugger can actually tap a phone without any installation other than proper placement. The problems here are that the pick-up should be placed near the side tone of the phone itself (or an extension phone) and the output must be amplified before recording or transmitting. This type of tap is also much more likely to pick up hum and be generally hard to understand.

The commonest method of phone tapping is to simply connect a set of high impedance earphone through a capacitor onto the phone lines, or add a matching transformer and go right into a tape recorder. This set up will record both sides of a phone conversation with amazing clarity. If a drop-out relay is added (or a voice operated relay) to the tape recorder, it will only operate when a call is being made, thereby conserving tape and power.

There are a number of things one can do to help eliminate the chances of phone conversations being overheard by outside parties. These range from the simple, and as one might expect, up through the very complicated. The chances of detection increase with the complexity, BUT if the bugging is a fairly amateurish (non-FBI, that is to say) job, a few simple approaches will probably turn it up.

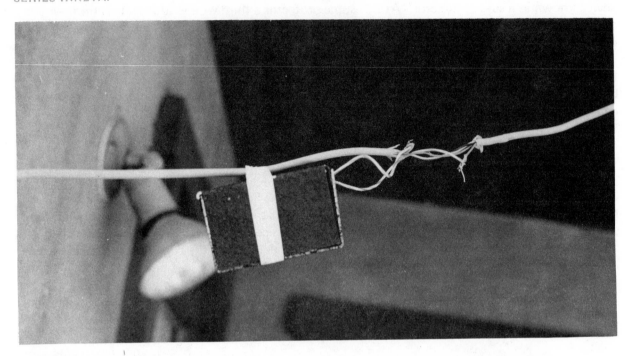

These two photos show a series type (line powered) bug in place on a phone line and also installed inside the instrument itself. In the first application the tap turns on when the phone is in use, transmitting all calls 1-2 blocks. In the second application the bug has been designed to act as a "third wire" type bug as well as a phone tap. When the phone is NOT in use it uses its own mic to pick up all room conversation and transmit it, when the phone is picked up, it acts as a normal wiretap.

This type is quite popular with law enforcement agencies as it gives double the pleasure, double the fun.....

Two Cordover modules ready-to-bug. The first (FMT-1) is hooked up to a pick-up coil and battery and ready to be dropped inside of a phone, or placed next to an extension phone. Second is their FMM-2 Wireless Mic module with microphone and battery ready-to-go....The range is limited to a hundred feet or so (adding wire to the antenna lead increases this a bit but lowers the frequency, if you're brave you can try doubling the battery power for a added kick also), the batteries last about 80 hours, but for a $5 bill (give or take $1.00) you're in the business, not bad, say what?

PHONE COMPANY

The Phone Company will help to some degree (assuming they are not the ones doing the bugging - Ma Bell has done more than her share of this sort of thing, either for her own records or by leasing equipment and lines to law enforcement agencies . . . . .)

If a bug draws more than 40 milliamps of current it will automatically trip the central office relay, alerting Ma to some problem which needs the attention of a repairman, however, no pro or even semi-pro is going to install anything that will eat up this kind of power. You can call the phone company and ask them to run a check on your line for possible bugging and they will run a current check (anything over a 1 milliamp loss makes them suspicious) and listen for hum, unusual crosstalk, or other alarming symptoms. A simple check like this will often do the job . . . and best of all, it's free.

Telephone company will also often dispatch a special investigator to check out a line in person. If a tap is discovered, the telco will remove it, restoring the customer's privacy, but will not help in finding, or the possible prosecution of the tapper(s).

If the tap does not trespass on telco property (i.e. an inductive tap) they may not even wish to re-move it, but will show it to you or refer you to local law enforcement bodies, assuming LOCAL LAW ENFORCEMENT BODIES DID NOT PLACE THE TAP . . . . . THE PHONE COMPANY WILL NOT FINK ON ITSELF OR LEGAL, "AUTHORIZED" AGENCIES. . . . .

Whether you elect to utilize the services of the friendly phone company or not, you should also plan on a self-search. This is done by examining the phone and its wires with a deft hand. Start with the wires. . . . .

Trace your phone wire to its wall plug and then from there throughout the basement, or wherever to the surge protector. See another little wire attached along the way and running into boxes or cabinets? Anything placed against the wire that could be a tap? Check out your "pair" into the junction box if possible (this is especially easy if you live in an apartment where the junction box can be quickly located). Any funny little wires or little gizmos hooked onto your pair? Also read bugging section to familarize yourself with the possibilities.

INVOLVED

If you have any slim knowledge of electronics or feel you can follow directions well, there are a couple of more advanced tests you can run:

1. Get a field strength meter or good receiver and follow the procedures outlined in general surveil-lance countermeasures, on and around your phone. REMEMBER the phone must be in operation for most transmitters to work (and give an indication on your equipment) and a clean sweep today does not mean it will still be clean tomorrow. . . . .

2. Get a good volt-ohm-meter: now disconnect the phone line AT BOTH ENDS. Undo the phone instrument from its little wall plug (remembering, wait, better yet, write it down, which color wire went where) and ALSO disconnect the line where it leaves the surge protector box and heads out-doors to the main cable. BOTH these connections MUST be undone or your measurement ain't gonna be worth the paper this book is printed on . . . . .

Wait a minute. Come to think of it, before you disconnect the line, measure the voltage of the line, should be about 48 volts. (If you are new to the VOM, it will have instructions for use, or the salesman can explain it to you; quite simple really).

Now, with the line disconnected on BOTH ends, set the VOM to high resistance and read the line. Should be around a million ohms or so, if it is considerably less than this, say 75,000 ohms, you gotta problem, probably in the form of a parallel bug on the line.

Now, twist either end of the disconnected wire together and set the resistance on the lowest scale. Read it again. It should be less than an ohm for normal homes, maybe one or two ohms for a long, long connecting wire. If it reads a few ohms again, you gotta a problem, probably a series bug.

If the line goes through several phones and pieces of equipment (as in a large office) disconnect each segment and test, then re-wire and move to the next segment. One can secure a whole building or large area with this procedure in a short period of time.

If you are aware of the area you wish to protect, you should make a measurement when you feel it is clean and then continue to make them on a periodic basis. Any change will show up dramatically.

For those among us who are more technically minded and/or of a more determined nature, there are a couple of further test procedures which can be conducted.

Many professional sweepers employ an audio generator to "sweep" a phone line. This procedure measures the impedance of the line and should be done on the line in question WHEN YOU ARE SURE IT IS CLEAN. After this initial sweep, any additions of any sort will show up as changes in the recorded characteristics.

To run said test procedure, an audio generator such as the ones sold by the various radio/electronics supply houses is used. Install it as shown in the diagram. Use any VOM of 20,000-ohms-per-volt or better sensitivity for the monitoring meter.

Set generator for 80 cycles. Now with the line disconnected, set the audio generator to read about 12 volts, set the AC volt reading on the VOM to a low scale, and adjust the generator downward until the VOM hits about 4 volts. Now, connect the line and notice the reading on the meter.

Compare the difference in the disconnected and connected readings. Repeat this procedure for many different settings up to 50,000 or 100,000 cycles, noticing the readings each time. Once you have done this on the CLEAN line, you can periodically repeat it on the SAME line to get a good idea of the bugging probabilities, as any device installed on the line will alter its impedance, ESPECIALLY as you pass through the resonant frequency of the installed device. When this frequency is approached, the meter will show a dramatic change from its previous readings. Now, if you are really clever, you can substitute an oscilloscope for the VOM and get a visual look at the sweeps. . . .

If you think someone might be employing a version of the infamous "infinity transmitter" (see the phone surveillance section) on your phone, simply dial it from another phone and feed the signal from your audio generator into the mouthpiece, while you slowly run up through the entire audio spectrum. If the device is installed, the phone will answer itself somewhere along the line . . .

USE OF THE VOM FOR CHECKING PHONE LINES

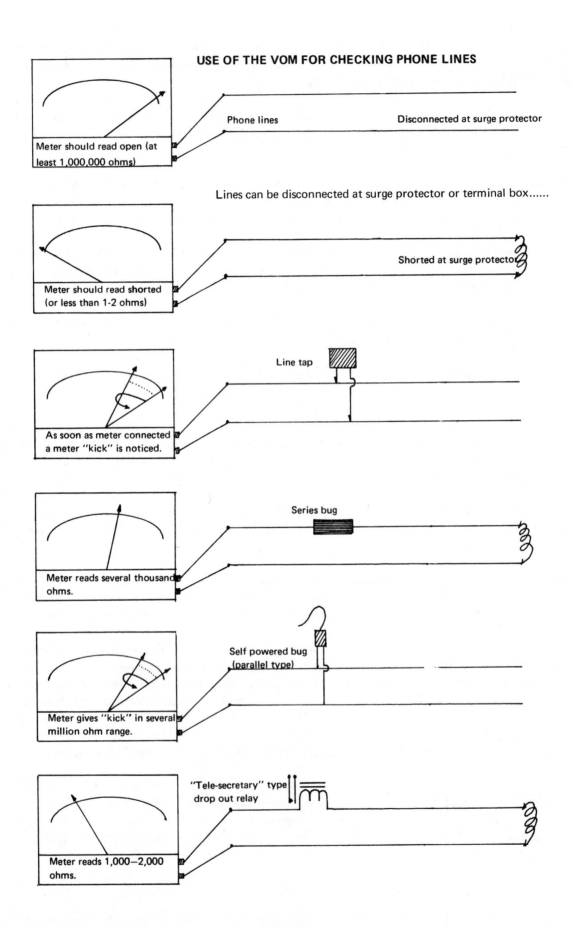

Meter should read open (at least 1,000,000 ohms)

Phone lines

Disconnected at surge protector

Lines can be disconnected at surge protector or terminal box......

Meter should read shorted (or less than 1-2 ohms)

Shorted at surge protector

Line tap

As soon as meter connected a meter "kick" is noticed.

Series bug

Meter reads several thousand ohms.

Self powered bug (parallel type)

Meter gives "kick" in several million ohm range.

"Tele-secretary" type drop out relay

Meter reads 1,000—2,000 ohms.

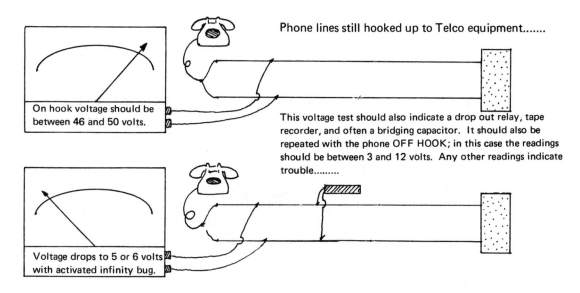

Phone lines still hooked up to Telco equipment.......

On hook voltage should be between 46 and 50 volts.

This voltage test should also indicate a drop out relay, tape recorder, and often a bridging capacitor. It should also be repeated with the phone OFF HOOK; in this case the readings should be between 3 and 12 volts. Any other readings indicate trouble.........

Voltage drops to 5 or 6 volts with activated infinity bug.

USE OF AF GENERATOR FOR IMPEDANCE TESTING

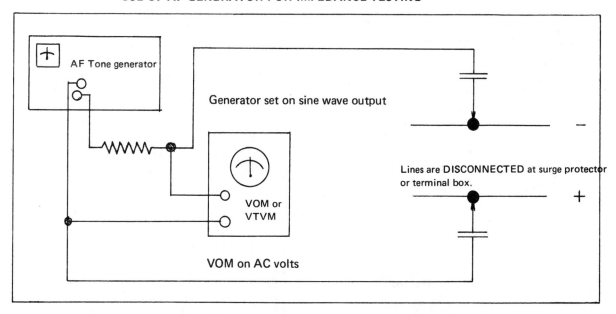

AF Tone generator

Generator set on sine wave output

VOM or VTVM

VOM on AC volts

Lines are DISCONNECTED at surge protector or terminal box.

To test impedance (technically impedance may be described as the opposition of a circuit to an AC current) of a pair of phone lines use the circuit shown above. The VOM should be 20,000 ohms-per-volt sensitivity, the resistor should be 20,000 ohms (half watt will suffice), the two capacitors are .25 ufd, 400 volt MYLAR types (may be paralleled to reach the voltage).

Start generator at 100 cycles, with its voltage meter reading about 10 volts, set the VOM on AC, 6–10 volt scale (depending on which model of meter you are using). Disconnect the phone lines at this point and reduce the generator's output until the VOM reads about 4 volts; reconnect the phone lines to Telco and record the reading. Note any difference in disconnected/connected readings. Repeat this procedure every couple of hundred cycles up through 50,000 cycles. If a device is connected to the lines a change will occur in the VOM reading as you pass through its resonant frequency. This particular frequency will be different from device to device, and this test is not a positive indicator of a bug UNLESS you have done the test and recorded the readings WHEN YOU WERE CERTAIN THE LINE WAS CLEAN. Any variation from the CLEAN readings does indicate trouble........

A scope can also be used but the readings should be photographed; expensive, difficult..........

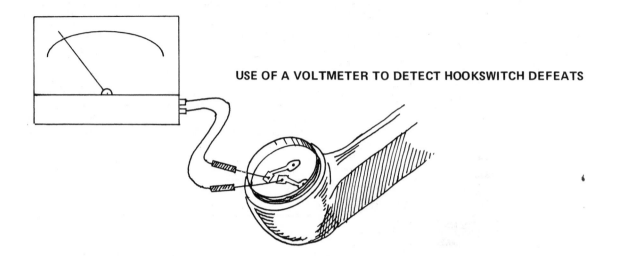

USE OF A VOLTMETER TO DETECT HOOKSWITCH DEFEATS

Any voltage present at the microphone terminals while the phone is in a hung-up mode, indicates some sort of bypass device in operation.

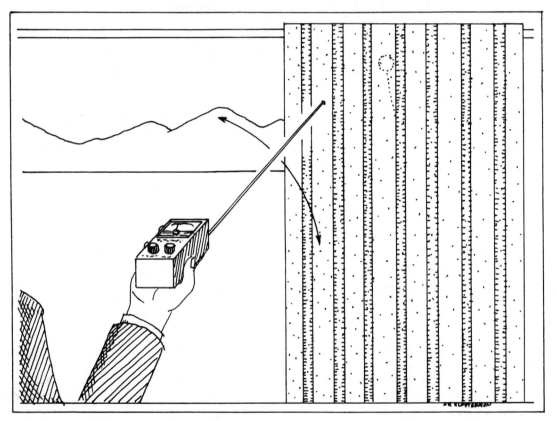

Sweeping curtains with a field strength-type bug detector. The probe MUST be slowly swept over every inch of the material. This should be coupled with a physical and possibly with a metal detector search.

YOU VS. THE MACHINE

Several companies manufacture telephone analyzers (CCC, Mason, Dektor, among others...) that perform a number of tests on telephones and phone lines. How good are they? Exactly what do they do?

Generally these analyzers run through several tests on a semi-automatic basis. They will test single line phones as well as key sets and call directors (in fact, they do more on the more complicated phones than on the single line types).

The usual tests available are:

Line voltage off hook-A digital voltmeter registers the exact voltage when the handset is lifted from the cradle. If the voltage is higher than normal it may indicate a series device (transmitter or tape recorder) is on the line.

Line voltage on hook-Same as above with the handset in the cradle. Here a voltage lower than normal may indicate a parallel device such as an infinity transmitter or drop out relay across the line. (Note: not all drop out relays, especially if the device has a high impedance input.)

Tone Sweep-A tone, usually automatically, sweeps from the low end of the audio spectrum up through the inaudible high frequencies. If an infinity transmitter is installed in the phone it will activate somewhere along the way and the device will sense the voltage drop and give an alarm. If an extension phone is picked up the same reaction results.

Line listen on hook-The telephone is disconnected from the Telco lines at the pin plugs or the instrument itself for single line models and placed into the analyzer's case with a small audio oscillator. The device will now check each wire against each other wire automatically for its own tone. You listen in on ear phones. The presence of a tone means the hookswitch has been defeated, or a third wire-type bug is installed, or that the phone has been re-wired to allow its own mic to pick up and transmit room sounds. This particular test is performed in several fashions to be certain all active and inactive lines are hit.

High voltage pulsing-A large charge (yeah, yeah, I know it sounds funny) is allowed to build up and then suddenly fired hard and fast, into the phone. If a diode, SCR, neon lamp or capacitor has been used to allow command shorting of the hookswitch, this high voltage pulse will set it off and indicate a problem on the machine.

Are the devices worth $2500—$6000? Well, they do successfully run a number of important tests, they are compact and show exactly what tests are going on in fancy LED readouts and number wheels, and they do save a hell of alot of time, especially on multi-line phones where you could literally spend hours searching out every possible wire combination for audio.

Besides which, they look neat.

Can you do the same tests?

Right....A good VTVM, preferably a digital type, will measure on hook and off hook voltages. This very same VTVM can be hooked up to the microphone terminals (as shown); hold the hookswitch down and check for any voltage. Any indication means a hot mic due to some sort of third wire or hook defeat system in use.

To conduct the wire listen test you need to hook an oscillator or AF generator up to both wires of the microphone and earphone terminals. Now go to the pin plug (multi-line sets), or the wall jack, or to the surge protector or box and hook up your handy-dandy spy amplifier and listen for the tone WITH THE PHONE IN A HUNG UP POSITION. Each and every possible wire combination must be tested in this fashion. Now you can leave the AF source in place and add a current limited (say 8-10 ma) high voltage source (1000-1200) of AC is suddenly applied to every possible wire combination while the output is read on a milliammeter. There should be no current flow in any of the pairs unless a SCR, or diode is triggered (which, of course, should not be there) indicating a third wire type bugging job.

Whether you use an automatic analyzer or do-it-yourself, remember to run RF sweeps and other wiretap checks.......

The very most important part of telephone de-bugging is probably also the simplest, i.e. the hands-on search. In the common (Western Electric model 500) home type telephone, one starts by disassembling the cover by removing the 2 screws on the bottom plate. Also remove the dial by loosening the two or three screws holding it in place. At this point one should thoroughly examine all exposed portions of the mechanism being especially aware of wires which do not match in color, any devices which do not seem to belong. The worst offender is anything which resembles a small plastic (usually black) ice cube with two or more wires coming from it.

Check the action of the cradle switch to make sure it does shut off when pushed down. Any wires not connected in the phone should end in a telco terminal.

Unscrew both the mouthpiece and earphone. The earphone is connected by two wires across which a small disc or tubular device is often connected (this device is a varisistor for reducing click noises). The microphone is of the carbon variety and should drop out when the handpiece is turned over. Examine this device carefully; as noted, some transmitters are built directly into this device, but the workmanship usually leaves a little to be desired. If the device appears to have been soldered, or appears much thicker than normal, you may have a problem. A final test is to shake the microphone and listen for the rattle of the carbon granules (in a transmitter mouthpiece these are removed and replaced with a small dynamic microphone).

Be certain to remove the wall box cover where the phone line enters the wall and search this for suspicious appearing devices.

If you have a touchtone phone, the procedure is a bit different. First, remove the outer shell as before, now loosen the touchpad screws and remove it. Turn this pad over and check for any extra items such as diodes, or transmitters. All wires leaving the touchpad should go to either one of the front two terminal blocks. These wires should be: Blue (goes to a number 13), Brown (C), Green (2), Gray (B), Pink (A), Red (D), and White (1).

Loosen the screws holding down the transformer and printed circuit board located underneath the touchpad. Turn the printed circuit board over and make sure no components are mounted underneath this board. THERE SHOULD NOT BE ANY. Check under the ringer mechanism and be certain only four wires go to it: Black (goes to 9 on terminal block), Green (16), Red (15), and White (16).

Check over the cradle switch to make sure it opens the contacts when pushed down and that nothing has been attached across one or both sides. Check the mouth and ear piece.

To check the 6 button office phone, (Western Electric 565) undo the phone wire where it enters a 50-pin connector pod, or check to see it is properly connected to the junction box, if no pin-pod is used. Now, take off the cover and dial as mentioned previously. Check the phone for all wires, extra devices etc. Make sure the cradle switch is working and has no added parts.

Check out the printed circuit board network, especially terminals marked F, RR, and C, as all wires can be bugged at this point. F should have two leads coming from it, RR one, and C should have one soldered wire attached to it. Check in and around the lamps for weird devices. Check out the ear and mouth pieces.

If you have the 6-line touchtone phone, remove cover and touch pad CAREFULLY. Check the bottom of pad for extra devices and wires. You should count 7 wires (blue, white, red, gray, brown, green and pink) going to and from the touch pad. Check out printed circuit network under the pad by loosening the transformer screws as mentioned before. Lift the board and check for devices or components underneath the board. Hopefully you will not find any.

Look at the ringer and make sure only 4 wires go to it (blue, green, red and black). Look under the large terminal block. There should be no components or wires on the bottom side.

Check hookswitch and mouth-earpieces. Check out terminals A, R and 6 on the terminal block. Here is where all of the lines can be tapped, a favorite with professionals. A and R should have one wire on top and one on the bottom. 6 should have 2.

If you are in doubt about anything, check out a similar model phone which you presume to be safe. Be very suspicious of any added components . . . . . .

ZEN AND THE ART OF DE—BUGGING.......

A good counter-surveillance expert will always attempt to determine who the enemy is in advance of any sweeping operation. A private operator, jealous spouse, cheap private detective are all going to use certain techniques in their bugging operations. Usually their operations will be limited to a drop-out relay in the basement, a transmitter installed in the phone or between the phone and the box, or either a transmitter or tape recorder attached to the terminal box itself. Of course, a commercial Tele-Ear "burglar alarm" infinity transmitter is also a possibility.

If you are going against a top private eye or good police intelligence unit you may find that a transmitter has been installed up on the telephone pole, usually at the pole terminal box.

If the adversary is the FBI, CIA, DEA, IRS, a top police unit or ultra-good private eye, we gotta problem; you see, the phone company, being what they are, does not run your wire from your own phone directly to their central office. First, of course, it goes to a 26 pair terminal box, from here it joins a cable containing other wires and then the trouble begins; the pair is numbered at the terminal box, after this numbered pair leaves the terminal box it goes to another larger box which may be several blocks away, known as a "B" box (in New York it is called a "bridging head", in Washington D.C. one says, "multiple" and in some other areas the box is known as an "appearance".) In this B box the pair re-emerges, and is again usually numbered. After leaving the B box the pair may re-appear in several more B boxes before reaching central office facilities.

After leaving the B box the line is enclosed in a cable with several hundred other pairs. The telephone company keeps a line card on each user with his telephone number, pair number, cable number and B box appearances. These B box locations and pair numbers may be learned by bluffing the phone company by posing as a repair person and convincing the repair clerk that you are checking out a problem. If possible you can get right to the source and learn the number of the Cable Records Office and call them (once you have the pair number) and ask for the B box locations. The problem herein, is of course, you must know the various telephone numbers and be able to talk the area Telco nomenclature to a "T".

One way to do this is to, as one handbook on police surveillance techniques suggests, "develop contacts within the phone company". Outside of police handbooks this is often referred to as bribery.....Most police units do have such contacts, as do many top private eyes. Even you, can learn to "develop" such contacts as many Telco employees, especially the younger set, do not love the phone company and will be happy to show you how to call, or do it for you, for a small "consultants" fee....

At any rate, most federal agencies and some top police/private detectives will use a B box pair terminal for bugging purposes. A real top priority case will find the unit running a Telco line (easy to get and match the color code) from a B box into a room or apartment where a special team will monitor the subject's calls at will. A lesser case will find the bug installed at a B box, making it much harder to locate.

If the subject is located in an office building or hotel, there may be a box on each floor, or couple of floors, if the spy can get a room on the same floor he need only locate his phone's pair posts and his subject's phone's pair posts in the box and run a jump wire between the two. Voila! Instant extension phone....

If you are planting a bug, or sweeping for a semi-professional/professional bug you can follow the cable and find the B boxes by other methods. If you know the number in your area (as mentioned, in the San Francisco Bay Area it is 640) to talk to the Telco computer, you can attach your little phone company headset, or purloined phone to any wire or set of posts and dial the computer whereupon the phone number will be read back to you.

It is also possible to attach an audio generator set for 400-800 cycles to the subject's phone wires (or instrument) and then trace it out with a banana probe or inductance coil (the former connected to a Telco handset, the latter to your little spy amplifier). In this operation you will be able to follow the tone down any wire or cable, or test any terminal box post without actually making connection (it should be pointed out that you can also hear any other things going down the phone wire such as conversations in this manner).

Most good surveillance experts, and some good counter-surveillance experts will have a Telco handset, banana probe, lineman's belt, fake id, etc. If you are going to dabble in this business from either end, it is wise to develop phone company contacts as soon as possible.

Of course, if it is a LEGAL recorder-type tap, the phone company will supply this information gladly and lease lines from a B box, or better yet, directly from a central office exchange. However, only a couple of hundred legal taps were authorized (this does not include the unreleased figures for "national security" taps) last year, and with the heat the phone company has gotten into in the past for giving away unauthorized leased lines, and the difficulty in obtaining a court order for a tap, most law enforcement agencies are advised to "avoid contact with the phone company [in a above ground manner, ed.] whenever possible".

What can you do if you are looking for a possible pole or B box tap? Well first of all you can trace the wire down by using a tone generator and banana or inductive probe looking for any taps or extra lines (in most areas you can dial a certain number [first three digits and then 0020 in San Francisco] and the phone company will automatically put a tone on the line for your use) as well as doing an RF sweep.

Once you have located the terminal box and B box (es), you can use a bit of clear varnish or a commercial skin covering available at drug stores known as New Skin, to form a seal over the corner of the box. Checking this seal every so often will give you an idea of whether the box has been opened for any reason. In fact, one neat trick is to climb the pole with the terminal box in question (a good agent will have a pair of pole climbers....) and open the terminal box just a hair. Now check it every day with a pair of binoculars; if someone tampers with it chances are good that they will close it afterwards....

You can follow the procedure for impedance sweeping WHEN YOU ARE CERTAIN THE LINE IS CLEAN, and then re-check every so often.

You can perform resistance measurements with a good (hopefully a digital) voltmeter. The resistances will vary somewhat with regard to cable type and weather conditions, but the following table will give you approximately what you should expect. Any serious variation from this table, or from sweep to sweep means trouble:

Gauge	Ohms per 1,000 feet	Ohms per mile
22	32.4	171
24	51.9	274
26	83.5	440

Remember, all resistance testing must be done with all equipment disconnected and the pair ends shorted together.

It is interesting to note that the top level buggers have recently borrowed a technique from ham (amateur) radio operators; they will place a low powered, hard to detect bug, with a short range, in an office and then park a car nearby with a sensitive receiver, high gain antenna, and a carrier switch which only turns on when a voice is present.

Turns on what? A high powered (say 10 WATTS, or more) transmitter which re-broadcasts the mini-bugs transmissions on a different frequency (usually in the VHF band). This means the operator can sit in his house/car/old lady's apartment 10 miles away and hear every word spoken in the target room.

This sort of a device is known as a repeater.

COUNTERMEASURES

If you suspect you are the victim of an unauthorized telephone surveillance campaign, there are a few things you can do to lower your risks:

Keep your phone locked up in a drawer when not in use and deny access to your premises to anyone, including cleaning people, without your constant surveillance. Always check any "repairman" and call to verify it with the phone (or gas - whatever) company.

Limit your non-critical calls to one phone and occasionally, only when it's important, use another phone on another line. However, if you make a habit out of this sort of thing, the other phone will get the same treatment. Even pay phones have been bugged near a subject's house or place of business by over-zealous spies or law enforcement types . . . . .

You can use a commercial scrambler; these devices employ several methods to make the human voice unintelligible to anyone not equipped with a like device. They have the advantage of screwing up all eavesdropping, including switchboard operators and chance listeners, HOWEVER, cheap scramblers simply remove a sideband of the conversation, or invert the speech patterns and can be defeated with a simple device and even expensive $500-a-set-jobs can be defeated by anyone with the time and equipment to crack the scrambling mode. Large spy outfits, (i.e. governments) employ computers to figure out the code and descramble with only minor hassle . . . .

You can feed some sort of noise (radio would work fine. . .) into the phone when not in use if you feel the conversation is being recorded. This will actuate any voice operated or line-tripped tape recorders and cause them to waste their precious tape recording the top 40. This is especially good with the mini-jobs which can deal effectively with a maximum of 45 minutes worth of recording before the tape has to be serviced.

It is also possible to mess up a tape recorder by inserting some sort of blanket noise into the phone along with your voice. The poor quality mics and earpieces used in the telephone itself will not respond to much over 3,500 cycles per second, while tape recorders will often to 100,000 to 15,000 cycles with ease. If you take your trusty signal generator and feed a sine wave of about 8,000 or 9,000 cycles into the line (by direct connection) along with your voice (at, say 10 volts or so) it will often completely overload the tape recorder and saturate it with the tone, but still allow you to understand the person over the phone . . . This is best employed only at critical moments, not during whole conversations, to give the bugger less time to figure out what is going on.

However, the only real, sure countermeasure is not to say important things over the telephone. Loose lips sink ships . . . . .

DEFEAT DEVICES

There are numerous types of telephone security devices on the market. Some are designed ONLY for defeating devices which use the telephone to transmit room conversation down the wire (such as the infinity transmitter). The key wording in these ads is "telephone comprise defeaters" or "infinity transmitter defeaters".

These devices are quite simple and usually consist of a white noise (static) generator and an induction coil. They are placed on or under the phone and load the sidetone coil and/or microphone with a large dose of random noise, effectively stopping most room bugs. A real pro might be able to filter out much of the noise with an equalizer, particularly if the noise is concentrated in one portion of the spectrum and does not contain many harmonics. However, the static is going to be of FAR greater volume than the feeble room conversation, so it is fairly effective against these sort of bugs.

Communication Control Corporation sells a number of defeat devices; their Wiretap Defeat System (Mark IV) is attached to the phone and adjusted for proper balance. The device then alters the basic impedance of the phone line so when you lift the receiver to make a call the line does not change enough to start a automatic recording device or phone transmitter (in effect, the bug "sees" the phone as still being hung up).

This device will also give a voltage reading and indication of a bug being on the line. If this on-line condition is in evidence one can select to place the Wiretap Defeater in the "operate" mode and make undetected calls, or switch it to "off", and feed fake information down the wire......

CCC also sells several telephones with a built-in "wiretap-trap". This is much the same sort of circuit mounted inside a phone. It will interface with any phone system and provides the same sort of protection as the Mark IV. It will not give an indication of whether a bug is in effect, most models do not have the choice of defeat/non-defeat, and it is not quite as sophisticated as the Mark IV, but it is easier to install.....

Ironically, the only type of device this does not even bother is the super cheapo, always-transmitting-easy-to-find module type bug, say what?

Dektor sells a "loaded" phone which puts more emphasis on detection and has internal RF sensors, line testers for most other bugs, and separates the internal sections of the phone by isolation so it is quite hard to use any portion of the phone for room bugging.

SCRAMBLERS

Any data that is transmitted over radio or wire, be it voice, Telex, or computer data is susceptible to interception by a third party. One way to circumvent this is by the use of a device which changes the data into a different format, transmits it, and then recodes it back to its orginal form.

Early scramblers utilized a couple of different methods of encoding; usually speech inverting or side band splitting. Either type of scrambler can be broken in a matter of minutes with inexpensive gear. In fact, almost all police radio scrambling is of this variety and several companies (see the suppliers section) sell defeaters......

State of the art scramblers utilize the theory of random-control; that is speech, or other analog information is broken down into simple parts (either by frequency, amplitude, or time) and then these "parts" are rearranged under the control of some random-like control factor.

This control factor is known as the key generator and produces a stream of "ons and offs", or 1's and 2's in an almost random fashion. The receiving end of the system must be fitted with a like device which produces the same "random" stream of 1's and 0's.

The receiver must then establish synchronization between itself and its mate before the data bits can be matched with the stream produced by the key generator and the whole mess unscrambled.

If Telex or data bits are to be scrambled the job is already half done; the random stream is simply mixed with the already existing bits and a coded test results. The only hassle, herein, is the fact that some computer communication systems may not accept certain types of coded data.

If you are considering the purchase of a scrambling system, consider several factors: the ideal scrambler must offer a high level of security, be simple to install, portable, require no special training to operate or complicated instructions that might cause errors when utilized by a non-technically minded personnel and be versatile enough to be used with phone systems, inter-office systems, Telex and even radio or computer if needed.

The key factor, to coin a phrase, in the security of the scrambler is the key generator. A good key generator has a random start capability so the same key stream is not used to encode more than one message, it should have a long series of non-repeating bits for each code as well as several user selected codes for you to chose from (hopefully on two levels, for primary and secondary changes). The generator should be fairly complex to resist computer efforts to break its code, but still offer fail safe operation. A nice added touch is a mechanical lock for the encoding selectors.

A good scrambler can do much to enhance the security force of any operation. It eliminates all amateur efforts at simple data theft, and makes it damn hard for a trained pro with access to a computer to eavesdrop on telephone, Telex, or computer conversations.....

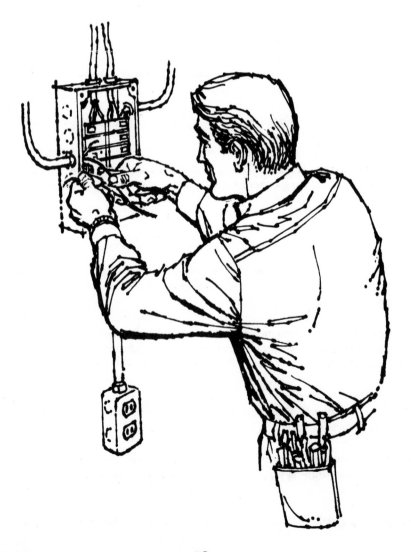

GENERAL DETECTIVE

One of the "hobbies" of the late J. Edgar Hoover, head of the FBI, reportedly was to collect data about the private lives of movie stars and sports figures. One of his favorites was alledged to be a file on the sexual conquests of Joe Namath........

GENERAL DETECTIVE

Often an agent can ascertain much information about a person without resorting to illegal and/or dangerous means. A whole mountain of information is lying around on any person in this computerized, credit-based, nosey society we have here.

Most people do not realize how much of their background is public knowledge for anyone who cares to ask.

To discover what you want to know, it's best to borrow upon some of the techniques of the private detection business.

Many public records are available to anyone who comes calling. Most are filed on a county or on a state basis, rather than in each city. Some good bets are:

Registrar of voters -

Names, addresses, place of birth, occupation, and signature

County felony and misdemeanor files -

Contains information on all convicted criminals, what the disposition of the case was, where it was tried, and often a probation report which contains a complete personal run-down of the subject.

Superior court files -

All civil, and divorce cases and information. Often cross filed.

Small Claims court -

Information on small claims suits.

Corporation files -

Names and information on incorporated business in the area including names of owners.

Federal Files are kept in a federal office, also open to most anyone.

Federal criminal cases -

Civil files - information on cases between the US and certain people. Bankruptcy files - information on those who file for bankruptcy.

Marriage files -

Information on those who have filed application for a marriage license; including names, addresses, birth place, parents, etc.

Birth Records -

Name, address, place of birth, names of parents, etc.

Death records -

Time and place and cause of death.

County tax files -

Real property files - name of owner and address where the tax is mailed to. Often employed by realtors and others wanting to talk with home owners.

Personal Property files -

Name and where the tax bill is sent on non-real estate, but still taxable property.

Mapbook -

Shows location of real property.

County Recorder files -

Information on leases, loans, deeds, etc., with both the lender and the borrowers rundown.

Department of Motor Vehicles -

Both the names and addresses of licensed drivers, as well as registered automobile owners. Not always open records, but can usually be approached with a good cover story.

Newspapers keep files on many people who appear in them. These files are private but, can often be reached by convincing them you are a bona fide book researcher; or a licensed private investigator, investigating a case.

The library contains some invaluable records:

Reverse directories - the telephone company creates a reverse directory wherein one looks up the address and the telephone number and the name is listed. They rent them to businesses such as collection agencies, on a monthly basis, but some public libraries have them.

Occasionally a phone company may let you come in and use theirs, or you can ask a collection agency, answering service, credit bureau, etc. if you can look something up in their copy.

Listing directories - Are directories with the telephone number listed in order. Rented from SOME telephone offices.

City directory - At the library. A listing of names, address, telephone numbers, occupations, etc. in your city. Usually cross-filed, but often will not contain listings that are unlisted by the telephone company.

Civil Lists - Some cities publish a listing of all their employees.

Who's Who - (In America), lists information including addresses of famous or important people, also a Who's Who in business, literature, law, medicine, finance, journalism, etc.

Great for finding corporation officers, lawyers, etc. Some states also publish a localized version.

Armed forces Registrars - All branches have registrar of active and retired officers.

Business directories - Standard and Poors, etc. Stocked by libraries and stock brokers, these directories give much information on companies, including their officers.

DETECTIVE

It is sometimes possible to gain access to various semi-secure records (such as hospital records, accident reports, insurance company files, etc.) by producing a release, signed (or, of course, forged) by the party(s) involved.

Said release should contain the wording; This form authorizes   , or their agents, to examine, inspect or make copies of all   (medical, accidental, etc.) REPORTS of any kind or nature pertaining to   sustained by   on   when   was involved in (accident, etc.)   with

Signature.

Always best to throw in a witness signature here also.

If you are going to appear in court (God forbid) on any charge, it is always best to document any and everything as much as humanly possible. This is always enhanced by the presence of scale drawings, photos, etc.

If you are involved in an accident or personal liability suit with a party whom you feel may be, well, faking it a bit - you can often get added tidbits by approaching an index bureau. These bureaus keep computerized cross files on persons who are known to indulge in the habit of defrauding Insurance companies.

The files are maintained for the insurance companies themselves, but sometimes can be opened to a "private detective" with a problem, or your insurance agent can access for you.

Private eyes operate on the general theory that in every phony story there is usually a grain of truth. When a person runs, or makes up some bogus cover story for one sort of con game or another, he/she/it generally uses a common fact or two. Names given can be names of friends or relatives or friends. Towns are often past residences or addresses of relatives, addresses and phone numbers are often transposed digits or simply slid one way or another a couple of key points.

Skippers never make a total transformation. More unwary victims are found through Wednesday night bowling leagues and karate clubs than names or employers. Anyone can change modes of employment and style of living, but who goes to the trouble of changing even his hobbies?

Private detectives are only as good as their contacts. While any of us can get access to numerous public and private records (as previously detailed) a good private eye will have contacts in the phone and utilities companies to get access to unlisted numbers and computer readouts of utility users and so on.

Telephone companies have a universal problem with lack of loyalty among employees. Justified or not, this opens the door for many unscrupulous operators (credit bureaus, collection agencies etc.) to convince said employees to sell copies of the little black book (a book with all unlisted phone numbers in a certain district), occasionally help install taps, sell locations of multiples (places where phone pairs re-emerge at some distance from the original junction box), etc.

While this sort of thing works out fine in the detective's home area, or for those companies with national organizations, what about the private operator who follows up a lead and ends up in Kansas City where he knows no one, except his third cousin on his mother's side who is always asking for a loan. What does he do?

Well, as one might reasonably expect, there is a world wide organization of private detectives, known oddly enough, as World Wide Detectives Organization. This "union" of private eyes hold annual conferences where new contacts are made and ole ones re-affirmed and generally provides a springboard for inter-cooperation.

When a private eye finds himself in a strange city, or needs information from a certain city, he can contact a fellow member of WWD and be assured of cooperation, thus effectively opening a series of successful contacts, virtually around the world . . . .

The detectives' role is often of master puzzle-solver. He must take any/and all available pieces and begin reassembling them into a master picture. He must be able to take, no matter how minute, tension, and patiently follow it up into a full-sized puzzle piece.

Most private eyes are seldom called on to use a gun, (many simply do not have a gun license) deal with beautiful women (except for such special occasions as WWD conventions . . .) worry about stolen gems, or perform any of the other MGM detective duties.

Detectives rarely do their own lab work. Many may have some or more police, CID, or formal police science background, but few ever get to make a tire moulage like they learned in police science 401 . . . Most of today's private eyes come up through the more direct routines of insurance claims investigation, or credit bureau work.

A good detective is familar with lab work, lifting finger prints, ballistics reports, etc., but he rarely gets into such work himself. Instead he is aware of where to go to have such work expertly accomplished, both to make sure it's professionally done as well as having the option of expert testimony in court. These labs and specialized organizations are generally available to the average citizen to make use of as well as the pro, and can be located with a minimum of trouble through the vestiges of the good ol', every-day, yellow pages.

STATEMENT

For various reasons, you, as an agent, may find youself in the position of needing a statement, either for your own records, or for a court case.

When interviewing someone, bear in mind they are a bit nervous and may not wish to cooperate. One can circumvent this reaction in many cases by appearing to be on "their side" or simply seeming to be interested in their opinion of a certain event of a person.

If it is an informal interview, i.e. for your own information, it is often best to act very informal. Instead of taking notes, use a mini-cassette recorder secreted about your person for the recording of information.

It is often helpful to employ one of the agents favorite techniques; the lie.

If you feel the person will respond well to authority; be one. A special investigator or private detective is less risky than an actual police is (police, generally, do not hold the view that imitation is the sincerest form of flattery).

Obviously, it would be unwise to spring an ID on someone who does not agree with the law and order philosophy.

Should you need a statement or a court case DO NOT LIE. Judges take a dim view of information gained under false pretenses. Prepare a written statement of the subject's statement which will contain (in the first person) all the facts you need, along with the date, subject's name and address, how you identified the subject for the statement, and a statement to the effect that this was all given under his free will and that it is all true.

Have him sign it and get a witness (probably you) to sign it also.

If the statement will run over one page, add a paragraph that the person will sign, telling how many pages the statement contains.

INTERROGATION

There are several methods and schools of thought on interrogating a person. Of course, various degrees of force tend to show the highest return in information, but these methods are always a bit gruesome and tend to outweigh any possibility of future cooperation from the victim, er, subject.

Besides, this is a family book and we shan't go into any great detail on forceful methods. You can watch a day or two of television and pick up anything you need to know on this subject.

One method usually employed by the police is the hard/soft (yin/yang?) method of having one hard, tough, mean, ugly type, berate the subject for a while to lower his resistance and then to have a "sympathetic" officer talk and question the subject in a friendly manner.

Once the subject gives you something to work on, it is customary to make him repeat the story over and over again, often to other people. If a story is hastily construed, the subject will often mess up the details as he goes over it again and again.

Needless to say, always record any information, preferably with a hidden tape recorder.

If you are on the wrong end of the interrogation, remember a few important procedures:

FINGERPRINTS

Fingerprints are the first thing Mr. TV detective looks for after any crime. In heavy crimes, they are the first thing real-life enforcement types look for.....Fingerprints are best gotten from hard, smooth surfaces such as wood, paper, etc. They do not take well on cloth or other rough surfaces.

Generally, to find a print, the searcher treats the area with one or more powders which cling to the oil left behind by the person who touched the object. These powders are easily purchased from any police equipment supplier.

If the prints are older than a few hours, they are often treated as latents and are treated by placing in a special chamber, or "shooting" with a special gun that exposes the object to fumes created from heating iodine crystals. The object can also be sprayed with silver nitrate solution and exposed to black light, where any prints will show up quite well....

A new type of print developer has been developed, if you'll excuse the english, which does not react with the bodily oils as all other methods, but which reacts to the amino acids left behind by the finger, rather than to the oils, or salts, as the older methods do. This developer is known as Ninhydrin and sells under the trade name of Nin Spray and can be ordered from the various police suppliers mentioned in this book.

Any print that is developed can then be lifted by means of sticky tape (Scotch will do in a pinch) or special lifters, and recorded for posterity. A latent print can lay latent for hours, days, or even years and be recovered by a good fingerprint expert. However, it must be there in the first place.....

Once a print turns up, or more correctly, a set of prints turns up (one print, or a partial set cannot always be traced), the F.B.I.'s new computer system can run a ID check and come up with the prints (if they are on file) in about 5 seconds......

The only sure-fire methods to beating prints are to wear gloves, wipe every surface VERY carefully after handling, or spray any surface you are likely to come in contact with, and do not want to retain your prints, with a common chemical sold under the trade name WD-40. This oily substance puts a very light coating on any object which will last for one month to one year, and which breaks down the surface tension of the object to the point where it will not support fingerprints.

Fingerprints are usually taken as definite proof of performance; meaning you did it Charlie....However this should be taken with a grain of salt, especially in government or large, syndicate-type of crime, as there is a technique for transferring prints supposedly developed in England which can take any lifted print and re-deposit it wherever the user wishes.

Work all possible details of the story out in advance.

Stick to as many true details as possible.

Make the lies based on another true situation if possible (if describing someone, use someone else that you are familiar with for the details).

Don't be too able to recall every little detail, pause to think sometimes and use "I think" occasionally.

RELAX! NEVER rub your hands, ask for a drink of water or indicate other signs of nervousness. Pause a second before every detail to get it out slowly and correctly.

SURVEILLANCE

It may become necessary to do some in-person surveillance on a subject. This can be either moving (tailing) or stationary (stake out).

One overpowering rule holds true whether you are on a mobile or fixed surveillance/stake out - It is always better to lose your victim than to let him know you are on to him.

It is far better to remain as natural as possible when tailing someone. If you have been tailing for some time and wish to change your appearance, a small natural change, such as a pair of glasses, or at the extreme, a well fitting wig, is far better than fake beards and makeup.

Attempt to fit your situation - wear the type of clothes your victim is wearing to give you freedom of movement for any place he may go.

Never carry any extras that would tend to remain in one's memory.

FOOT

Always keep your subject in sight. It is usual to remain about 10 - 15 feet behind him in crowded areas and half a block in sparse areas. In uncrowded situations, it may be best to remain on the oposite side of the street.

In heavy crowds, change position constantly, using other people as cover. If the victim turns in your directon, DO NOT use a TV move and jump into a doorway or behind a person. Simply glance into a store window or talk to another person. This is best accomplished by asking directions or some other non-offensive question. Never look at your subject when he is facing you.

It is far better to utilize at least two people in any tailing operation. Your suspect may be on the up-and-up for people following him, and may even have a person on his side following some distance back to spot tailers.

If you are foot-tailing with another friendly agent, have a series of pre-arranged signals to communicate with him. Hand and arm positions, especially when emphasized with a newspaper, can be quite effective. An old favorite of the "I led three lives" variety is to pull out a handkerchief.

Should your victim go into an apartment or store, follow him. If he gets on any elevator, you get on also and press one floor above his. Hopefully you can run back down the stairs and cautiously open the door to see where he enters.

If he goes into a restaurant, and you are reasonably sure he has not spotted you and is going to come out a back door, you can remain outside or go into it also and sit behind him. As you see him preparing to leave, it is wise to check out first and re-establish surveillance outside the premises.

If he/she/it enters a bus, train, etc., try and use another entrance and exit, always remaining behind your victim.

Should the bus leave before you are able to board, grab a cab, steal a car, or some such, and follow the bus until he departs.

It is a wise idea to carry a sufficient cash reserve to meet any emergency. Suppose you trail a prospect to the airport where he boards a plane for Delcyville, Georgia?

You should be able to hop on board . . . .

If a suspect feels you or someone is tailing him, he may reverse his direction suddenly, glance in windows for your reflection, drop something and pick it up, turn to light a cigarette, etc.

Another popular ploy is to turn a corner and stop suddenly. If this occurs, one should keep on going past the subject without turning around until you are past the danger point.

The suspect may get on a bus and then get back off before it leaves, hoping you will blow your cover by jumping back off also. If this occurs, stay aboard for at least one stop and try to re-establish contact.

Entering a building by one entrance and leaving by another is a good method of separating you and your victim. The best procedure here is to have more than one person on your side. While you go in, they watch the other exits.

If you are lucky enough to have at least one or more accomplices on the trail with you, you can use visual methods of signaling, or better yet, employ a CB walkie talkie. It is best to switch off every so often, with you turning a corner and the other agent picking him up for awhile before you return.

Always have a phone number where either of you can call and leave a message, should you become separated for any reason.

AUTO SURVEILLANCE

Utilize a non-flashy, medium-priced car. It's seldom you will need to outrun anyone and a Pantera is sure to attract more attention than a Chevy . . . .

Always keep your tank full of gas and the car in proper working order. If you are serious about this sort of thing, you should practice quite often to get the feel of it.

As in footwork, it is far better to use at least two cars, and it's helpful to have two people in each car. In this manner, one can watch, and one can drive, also one agent is instantly accessible if the victim parks suddenly.

Keep a few cars between you and your victim, and change lanes every so often BUT never at the same time he does. If your victim suddenly turns, go on for another block and turn the same direction.

If you are on uncrowded residential streets, you should stay much farther back, at least a block or two. You can also parallel trail on residential streets by turning one street off your victim and attempting to match his speed before turning back on to his street.

This gives him a break where you are not behind him.

Probably the best all-around method is to utilize three units, whether cars or foot agents. Two stay on the same street as the victim is in different spots (although both behind him) and one stays a street over, paralleling everyone else.

Every so often one of the two turns off to be replaced by the parallelee. In this fashion, the victim doesn't have a chance to concentrate on any one vehicle for any period of time.

If you are on the trail for a period of days, it is best to change cars as often as possible.

CB radios are almost a necessity for car trailing.

It is wise to keep your car(s) stocked with maps of the area, a camera, change of clothes, a flashlight, binoculars, etc., for short notice jobs.

If you are using a fixed stakeout point there are several rules to observe: never tell anyone involved that you are watching anyone, a fake "special agent" trip may get you in the building, but it is sure to attract more attention than it's worth.

Always pay in cash, never checks or credit cards.

If you are using an apartment, it is wise to make up some sort of story about your wife arriving with the furniture or such. If you are using a motel, carry NOTHING in your luggage that can identify you.

If you are using optical equipment from a window, do not stand too close, and, of course, never use a back light. Always be sure it is very dark.

DIVORCE

Oh boy, some states have passed no-fault divorce laws which have pretty well taken the fun out of divorce trials. In such no-fault cases, neither party has to have proof of any wrong-doing to get a divorce.

If you are involved in a possible divorce situation in a non no-fault state, or if you're just curious; there are a few things to remember: state laws differ on what is needed to get a divorce, but in most cases, at least one good, proven case of: adultery, desertion, extreme cruelty, drunkenness, insanity, bigamy, impotence, etc., will do for the necessary requirements. In any case, this testimony must be collaborated with a "disinterested" party. The husband's/wife's word is just not enough. A private detective, even though employed by one side of the case, is usually considered a reliable

TAILING, MADE SIMPLE. . .

Several companies have marketed electronic tailing devices. These systems differ a bit in surface features, but most all work on one set of principles:

A small "beeper", usually a metal box about 4" x 2" x 1½" with a couple of powerful magnets attached to its top. A small, center loaded antenna projects from one side. The device puts out moderately high powered pulses in all directions. The beeper is normally self-contained, but can be plugged into the target vechicle's own power supply.

The receiver is mounted in the tail car. It is so designed as to internally produce several different tones. The receiver normally has a three position range switch, a squelch control, and sometimes a null switch.

The receiving antenna system usually contains two carefully matched antennas which are mounted on either side of the tail car (although some models use a vertical loop instead).

To utilize the system one simply turns on the beeper and slaps it to the underside of the target vehicle; this is a 5 second operation and can even be performed at a stoplight, if one is careful.

The receiver now picks up the pulses and converts them into an audible beeping tone. The tone increases in volume as you near the target vechicle. If you were to pass the parked target car, the tone would turn into a scream....If you are tailing a moving vehicle, or trying to locate the vehicle within a city, you start with the range switch in the "long" position and gradually switch in into "medium" and "short" as the tones become loud and then merge into one long tone.

In the long range position, you are searching an area of about 6 miles (three in front and three in back), in the medium mode this drops to about 1½ miles in either direction, and in the short end of things one can expect about ½ mile.

If you are using the null switch another factor comes into play; if you are parked, and the target vehicle is also parked directly in front of you (i.e. directly between your two antennas) a null, or lack of any sound will appear. If the vehicle is moving and you are utilizing the null feature, a turn to the right will produce a slightly different tone in your receiver than a turn to the left will. Of course, the range/volume relationship is also operational in the null mode.

Electronic tailing offers several possibilities: You can locate a tagged car within a normal city in a fairly short time. It is possible to maintain a tail without ever actually seeing the target car (or, conversely, him seeing you....). This is accomplished with a little practice and a basic understanding of the system's capabilities; if you are both on a freeway, for instance, you can maintain a steady tail a few miles behind the vehicle-if he slows down, or stops (to see if anyone is following him) you will get a sudden increase in volume allowing you to do the same damn thing. Using the null feature you can tell if he suddenly turns off onto a exit ramp, and which way he has turned.

It is also possible to keep surveillance on a parked car without ever "seeing" the car: simply put the null switch into operation, park nearby and in a direct head-on line so you get your null and wait....When the car starts up and pulls away from the curb, the beeps will begin. By listening to the type of beep you can tell which way he has started, or if he is coming toward you or going away from you by the volume feature.

These tailing devices are legal and available to the general public at this time.....See the suppliers section.

VEHICLE FOLLOWER model 1012

The LEA Model 1012 Vehicle Follower System features the latest innovations for complete vehicle surveillance. The system consists of an all solid-state total-power degenerate interferometer receiver, a pair of quadraloop antennas, and solid-state crystal controlled transmitter.

The interferometer receiver is the type used in many of today's rocket tracking systems, featuring meter read-outs as well as an audio signal. The Relative Direction Meter continuously indicates the direction of the vehicle under surveillance, left or right of the following vehicle. For example: when the vehicle with the attached transmitter bears to the right, the receiver meter will indicate this by pointing to the right. Accurate boresight calibration one degree off center produces a 12% full-scale deflection.

Distance from the transmitter is determined by two methods. One by a Relative Distance Meter (field strength) located on the front panel and the other by the tone of the intermittent signal of the transmitter. This tone is relative to the distance between the transmitter and receiver. The duty cycle of the signal can be varied to meet special operation conditions on request. The range of the system depends on the terrain. In most cases it is two to six miles nominal.

The receiver has a three channel capability, i.e., three transmitters may be operated simultaneously; however, only one channel can be monitored at a time. All channels are crystal-controlled and switch-selected. (More than three channels are available on special order.)

The quadraloop receiver antennas are low profile antennas similar to the type used on sounding rockets. Their low profile, 1 inch high, allows them to be mounted on the hood of a vehicle with the guise of a hood ornament, or painted with acrylic paint to match the vehicle. The antennas may also be mounted on the vehicle roof or, for complete concealment, incorporated into a luggage rack atop the vehicle.

The transmitter is available in three different models: a 100 milli-watt unit with a 7 inch vertical whip antenna, a 200 milli-watt unit and a 1 watt unit that operate into a 50 ohm load. Power for the 100 milli-watt transmitter is supplied by two 8.4 volt batteries mounted on the transmitter or by the vehicle's 12 volt battery supply. The transmitter is magnetically mounted to the vehicle under surveillance.

The antennas can be permanently mounted or temporarily attached in many different configurations. The receiver is completely portable and may be moved from vehicle to vehicle. A special bracket adaptable to most vehicles is included for dash board mounting of the meter for eye-level reading convenience. A non-glare lamp illuminates the meter face for nighttime operation.

The receiver is supplied with a cigarette lighter socket adapter. Power can also be supplied by using any other negative-ground 12 volt d.c. power supply. The antenna leads are connected to receptacles on the receiver front panel.

The LEA Model 1012 is custom tuned to frequencies between 173-174 MHz specified by the customer. Special frequencies, not within this band, can be requested for individual requirements.

Each unit in the system is available for individual purchase. Requests for special requirements may be subject to additional cost. Pricing will be supplied on request. Inquiries are invited.

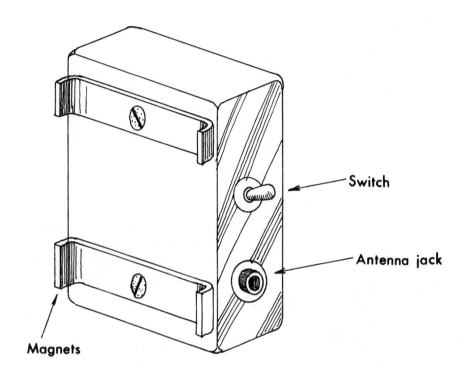

Switch

Antenna jack

Magnets

Receiver

VOLUME

NULL
REG
OFF
AUTO

RANGE
S
M
L

PULSE

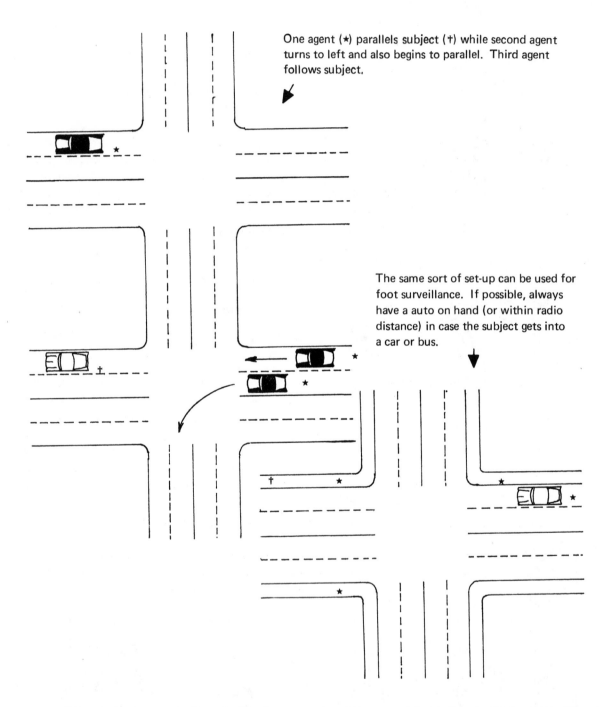

One agent (★) parallels subject (†) while second agent turns to left and also begins to parallel. Third agent follows subject.

The same sort of set-up can be used for foot surveillance. If possible, always have a auto on hand (or within radio distance) in case the subject gets into a car or bus.

This method is known as parallel tailing; the idea is to use two to four agents (★) to follow one bad guy (†). The advantage to parallel tailing is that you can keep the subject (or bad guy) under constant surveillance while having the agents constantly alternating positions. This sort of switch-play makes it very hard for the subject to get a make on the people following him.

It is just about absolutely necessary to have the cars equipped with some sort of radio communication.

83

source of collaborated testimony.

Bigamy is a hard one to prove. Unless the person slips up and in a drunken fit of ego tells the details, it is usually near impossible to find a divorce record (as any state and quite a few countries will grant them). If a former spouse can be located, the situation can usually be straightened out in a hurry.

Desertion normally requires one spouse to leave for a varying period of time (up to a year) and refusal to return. Either drunkenness or extreme cruelty must be proven on some sort of habitual basis, not one fling and an argument. Normally, it will require some form of physical violence to be considered extreme cruelty.

Adultery is the fun one. Actual proof of this evil deed can come from a couple of different directions. A closing (where one party is surprised in-flagant . . .) or by probing intent and opportunity. The latter method is rarely understood by the general public Put simply, intent can be written notes, recorded (or witnessed) signs of loving emotion (kissing by the water cooler, and so on). Opportunity is a bit trickier. Simply having the two people alone in a situation where it could conceivably occur is the letter of the law, but a motel room is going to stand up a lot better in court than is a hospital waiting room, for instance. The period of time they can be PROVEN alone (this means all exits must be covered, they must be seen and hopefully, photographed, entering and leaving together) should be of sufficient time for the act to occur. All activity (people entering and leaving, shades pulled, etc.), should be recorded along with all details such as time, room numbers, etc.

In a couple of states, one slip of the marital bonds is not considered enough for a divorce, and a pattern of such activity must be proven.

Should you need such records as hotel register copies, it is wise to play it pretty straight. The manager is under no compulsion to give you said copies, but the word "subpoena" will often work wonders. (I mean, an explanation of the manager having to show up in a dreary courtroom, getting adverse publicity, etc., will often turn the trick). If the records are simply to satisfy your own base curiosity and not for court purposes, a fake badge and "private detective" license often works well. This last idea, of couse, is illegal. If you decide to go the raid route, beware of a couple of things. If you are helping a buddy, while you are on his (or "their") premises, you are an invited guest and can help participate in the fun, but should you decide to break down a hotel room door, be aware that everyone involved is probably going to get hit with a trespass and/or break and entry charge.

Any form of enticement whereby a spouse is led into a situation where adultery is likely to occur by the other side of the marriage, or any sort of pre-arranged situation is trouble. Not only will the divorce not be granted, but people may find themselves with other charges.

Collusion, i.e., a certain party or parties offer false testimony in court as of the doings of one spouse is also a no-no known as perjury and jail time. . . . .

While not legal in court, wiretaps are often employed for prospective adultery cases. A drop-relay recorded on the phone is a good first step, as most devious plans are first laid, (or verified) by phone. A back-up unit is a room bug in the likely premises, and possibly an automatic camera if you are REALLY curious.

A firm cleaned up some years ago by offering a "special" kit that consisted of a movie camera set to take only one frame every couple of seconds and a tape recorder that was turned on by a spring controlled pressure plate.

The camera was equipped with a mini-wide angle lens and designed to be hidden behind some sort of room furnishing, while the recorder, it was pointed out, worked very well under a bed where any pressure on the bed would turn it on . . . . .

One should bear in mind that haste makes waste, and lack of God-given patience is the enemy of all agents. The victim must not feel you are pushing things in any way (well, I've got to go out now, dear, why don't you go ahead and make any phone calls you have to make . . .), or he/she will stop and resist, or at least change the base of operations.

Remember, the victim is probably (hopefully) already saddled with some guilt pangs and may actually be a bit sloppy, subliminally hoping to be caught, and punished for his or her evil doings.

LEGAL PAPERS

Legal Papers are served by persons not involved with the case in question, a commercial process server, or the sheriff of the county involved. Normally, the first approach is to find out where the person works and approach him there. The secondary method is to stake out the person's residence and hit him there. The person named does not have to accept the papers in any way, they must simply be handed to him (or even dropped within a certain radius of him) while he is told what is transpiring. The server must then sign a witness sheet that the papers were so delivered.

Sheriff departments will make one or two concentrated efforts at service, then will move on to other, more pressing matters. Legal servers will take whatever steps they are paid to take. A smart legal server does not admit who he is to either the person or the person's neighbors etc., until the evil deed is done. Legal servers always try for a physical description of the person to be served, along with all other details that may be available.

If you are questioning neighbors, etc., about someone you wish to serve, it is a good idea to lie and become someone beneficial (one that always conjures up the American dream coming true is to be from the legal estate of a relative . . .) as not to unduly alarm them, and in turn, your victim.

THE MOBILE LABORATORY UNIT

It has already been suggested that one of the most important functions of the criminalistician is the examination of the scene of the crime for physical evidence. After any serious crime such as murder, robbery, or burglary, the nature of which is such that traces of the criminals may reasonably be expected to be present, the scene should be guarded and the laboratory summoned. The detective without laboratory training is frequently unaware of many possible traces. He is often ignorant of the significance of seemingly unimportant details. In addition, his slight knowledge of the handling and preservation of evidence may lead to serious errors.

At the scene of the crime the laboratory investigator will often be required to make quick judgments. For example, his opinion will be requested concerning the possibility of certain stains being blood or semen. These tentative decisions are necessary to the work of the local detectives who are in charge of the case. Frequently they are confronted with circumstances which would permit suspicion to fall upon a number of persons. The eliminative aspect of the laboratory's work in these circumstances is of great value. In addition to suggesting the possibilities

that may arise from the first examination of the evidence, the laboratory man must decide what evidence should be removed to the office for further study, and what method should be used for its preservation.

It is necessary, then, that a laboratory be equipped with facilities for making preliminary analysis and then collecting and preserving the evidence at the scene; hence it must possess a mobile unit. This unit need not be as pretentious as the term would seem to imply. The extent to which the unit is equipped will depend upon the budgetary resources and the size of the area in which the laboratory operates.

We of Criminal Research Products, Inc. have designed the basic Model 700 POLICE MOBILE CRIME LABORATORY that is available to law enforcement departments. This unit was designed and constructed to meet the need of every investigating agency. This unit is equipped with professional and scientific equipment of the latest design.

This unit is being used by law enforcement agencies in the United States, the Federal Police in Mexico City and other foreign governments. Write for additional information.

Cat. No. 116-574 . . . . $24,500.00

Of course, if you really want to make full scale investigations..........Give Criminal Research a call..........

PRIVATE ESPIONAGE:

INDUSTRIAL AND PERSONAL

From the Watergate hearings:

Q. "When a man undertakes to disguise himself he is involved in undercover work, isn't he?

A. "Well, we run into a definitional problem, sir."

Q. "Well, you didn't think he applied for this voice alteration device in order to sing a different part in the choir, did you?"

PRIVATE ESPIONAGE: INDUSTRIAL AND PERSONAL

Industrial espionage offers one of the rare chances for the free-lance spy to actually make a bundle of money; or of course, get into an equal amount of trouble. There are a number of factual, organized IE rings/operators in existence today. Besides these professionals, any number of amateurs are constantly kicking around, trying to sell one or more gems of stolen information.

IE is an unusual field, in that the IE agent invariably commits one or more felonies while getting his information, the cases rarely come to court, and even if they do, the courts are a bit unsure exactly what sort of crime has taken place ......

In the first place, a good agent never steals anything directly. Information can be recorded or photographed, leaving the originals in an untouched condition. This method means you did not actually steal any physical object, as well as not tipping the victim that any leak has occurred. Unless an IE agent is apprehended in the midst of performing a break in or wire-tapping episode, the courts seem to be a bit unsure as how to prosecute the supposed theft of information. Even complicating this dilemma is the fact that to prosecute the victim, one must first prove there really was a secret, by divulging same in court. This, would, of course, let any competitors who cared to listen, have access to the very thing the victim is trying to protect.......

To get the real, honest to God low-down on the industrial espionage game, we managed to delve up an honest-to-God Industrial Spy. No easy thing, this. *

Our spy was/is named Don Duch, and he operates on the West Coast, primarily in California. Mr. Duch is a licensed private investigator, but he rarely practices the gumshoe game anymore, because "the no fault divorce law has taken the bread and butter out of the investigation racket. . . ".

Instead, D.D. leases his talents to any number of businesses who have problems, or who simply want to know what the opposition is doing. Some of his contacts come from referrals from other detectives, some from tips from a friendly security corporation who passes on its requests for spying to Mr. Duch, and some D.D. digs up for himself.

He is an avid reader of all the local business journals and business sections of the daily papers. When he spots a firm that has just developed a new product/process that is sure to put it far ahead of its competition, Mr. Spy starts looking around at the competition . . .

Another avenue of approach is to find a firm that is in trouble, let's say it's being sued by someone, something for infringement of patents, or some such, and is in pretty deeply. This firm might also be in the market for a bit of dirt on the plantiff.

Okay, now he's got a possible client, now what? Let's pretend YOU are a talented amateur industrial spy, what would you do?

First things first, as they say, you need to know whom to contact in the prospective clients firm.

*We do not cop out like those other books, this is his real name, I hope he gets busted . . . . . .

One approach is to look up the company in one of the various business registers and start with a list of the officers that might be in a position to use the information.

These names are then investigated (with the procedures mentioned elsewhere in this book) to see if anyone stands out as a bit on the underhanded side. This would be the first place to start. A quick phone call to the person involved will tell you if he is interested or not . . . (many will NOT be, but some will be very, very, interested . . .).

Now that you've got your client interested, it is best to proceed with a bit of care. Perhaps you should sit still for a few days after discovering what exactly your client needs. Figure out exactly how hard it is going to be to get the information, and how much it is going to help your client before your next meeting. This sort of estimating will give you a good idea of exactly what to charge for the job.

GETTING THE JOB DONE

In many instances, the client will be able to help, or nearly even do your job for you. Extensive, careful questioning will often reveal exactly where the information is stored, or who is most likely to be bribed, or at least physical facts such as secretary's names, office layout, etc.

It is interesting to note here, that, contrary to popular belief, the most common technique for obtaining "secret" data IS NOT the use of surveillance devices. While they are used, no doubt about it, there are often much easier ways to dig out information than the risky implantation and tedious maintenance of electronic devices.

The most common method is the utilization of a person within the victim's firm who already has access to the necessary information. The quickest method here is simple bribery, or as it is known in the trade; simple bribery.

There are several workable methods to choosing a "helper" in a target firm. If possible, the list should be narrowed down with the client's help, he will often know who has access to the knowledge in question and who doesn't.

If even this method is unlikely, or just about anyone in the outfit can help you (this is especially relevant if the person is simply going to be used to unlock doors, or gather data he may not normally have access to) a good place to start is simply copy down all the license plates in the company parking lot. In most states, the DMV will look up the owners name and address, although they may require a small fee for this service.

Once you have a probable list of suspects, the next place you would be likely to turn to is your friendly credit bureau, or two. Any good industrial spy worth his salt will have joined, or have access to (from a friendly store owner or some such) at least one credit bureau.

A quick run-through will often turn up at least one or two names of people who have a bit of difficulty managing their affairs . . . these people are your prime suspects.

If you're still shy of prospects, you can often bet on technical writers to be underpaid and quite knowledgable. Junior executives (or even seniors for that matter) who were just passed over for a promotion (once again, the business journals are a necessity) are also viable shots.

Any executive who has just "resigned" (business journals, again) may be pissed off enough to cooperate for a fee.

So you've got your possible mark, now what? Well, certain factors must modulate your approach somewhat. If you are shooting for a minor type exec. or tech. writer, or even "maintenance engineer", you probably can lead off with a strong "private detective" role.

We have the miracle of television to thank for this one, you'll be surprised how many people will want to help out a real, dyed-in-the-flesh private eye. You can either flash some phony identification badge or just imply you have been hired to do an investigation.

What sort of investigation? My first choices are the "management wants to know what certain employees are up to and wants your help" approach, or the "I've been hired by a company who is thinking about buying this company and wants a friend on the inside". In either approach, you must convince the guy he is an "investigative consultant", or even assistant detective.

The first thing is to put him on "retainer". Lay a couple of hundred on the guy and ask some idiotic questions about what he has noticed, or how to boost output, or who's doing his job and who is not. Get the guy thinking the management (or new management) is putting a lot of faith in his opinion, get his ego as large as possible.

After a few weeks of listening faithfully to his "reports" you change his "retainer" over to a check.... after he cashes a couple of your checks you lay it a bit heavier .... he is to steal, get, photograph, or just help you get into the plant/office alone some evening. Once you're inside, of course, your friend is politely told to get lost, or go "guard" the door. If he balks at any point you lay out a double payment and remind him of the checks he has cashed. A few prudent words here about what his employers would do if they saw the checks, or about the fact you are both going to jail if necessary, will destroy most morals faster than you can say Shazam.

Now suppose you've got to attack a heavier prospect; a fairly senior executive or some such. If you think the guy is not happy with his employers (passed over for a promotion, etc.) you can use the "head-hunter" bit; you've been hired to find a man who; now read off a list of qualifications that seem to fit the man to a "T", for some unnamed client who wants to pay a much higher salary than the guy is holding down now. It is even possible to run a phony "tailor" ad in a business journal listing the qualifications (which of course, fit the victim to his eye color) and have him call you.

The bit here, of course, is that the client wants you to be sure the man has the qualifications for the job . . . a few dinners, cocktails, detailed questions about his part in the new operation/proposal /product and you will often have the information you need painlessly . . . . and, needless to say, the "client" finds someone he likes better for the job . . . . .

If the target (sounds so much more professional than victim, don't you think?) is a bit too sophis-ticated for this approach, there is always the tried and true call girl approach . . . it's surprising how many guys can be flattered to the point of talking about their role in this or that to some sharp girl . . . . if this fails they can always be approached later with photos, tapes and other memorabilia of that exciting weekend . . . .

One "notable" operator likes to pick nice young girls who could be just about any age between 17 and 24, right? Uh huh, then the girl is conveniently pushed off on the target . . car breaks down and needs a ride, frequents his favorite bar, is doing a thesis in school and needs to interview a successful executive etc. etc. . . .   A few days after the big event, the target gets a nice little letter from the girl's brother, uncle, father, protector, boyfriend - and lo and behold, she was only 17 years of . . . . . .

Sometimes it's not necessary to resort to bribery at all. One can borrow the big lie technique of the collection agency/skip tracer. Simply by taking any information you have and then using the expansion technique one can often get enough to get started.

If you know the guy's secretary's name, a call when Joe is out of the office with a "Hi, Peggy, is Joe in? No? This is Marty . . .   Is he still in a meeting with, a uh, yeah, that's it, Bill Samuels. I wanted to tell him I've got some new information on the deal . . Oh, it did go through? Gosh, I hope he didn't pay over $100,000. . .Oh, that's good. . ."

Another sure-fire winner is to approach the office in some other skin. Many execs are happy to talk to reporters from some trade or prestigious business journal, but be aware, a sharp exec will often call to verify you are a reporter for such and such . . . this means you've got to have some name of a buddy to verify your employment. Now, occasionally a set of "credentials" will delete the phone call, and once in a while the guy will talk to a freelancer, but a verification number is the real ticket.

While you're interviewing the mark, you can often dig out facts he wouldn't tell his wife . . . but to prove how sharp he/the company is, he'll gladly tell YOU . . . at the very least this is the perfect cover for a plant tour, and a good chance to plant a bug . . .

If the target area is quite large and diversified, one can sometimes just put on a worker/policeman/ or guard's clothes and wander about at will . . .

If you feel limited access is enough; a one-shotter as a Ma Bell repairman, air conditioner serviceman, power inspector or industrial safety inspector, may suffice. Just be sure to have cover ID and the proper attire.

A night time visit is often arranged with the janitor, guard, or maintenance man. These people have access to the entire facility and are often getting paid some outrageous sum in the neighborhood of $2.50 an hour. One can often bribe such a person to let you do a night time tour, but keep a couple of things in mind: convince him there is a quasi-legit reason for the visit, reassure him you are not going to steal anything and no one will ever know you have been there. Don't offer him too much (this rule applies to bribing minor personnel also) people seem to think the crime is far worse if the bribe is high.

In a clandestine approach, either by bribery, or by out-and-out break and enter, it is a wise idea to carry no ID, and a thousand or so dollars CASH on your person. If you are discovered by a janitor/ guard/policeman, you can sometimes pay your way out of it. Of course this is not foolproof, look at the $90 a week security guard that caught the Watergaters in full bloom, now those jokers must have offered him something, but man, he turned 'em in . . . . that's the kind of guard you want around YOUR place.

Another idea practiced by many such clandestine characters is to find out who the secretaries in the executive department are. These girls have knowledge of just about everything that goes down in top offices, and get paid $750 a month. HOWEVER, they are often very, very loyal to the boss and the company because they FEEL IMPORTANT. Bribe offers here are likely to get reported to

OFFICE ESPIONAGE

A good industrial spy can often get information from such unlikely spots as shipping departments or mail rooms. If a competitor has a good idea of your materials orders, he can often puzzle out when you plan on introducing new models, how sales are going, what your back-stock is like and so on.

Personnel files are another trouble area; it is easy to tailor a special employment package to steal a key employee if a headhunter knows exactly what you are giving in the way of pay and benefits. Often candidates for blackmail or bribery can also be gleaned from the personnel file department.

As many firms turn to computerized record keeping a new type of thief appears; the computer defeater. A computer is simply an overgrown adding machine with a memory-they do exactly what they are told (if they could only wash the dishes....) with little regard to who is doing the telling. With the proper entry coding and access it is a simple matter to learn anything one wishes from one of these beasts. As many computers are rented on a time share basis, virtually anyone with access to a terminal can get into the mainframe. Then it just takes a code....

Employees and agents are not the only dabblers in espionage; many an employer has placed a VOX operated tape recorder or mic in a washroom or lunchroom. A 10 minute conversation between two employees is often worth month's of research about internal problems, or at the least, shows who is goofing off and who is working.

The executive end of industrial espionage is probably the easiest sort of all. Most offices have literally no security beyond a easily defeated file cabinet lock, and access is often gained by joining or bribing the janitorial staff.

An amazing amount of material can be gotten by just going through the wastebasket each night. Even an office with a shredder will often leave carbon paper or carbon typewritter ribbons lying about in the garbage. Needless to say, this is as dangerous as the orginal.

Even without the aid of lost carbon paper it is easier to rub a pencil over the top sheet on a pad of paper and get a readable impression of what was written on the sheet which was above it then it is to employ weird surveillance devices.

Industrial espionage is on the rise. Many companies are only too willing to spend $5000 to get a half million dollars worth of SOMEBODY ELSE'S RESEARCH.....Much of this information is picked up and sold by amateurs, and the commonest method is simply keeping one's eyes open.

There are a few counter measures you can take if you feel you might be victimized by this sort of thing: if someone is snooping where they shouldn't be, you can purchase a variety of fingerprint powders and pastes that coat an object invisibly, but glow under UV light, or even that darken with contact with skin oil. These chemicals literally cannot be washed off for a week or so. They are available from any of the criminal research type suppliers we have listed.

A burn or shred schedule should be set up for all waste material. No less than 2 trusted employees who are not best of friends should carry out that procedure every day. All confidential documents should be kept under a good lock and key system.

A thin piece of metal should be placed under the top sheet of all memo pads and tablets to prevent the formation of impression marks. Carbon ribbons should be destroyed after every use.

Perhaps you should employ a sweep team to scour the office for bugs, and employ a jamming device to help guard against a "walk-in" bug. Never let repairmen or other unauthorized people into your office AT ANY TIME, unless you are there to supervise the "repairs".

What the well dressed private spy might wear:

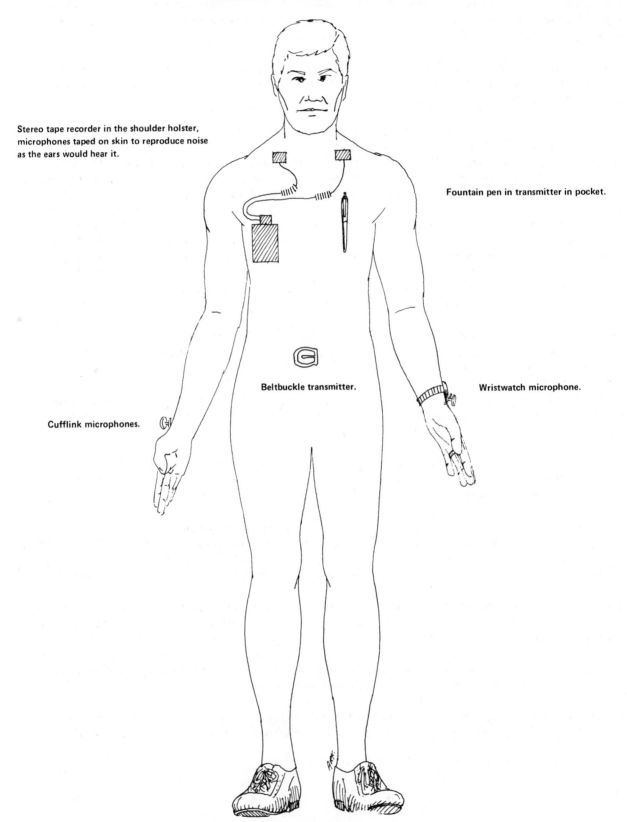

Stereo tape recorder in the shoulder holster, microphones taped on skin to reproduce noise as the ears would hear it.

Fountain pen in transmitter in pocket.

Beltbuckle transmitter.

Wristwatch microphone.

Cufflink microphones.

Transmitter in heel of shoes.

the very people you would rather not have them reported to.

The preferred technique here is, as it's known in the trade, the secretary-seduce . . . a quick affair, or even the real thing (not coca cola in this case . .) will often get mucho info. HOWEVER, (seem to be using a lot of those here, don't I?) it is still far better to ask her questions about her "career" and appear really interested, or con her with a cover story about writing a book, trying to get a job and want to know how to write a presentation, could she bring home a sample . . . is far and away better than the outright bribe. At very worst, hide a good bug in some portion of her effects, or give her a nice desk clock/picture/calendar with a built-in extra that will often get planted free of charge.

When a good private spy looks a job over he works up some sort of proposal; is it going to be a bribery bit, or just a secretary-ball, will he risk going to jail for breaking and entering, or does he have to plant a $600 Infinity Transmitter that he may never get back? How much leg and book work will be involved, how much "juice" will need to be passed around? All of these things determine what sort of fee to charge.

There are a couple of kinds of I-Spies that do not work on a contingency basis. One sort is the free-lancer, he does not work for anyone, just simply looks around for information that will be of value to someone else. This sort of thing is big in industries that thrive on large R and D budgets, such as the drug trade, or businesses that must bid for large jobs such as electronics or aerospace. The competition is often happy to spend $50,000 for a drug that cost its nearest relative 2 million to produce.

There are a number of professional freelance agencies in existence. Many operate outside the United States; Switzerland is reported to be a big spot for this sort of dealing. These agencies are usually well funded and quite professional. Any information they come up with is often put up to select people for bid, much as one might do on an object of art. Often an especially valuable chunk of info will be offered back to the person/firm it was purloined from first, or at least, they will be invited to bid also . . .

This sort of thing occasionally leads to someone (usually an amateur) stealing something and then selling it back to the original owner as well as to one or more of this competitors. No professional would think of doing this, as his business depends on his reputation for being an honest thief. Some spies will take the morality thing so seriously they will not steal from a former client, or even from someone who has purchased information from them at an "auction".

Some firms, in particularly sensitive markets, will employ their own full time spy. One can only imagine the job application for such a position . . . . .

Amateur or professional, a one-time shot or on an on-going basis, there is quite a bit of private business espionage going on today in all types of businesses from major pharmaceutical companies down to retail stores. A recent book even claims there are two full-time, private schools in California for training private spies.

We found this a bit hard to verify, but several times the same location was mentioned as a distinct possibility, and one surveillance expert summed it up with the explanation, "Well, I don't really know for sure, but one does hear rumbles every so often . . . ."

Okay, okay, enough of this hypothetical rambling, you mutter, how can an honest, God fearing, red blooded...*well you get the idea*, American, use this sort of knowledge? Well let's take a little jaunt into reality (dammit all, if you wanted escape you should have bought a Robbins novel...). Suppose you are considering going into business with someone. Either you or he has placed an ad in the paper advertising this great opportunity for the two of you to make enough money inside of 6 months to live in the Virgin Islands for the next 20 years....The other party, is of course about to invest his entire life savings, plus half of what he embezzled from his last job, into said scheme.

The first thing is to get as many facts as possible in a strictly businesslike fashion. If you really are going to invest some money, or time, into another person's ideas, he should expect to be asked a certain amount of background information. If he balks at answering these questions, well, you really wouldn't want a partner like that anyway, would you?

Where did he work last, or what did he work on last? Where is he from, where does he live-rent, own, or lease, always insist on has social security number and ALWAYS RUN A CREDIT CHECK by having your friendly banker or local merchant that uses one of the major credit services run him through. Find out exactly what he has in the way of collateral (whether it is going into the deal or not).

Once you have a list of this information CHECK IT OUT using the records and techniques shown elsewhere in this fine book. Everything should jive....ANY mismatches mean trouble.

Next talk to the BBB, State Attorney General, and the Commissioner of Corporations; investigative section, asking about your newly found partner by name AS WELL AS BY SCHEME. Many, many people have been, ah, taken, by the same con artist, and the same scheme, simply because they did not bother to see if any of the grand promises were really based in any foundation of reality as we know it today....

Okay, so far so good, all above board and legal. Now, we delve into the realm of just how far your moral principles hold up......The normal run through will probably suffice in 90% of all the cases...but.....if you wish to REALLY know what is going on, get the down and dirty, do a no-no (another trade vernacular), you can borrow upon the ideas of some of the more nebulous types around (used car salesmen, government agents, you know the type).

If you are facing a situation where you are applying for a job, asking for money from a group of investors, or just talking to someone in his office, you can pull the old, but far from dead, hide-the-recorder-in-the-briefcase ploy. In this little ditty one simply hides a battery powered recorder (with AGC, and a good mic) in a briefcase with the mic held in place behind the keyhole, or small pin hole, and the remote start feature rigged into the handle as shown.

Now, run through your bit and then excuse yourself, either when the interview is over, or to let them "think it over in private". Leave for a while and then return to pick up your "lost" briefcase which you thoughtlessly left under a chair.

"Thank heaven I found it".....

This is best done by bringing an array of several items, including the briefcase, into the conference as to create less chance of someone pointing out the fact that you are "forgetting" your briefcase.

If you can stick nearby during this period of private discussion, a bug will work as well as a briefcase, however the recovery can be a bit stickier........("Oh, there's my little black box, I've been looking all over for that, and here it was, stuck underneath the table all the time...").

If you are really, really concerned about what is going on behind the scenes you could always bug the phone BEFORE the interview, and collect a couple of days worth of before-and-after office lowdown...

Now, just for sake of something to write about, let's say you are thinking of taking the fatal plunge, no, no I mean matrimony. Now, she's a nice enough girl, right? No reason to disbelieve her, right? Then why the hell are you reading this?.....Uh, huh, sure.....Well, the same basic things apply here as in business, you've just got more to lose, that's all....

Instead of running a credit check, you may have to resort to more earthy (i.e., illegal) things right off of the bat. A bugged phone for a week or so will turn up things you may have never dreamed of.....Wonder where she goes, how about having a friend tail her, (or you in a friend's car)?

If you're really unsure the old tape-recorder-under-the-bed bit is a sure fire winner to see if she really snores in her sleep, if that would bother you....Or the infinity transmitter, excuse me, I mean Tele-Ear Burglar Alarm, installed in a bedroom phone or wall box, will always let you make sure she is safe and sound in bed, not being raped, or attacked or anything. After all, it's for her own good, right?

A favorite trick of your author's (Uncle Scott as we fondly think of him), back in the high school days, was to invite two close friends, or sisters, or what have you, out for a double date with you and a buddy. Now you do whatever comes natural, go to the drive-in, for instance, and lo and behold you and your buddy volunteer to get out and get the popcorn during intermission.

Any cheap bug, or even a walkie-talkie taped in the transmit position will then give you a good idea of what the rest of the evening could be turned into......

Of course, the ultimate tool for evaluating any business deal, marriage proposal, or what the hell, even a singles bar bit has just gotta be the good old voice lie detector, the PSE. . .

Remember, things are really rarely what they seem.......(did you know there's a doctor in Brazil who reconstructs hymens?, okay so that's a bit off of the subject, I was just trying to show you this concept of things rarely being.....)

96

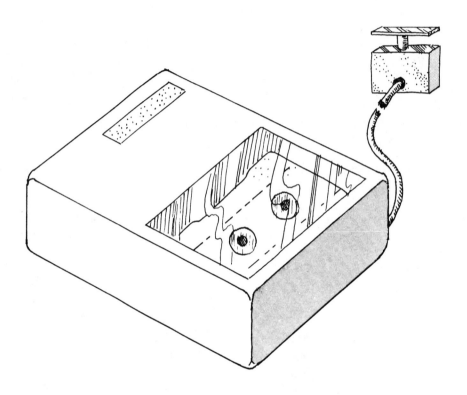

A modern tape recorder can be rigged into a Sunday Bedroom special by a couple of simple alterations: place the correct size of mini-plug (available at Radio/Hobby supply houses) into the remote start hole. Run wires from each side of the plug into a micro switch as shown. A light plastic sheet can be glued to the tip of the switch for added security. The switch is now placed upon a hard object (books, brick, 44 magnum, etc) so it just touches the bottom of the mattress in question.

Any downward movement of the bed will now turn on the tape recorder which will run until the weight, or movement, is removed...A bit of testing will assure correct switch positioning....

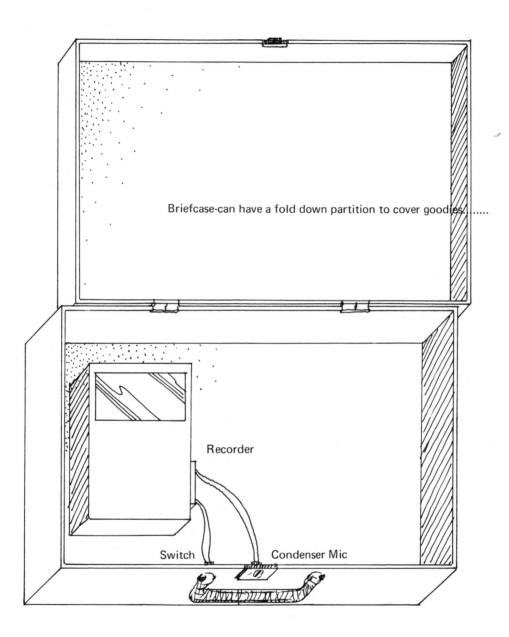

Briefcase-can have a fold down partition to cover goodies.......

Recorder

Switch   Condenser Mic

To make this magic beast you simply mount a tape recorder (usually a smallish cassette) in a briefcase. Now get the correct jacks for the remote start inputs. From the remote mic jack run a couple of wires to another, sensitive (usually condenser) mic which is hidden behind a key hole or minute hole you have drilled in the case. The remote start wires are run to a hidden micro switch, or simply to two small metal contacts which are mounted one on the handle and one on the case in a position where the handle mounted plate will make contact when you fold the handle up, but not when it is in a "down" position.

Now simply conduct your business and then unobtrusively reach down and fold the handle up. Leave the room and return sometime later for your "lost" briefcase. BE CERTAIN IT IS LOCKED! A super long play recorder can be utilized if you are not too concerned with fidelity. A nice leather case will help absorb any running sounds. . . .

Just for the sake of curiosity let's play pretend; it's sort of like playing doctor, you remember, the little girl next door....well anyway, the concept is the same. What if you could apply an accurate lie detector test to anyone you wanted, at any time, even over the telephone WITHOUT THEM KNOWING IT!

Think that stock option is really as good as the salesman makes it sound? Believe your job applicant really graduated from Yale, or stole from his last job? Think your old lady really played bridge until 3 am? Ever wonder if those politicians are embellishing things a little bit, or if your cashier is tilting the till? The possibilities for such a sci-fi device would be almost unlimited, right?

As you have no doubt surmised from my clever style of introducing things on a fiction basis and then hitting you with the heavy stuff just when you least expect it, such a device does indeed exist.

Our magic box does everything except make the liar's nose grow longer. . .It functions on the principle that the human voice is modulated by minute physiological tremors (in the 8-12 Hz range) when the body is placed under heavy stress; such as the stress measured by conventional lie detectors when a lie is recorded. These modulations are FM and too low to be heard by the human ear.

Now, take a device which records the voice and then filters out the audible portions, leaving only these stress tremors. At the same time the recording is made the stress tremors are charted on a strip print-out so later comparisons can be correlated between spoken words and stress points.

Now, if a carefully worded interrogation is used on the subject, stress induced by guilt, fear, anxiety and conflict will show up in areas of attempted deception. This aids in a variety of decisions based on any judgments concerning motivation, normal tension levels, and reliability.

The device in question is known as a PSYCHOLOGICAL STRESS EVALUATOR or PSE and is in use by a number of law enforcement agencies, private investigators, law firms, psychiatric clinics and private corporations. It is often used without the subject even being aware of its presence. . .

In fact, when the PSE first came out it was tested on such strange bedfellows as TV programs; in a run of 75 shows of "To Tell The Truth", wherein three suspects each stand up and say, "my name is...." the machine picked the right actor 71 times. Now, this is especially hard when you take into consideration that this is a programmed lie which produces little stress on the actor. Another test was conducted with 3 x 5 cards in which the subject read off neutral and emotional words in a random sequence. The machine picked the emotional words 52 out of 53 times, in a series of seven tests.

In a final demonstration of prowess, the machine was asked to work with the police in Maryland County using lie detection test questions to establish guilt as well as "guilt knowledge" in a number of cases. In 26 cases containing 162 elements of crime the machine scored 100% (corroborated by confession or investigation).

The device is housed in a briefcase and can be turned on during most any conversation without arousing anyone's interest. After the conversation, the tapes are replayed and compared with the chart recorded stress points using the PSE's chart interpretation criteria. As I mentioned, it is possible to even record a phone call and later evaluate the results....

The possibilities of a machine which gets better-than-the-average-lie-detector results on spoken (EVEN ON TAPES MADE YEARS AGO AND PLAYED BACK INTO THE MACHINE) are mindbending. You can be damn sure the CIA, FBI and such have PSE's, as can you be fairly sure many businessmen have access to said beast.

Now carry this another step or two and figure out what would happen if every VOTER had access to a PSE, or the device's findings......It is an interesting conjecture to note that the machine does not do as well on statements that are read, rather than answered on the spur of the moment, or cannot respond as accurately to "hedged" concepts; i.e. non-yes-or-no, but maybe, or if certain conditions exist.....It is also interesting to note, on a purely one sided, and probably dead ass wrong, angle, how politicians have been much more careful when giving public speeches in *the last couple of years since the inception of the PSE to utilize exactly these read-or-hedge techniques.....Paranoia? Who knows..........*

The PSE is available for a mere $4000 including a nice Samsonite briefcase. One can also get three day's training in the use of the PSE with purchase at the manufacturer's plant in Virginia.

A last passing fact, one writer, researching the PSE for a magazine, ran back network tapes in the Kennedy killing, including those of Ruby, Oswald, and damn near everyone else in the state of Texas. To say the tapes appeared to show most of the statements appeared to be pure and unadulterated bullshit, would not be an overstatement..........

Perhaps we will start to see PSE's appearing at Bridge parties, or maybe even on a rent-a-detector basis at marriage chapels in Las Vegas........."Do you take, or have you previously taken......."

PSYCHOLOGICAL STRESS EVALUATOR
Dektor Inc.
5508 Port Royal Rd
Springfield, Va 22151

Here the irrelevant question shows no deception and a relative absence of tension.

Note the difference in response to two approaches to essentially the same question The first shows an irregular wave pattern with

some cyclic rate change indicating some tension. The second shows a clear diagonal pattern indicating a deceptive answer.

Here again is a high-tension diagonal pattern indicating deception.

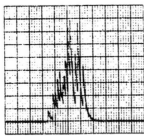

Q — Do you like beer?
A — Yes

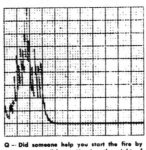

Q -- Did someone help you start the fire by ———— Rd. on Monday the night of the fire?
A — No

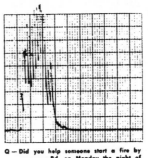

Q — Did you help someone start a fire by ———— Rd. on Monday the night of the fire?
A — No

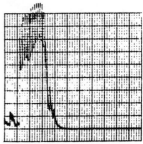

Q — Did you start the fire Monday night 8-14-72 by ———— Rd.?
A — No

These charts are taken from an actual examination of an arson suspect. All of them are in Mode III and clearly demonstrate the irregular wave pattern of non-stressed responses as opposed to the regular pattern displayed when the micro-tremor is suppressed.

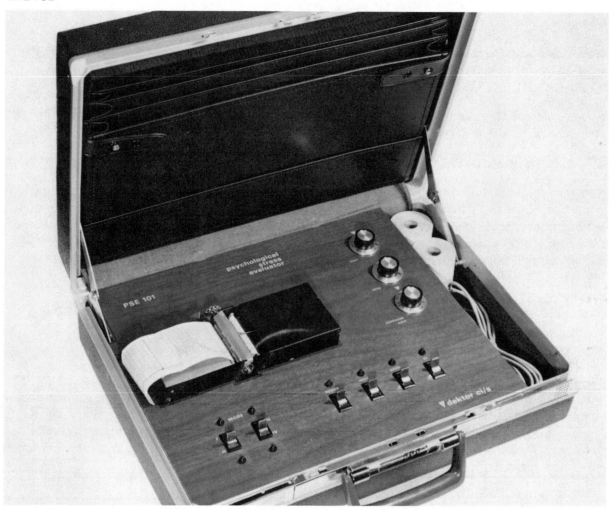

This instrument has been developed to provide a means of detecting physiological changes resulting from a psychological reaction in the manner of the electro-encephalograph and the polygraph, without the use of attached or visible sensors. It makes use of specific voice qualities which reflect visually or aurally undetectable changes resulting from small changes in the degree of psychological stress. By using the voice as the physiological medium, the artificial stress induced by the controlled environment and attached sensors of the polygraph is eliminated and much of the consequent pre-test required by the polygraph may be avoided.

The PSE-I is designed to be used in conjunction with a tape recorder (preferably a UHER 4000-series recorder), to exploit the full capabilities of the instrument. Chart runs can be made simultaneously with taping or from previously recorded tapes. Four modes of operation are provided to allow the optimum charting for different types of tests (e.g., Peak of Tension, General Questions, Zone of Comparison, etc.) and to suit the individual desires of the examiner. Used in conjunction with the changeable speed of UHER 4000-series recorder, the highest possible confidence level can be attained.

Either "yes" and "no" answers, narrative answers, or conversational utterances may be used to accomplish the evaluation.

Because the voice frequencies employed are well within the 300 to 3,000 Hertz frequency band, examinations can be conducted via local or long-distance telephone.

The chart recorder unit employs a heated (inkless) stylus which provides a trace of adjustable darkness to suit the desires of the examiner. In addition to mode selection, the front panel contains controls for adjusting zero level, gain (signal amplitude), and stylus heat; electrical editing to remove the examiner's voice or other undesired material and hold the chart run during the edited period; a below baseline event marker; and switches to control total operation, chart-drive speed, heating of stylus, and signal input.

The instrument is contained in a standard attache case and comes complete with all necessary cords and cables. It can be provided with or without a UHER recorder.

Also included are an instruction manual and a taped course of instruction which takes the student, step by step, through a series of actual taped examinations to allow the attainment of proficiency with this instrument.

The PSE-I operates from 115 volt, 50/60 Hertz commercial power. It carries a one-year guarantee against defective components or manufacture.

101

LIE DETECTION—POLYGRAPH AND VOICE ANALYSIS

No device can directly tell if a person is lying or telling the truth. All "lie detectors", whether polygraphs, PSE, or Mark II type analyzers, measure emotional stress patterns of the person under test. These patterns are then interpreted to tell how much stress the person is undergoing, and, hopefully if the person is being truthful; ASSUMING THE PROPER TEST TECHNIQUES ARE UTILIZED.

The trouble with science is that it must be interpreted by scientists. . .Any lie detection entails detailed interpretation by the operator. To insure the proper results, tests are constructed in such a fashion as to lend control to the test.

Anyone who knows he is undergoing a lie detection test is usually a bit on the apprehensive side. Most people show this nervous tension in the first few questions of any lie detection test, then they normally settle down. Persons who are lying are generally more tense than persons who are telling the truth, BUT THIS CANNOT BE USED AS A BASIS FOR LIE DETECTION. Each person has a seperate "tension index", this must be established and then variations from this norm can be used to show stress points.

There are several patterns of questions and responses which are used to decide if a person is being truthful or otherwise. Each particular method has certain advantages and disadvantages.

NEUTRAL QUESTIONS

In this type of test the subject is asked a neutral question such as, "Is today Monday?". The next question is then a relevant question, "Did you murder your wife?". The stress level should be considerably higher on the relevant question than on the neutral question. Usually a series of two or three relevant questions is asked and then a neutral question is thrown in and the stress level re-noted.

The problems herein are that some questions are not neutral to all people, and that a stress increase must be of a certain level to actually indicate a lie. This level must be determined by prior tests.

STRONG CONTROLS

Here the subject is induced to lie about something that is not as important as the issue at stake. Such questions as, "Did you ever lie in school", or "Have you ever told your mother a lie?" are typical of strong control questions.

Now hopefully, the subject will say "no", this is, in all probability, a lie. His stress reaction is then noted and a strong issue question is asked. If his response is a fair amount greater than the reaction on the control question, he is probably lying. If the response is about the same, or less, he is probably telling the truth.

Usually a strong control is followed by two or three real issue questions and then another strong control is asked.

Once again, the increase in stress must be of a pre-determined rate to indicate the stress of a lie. It should also be noted that a good operator leads the subject in the control questions; i.e., instead of asking, "Have you ever cheated in school?", the operator asks, "You've never cheated in school, have you?"

DOUBLE RESPONSE

In this method, each question is posed in a set of two; i.e., the person is asked, "Do you work for ABC Company?, do you work for ABC Company?". The subject is told to answer, "yes", to the first question, and, "no", to the second.

Now, the idea herein, simply stated, for those of you with short attention spans, is that one answer must be correct and one must be a lie. Therefore, a different stress factor should be computed for each answer. If one is considerably higher than the other, the high one, is, in all probability, a lie.

In this method no control questions are used as each set forms its own control. It is usually quite easy to interpret the results of double response question sets.

TEST PROCEDURES

Under ideal test circumstances, such as a criminal investigation, or pre-employment exam, certain test procedures should be followed to induce the proper control factors into the test.

PRETEST

The person under test should be brought into a quiet room and told what is about to transpire. He should be made to sign a consent form for the test, and then the examiner should read each question to the subject, explaining that if he has any questions, or anything to tell he should do so before the testing begins as any problems or misinformation will show up during the course of the test.

Once the person agrees to each question and signs the form the test should begin.

TEST

Each question should be asked in the same tone of voice. There should be a period of a couple of seconds after each answer before the next question is asked. The subject should be told to say either "yes" or "no" to each question.

The test should be repeated twice. Wait a minute or so after the first test is completed and begin the test all over again. After the second round is completed, you can compare the results of the two tests.

If a person shows a high stress level to the same question in both tests, it can be assumed that question bothers him and he has not told all he knows in the answer. If he shows a high level on only one test to a certain question, it cannot be assumed he is lying; rather he should be told that he registered a high response on that question and could there be any reason for it?

Never expect the same level of stress on any question to appear during both tests. The machine records changes in emotional levels and they can vary from test to test, or during the course of one test.

The question may have surprised the subject when it was first asked, or it may have triggered a response from something totally unrelated to the question. If a high level is shown on one test, and a normal level on the other, the subject should be informed of a "reaction" from the machine and asked about the question; it cannot be safely assumed it was a lie.

POST TESTING

The person should be left alone while the examiner goes over the test reactions. Then the examiner should confront the subject with any questions which gave a deceptive reaction on both tests, or showed a high stress value on both tests. He should be told the machine says he is not telling all he knows about those questions, and could he please explain why that reaction occured?

The idea in this phase is to convince the subject the machine is good and he should start giving out admissions......It often works.

TYPE OF TEST

There are a couple of different types of tests that are used for different circumstances. The commonest types are those used for pre-employment examination, and those designed to extract information about one specific incident (usually a crime).

Certain factors hold true in either type of test: the questions should be kept as simple as possible. They should always be able to be answered with a "yes" or a "no". If it is a question about a certain incident, it should be asked straight forward (i.e., did you beat up the bosses' wife outside the factory on Friday, July 4th?).

The first two questions should be "sacrifice" questions; the person may be a bit nervous about the test and will show stress on the first couple of questions simply because of the test. To combat this the first two questions are meaningless questions that are disregarded in figuring up the test results.

It should be noted that certain persons have a guilt complex; this sort of person may show guilt reactions even when he is totally innocent. To test for this condition, the subject is asked a question about a specific, but hypothetical, crime. For instance, "Did you commit the armed robbery at the Bank of California on Friday the 13th?" If he shows a high stress level on both tests, you have: either a person with a high level guilt complex, or just discovered a crime and captured the criminal in one swift move.

PRE—EMPLOYMENT EXAMS

Many large firms ask the potential employee to take a lie detection test as part of their pre-employment testing. In many states, it is illegal to demand that a person take such a test as a prerequisite to getting the job; HOWEVER, if you refuse to take the test, be damn sure they are going to find a reason for hiring someone else. . .

Pre-employment exams may vary from company to company, depending on what their uppermost concerns are, but a set of general guidelines would be:

whether you have stolen from your previous employers
use of alcohol or drugs
whether you do/have passed bad checks
arrests
whether you/have do participate in the fine art of industrial espionage
whether you are violent
whether you lied on your employment application
etc, etc.

SPECIFIC TESTING

Generally any sort of lie detection will show if a person is innocent or has what is known as "guilty knowledge". This latter condition could indicate anything from actually having committed the act, to having known about it, either before or after it went down.

Once guilty knowledge is established, the examiner usually confronts the subject with the knowledge in the hopes of getting exact admissions. Once something has been admitted, the subject is re-tested; his reactions to the heavy questions should be noticeably less stress-filled.

The test should be given after the usual pre-test going-over. Once again, you should use two sets of identical questions, given in two separate tests. Once the testing is over, the results should be analyzed for several factors: the first thing to look for is the item on each test which introduced the greatest stress reaction. Next, one should look for the items which give a high degree of stress on both tests.

Once these items are located, the subject should be hit up with both types of reactions and asked to explain his reaction (s).

TYPICAL TEST

The test should begin with two sacrifice questions. Usually questions like, "Do they call you XXX?" (rather than, "is your name XXX", as he may be using an alias or have a nick name), or "Are we in Detroit?" are used as sacrifice questions.

Now either a neutral or control question is asked (depending on which sort of test you are using) to get a stress control level. Neutral questions can be such things as, "Do you live in XXX?", control questions can be questions like, "When you were a child, did you ever steal anything?"

Generally the stress level in the control (or neutral) question BEFORE the relevant question (s) is more important in establishing levels as some of the guilt reaction may carry over into the next non-relevant question.

Now one relevant question is asked; Do you know who.......? Do you have any knowledge about......? Have you ever.........? Etc.

Occasionally a guilt complex question should be tossed in as aforementioned. Should the subject show a high stress reaction to the guilt complex question in both test he probably has a high guilt level and CANNOT be effectively tested with any lie detection methods.

The last set of questions on the test are often what is called a SKY sequence. This stands for: Suspect (Do you suspect someone by the name of.....?), Know (Do you know who ....?), You (Did you.......?). When the stress level of Y is considerably higher than the S level, it is a good indicator of the subject's active role in the incident. Each of these SKY questions should be asked out-of-order, during the earlier portion of the test as a control on the SKY sequence.

The only other little tip I can lend, is the fact that when the test is repeated in the second sequence, it is SOP to change the order of the first relevant question on each test EVEN THOUGH YOU ARE USING THE SAME QUESTIONS. This is done to prevent any reaction strictly because it is the first "guilty" type question on the test.

SAMPLE TEST

This test could be used with any type of lie detection equipment.

TYPE	QUESTION
Sacrifice	Do they call you XXX?
Sacrifice	Are we in XXX?
Control	Did you ever lie to your parents?
Relevant	Do you suspect someone named XXX?
Control	Did you ever cheat in school?
Relevant	Do you know who XXX?
Neutral	Do you live in XXX?
Control	Did you ever steal anything as a child?
Relevant	Did you XXX?
Neutral	Do you have a driver's license?
Guilt Complex	Did you beat up the bosses' wife outside the factory?
S-Relevant	Do you suspect someone named XXX?
K-Relevant	Do you know for sure who XXXed?
Y-Relevant	Did you XXX?

Besides these common types of tests one may also encounter specialized tests designed to find a reaction to a certain pattern or word. These tests are generally used along with a "normal" test, two of the most common are the PT, or Peak of Tension and the WA, or word association type tests.

In a PT test a certain fact is drawn from the crime, such as a number (say of money stolen), or a date, etc. These facts are worked into statements; in a WA test certain words are mentioned to the subject and he responds with the first word that comes to mind. Several of these words are connected with the crime. Look for tension peaks.......

TYPES OF "LIE DETECTORS"

Basically all lie detectors, or stress analyzers, fall into one of two categories; polygraphs or voice analyzers (although it should be pointed out work is being done in several other fields, notably eye movement, which may soon be utilized in other types of stress analyzers....).

The polygraph has been around in one form or another for a number of years. A good polygraph measures at least three bodily functions; usually breathing, heart beat rate or blood pressure, and skin resistance. This is affected by attaching a pneumograph, a cardiograph, and a galvanic skin resistance sensor to the subject. These particular measurements are chosen as they are known to be affected by changes in the emotional and stress levels of the subject. It is usually thought that the combined readings of the three sensors give a better indication of stress than any one alone does.

Good polygraphs feed the results of all three sensors into a chart recorder with three pens. As the stress level increases the chart shows an upswing in one or more of the indicator lines. Generally a polygraph is operated by a person trained in the operation and interpretation of such devices, in many states he must be licensed.

Cheaper polygraphs only measure one function, normally skin resistance (GSR). Such devices attach to the hands and measure the resistance levels of the body. As the emotional state changes the various glands (including the sweat glands) begin to secrete and the body's resistance to a minute electrical current changes. These changes are usually connected to a meter, rather than an expensive chart recorder. This type of polygraph can be found in smaller police departments and in toy stores, both models work approximately on the same level.......

Voice analysis as a means of lie detection, or stress level measuring was introduced a few years ago by Dektor Counter-intelligence and Security. They developed and market a device known as a Psychological Stress Evaluator. This consists of a device that analyzes the components of the voice spectrum and filters out the normal "speech", but saves minute FM changes imposed on these vocal "carriers". These FM changes are in the sub-audible band of 8-12 cycles and occur when the subject is in an UNSTRESSED condition, as stress increases these indiscernible modulations disappear. They are apparently caused by minute fluctuations in the muscles of the vocal chord and its surrounding mechanism.

The PSE is normally coupled to a tape recorder and a chart strip-recorder, in this fashion the presence or absence of these sub-audible indicators can be correlated with an exact word or phrase. To a practiced operator it is possible to pick out established stress patterns indicating a lie, a release of tension after the lie, and a return to the normal stress level on the next control or neutral question.

The detail of the recorded waveform allows the operator to make numerous judgments about the subject's reaction, or even his level of stress in any spoken phrase.

During this past year a new device known as the Mark II has been introduced (invented by one Fred Fuller and developed by Technical Planning, Inc, and nationally distributed by Law Enforcement Associates). This device is also a voice analyzer, but differs in several respects from the PSE; it measures an imposed modulation, or "tremolo" effect also, but goes for it in both the audible and sub-audible spectrum. The presence of this stress imposed effect is shown by adjusting the device for ambient noise and sensitivity and then depressing a button marked "analyze" after every answer, or word to be analyzed is uttered. The numerical result is then shown to the operator directly by a LED (like they use in hand calculators) display. The operator compares the number to the numbers received by posing the neutral or control questions and a level of lie probability is established.

The Mark II can also be hooked up to a tape recorder and chart strip-recorder to provide a record of the test. It is sold in two models; one desk-top, with LED display only, and one which comes in a carrying case with tape and chart recorders built-in.

On a polygraph the operator establishes a base line of stress and then assigns values to the various stress "spikes". A value of X is generally used to show a minor reaction to any one of the three indicators, a value of X_1 is given to a stronger reaction and, as you might suspect, X_2 is assigned to a strong stress reaction.

If an X shows on at least two indicators, or an X_2 shows on any one, it is usually considered to be a strong indication of a guilty reaction. Of course, these reactions should be compared with the control questions to get an accurate result.

In the PSE, the waveform is analyzed (Dektor has a training program for purchasers) for stress indicators and established stress reactions.

In the Mark II a numerical value must exceed that of a neutral or control question by a certain percentage to be considered suspect (this varies on the type of test between 20% and 30%).

How well do they work? Well most all of the polygraph operators claim the PSE and Mark II are invalid, this could be due, in part to a natural reaction called self-survival. Both Dektor and LEA furnish reports and testimonials that show their devices are at least as accurate as the polygraph, possibly more so.

Of course, it must be remembered that all three have to be evaluated by the operator, some discrepancy may show up from operator to operator, especially in the polygraph and PSE. The Mark II is easier to use, and, in fact, they claim most people can learn to utilize it correctly from their training manual and a couple of test tapes that they provide.

Another interesting facet of both the Mark II and PSE is that either can also operate from already recorded conversations, or over the phone, television, or radio. Or they can be used "live" without the person realizing he is undergoing the test. Of course, in either of these situations the test is not really a test, and the controls are almost totally lacking, but a general level of stress can be established and additional stress points picked out.

Numerous people have used the PSE on Lee Harvey Oswald's various conversations and almost universally come out with the findings that there exists a lot of unexplained phenomenon. . .The Mark II people analyzed Patty Hearst's tape where she tells of going over to the SLA on her own after the kidnapping. Their findings are a high stress level in general, but everything seems to be the truth. The only point of question is when she denies being "hypnotized", possibly indicating she does (did?) fear some sort of "brainwashing".

Personally I think either the Mark II or PSE have great potential in such unexplored areas as matrimony squabbles, poker games (especially the Mark II, just think what that would do to the art of bluffing), politics, used car sales, and just lots and lots of fun ideas.....

Of course, many are already in use by companies for employment verification, post-analysis of business meetings, checking on salesmen (even when they call in?), criminal investigations, and so on. You can bet your bottom dollar government agencies (CIA, FBI, or worse yet, maybe the IRS?) are checking these devices out, as well as a host of people wanting to use them for some personal gain........

108

EDITING

A word is in order about editing. Any good sound man can take a tape recording and change the meaning of the recorded conversation to the exact opposite of what was originally intended within a few simple operations. This procedure entails recording the words, syllables, and in some instances, letters, in the order desired, and can be done without a trace. For this reason, it is hard to take any recording at face value (a good example of heavy handed editing was the records which appeared shortly after the Watergate investigations, which gave a clear, concise recording of President Nixon admitting his guilt in a number of crimes).

There is little you can do about editing, except not allow your voice to be recorded by anyone you suspect to utilize it for hostile purposes. All TV and radio tapes are edited, this makes most things that appear on the 5:00 news subject to interpretation, to say the least.

If you find yourself in an interesting situation, you should demand the right to hear the EDITED version of the tape before it is released. It is also prudent to watch for trick sentences asked by the interviewer. Your answer may not be the same one given to that particular question. Be wary of sentences which can be reversed by dropping one "not".

It is sometimes possible to force the issue by simply replying to your own questions rather than the interviewers'. For instance, you want to announce a certain event and the interviewer refuses to ask the lead question. Simply reply to any question he puts to you with the proper answer to the question you wanted asked. If they want to use the tape at all, they will have to edit out his question and insert the proper one to make the conversation appear sensible.

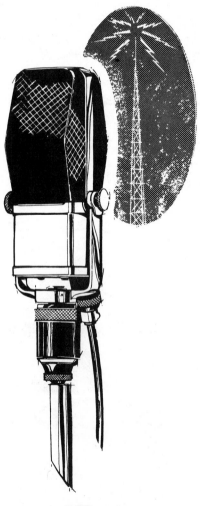

LOCKS:
AND THE OPENING THEREOF

If rules are made to be broken, are locks made to be opened? *Anonymous.*

A working knowledge of locks and their inner most secrets is a necessity for the active agent. Virtually all government agents are well versed in this sort of thing, most army intelligence officers are equally able to deal with most locks and even many private detectives could double as effective burglars if business falls off.

In times past, it was standard procedure to turn CIA type agents loose after training to break into government (and maybe private?) offices on their own and bring back proof of the venture without getting caught or having the B and E noticed the next day.

I cannot attest to whether this sort of thing still goes on or not .....

The advantages of picking or other skilled methods of entry are many: less noise and hence less chance of discovery, no tell-tale signs that a violation has even occurred, fewer tools are necessary than with most break and enter methods, and lastly, but not leastly, it has more class. . .

With any of the picking methods presented here it is necessary to practice, practice, practice. Any picking takes some time and lots of skill. Like most other things in life, it is seldom accomplished as easily as presented on television.

A good method for effective practice is to obtain a lock which lends itself to dismantling and remove all but two pins (one long and one short). Follow the techniques given until you have mastered the two pin lock and then try three pins, then four, etc. Once you have this down pat, replace the two pins with mushroom pins and start over .....

Before picking any lock, squirt a bit of graphite into the locks' innards to help free it from the binding effects of dirt and other contamination.

PIN TUMBLER

The pin tumbler lock is the most widely used lock. It offers medium to high security and is found in doors, cars, and a host of other applications.

The principle of the pin tumbler is a series of tumblers resembling small pins (usually 5) held in place by other pins resting on top of them, called drivers, which are in turn, held in place by springs.

The tumblers, drivers and springs are mounted in the shell of the lock and the tumblers extend down into the core of the lock. When the proper key is inserted the tumblers are raised to this shear line, or division between them and the driver pins. This shear line is located at the top of the core. When this transpires, the core may be turned freely with the key.

If a key is cut too low, the driver pins will extend down into the core; too high and the tumblers will extend up into the shell of the lock. In either case, the core is held stationary and the lock stays locked.

Pin tumblers require a high degree of tolerance in lock and key making. About .002 of an inch is required for correct functioning.

PICKING

Picking locks requires two intrinsic items: A pick and a tension tool. The pick is a thin tool cut from spring steel which ends in a slight upward curve, or a number of other tip shapes ranging from diamonds to balls and squares. The pick is used to raise each pin to its shear line. The most popular pick is probably the curved pick, although you should have a variety of alternatives on hand. There are many sets on the market containing anywhere from 5 to 200 picks and tension tools in some sort of carrying case.

The tension tool is an "L" shaped (usually double ended) piece of spring steel. The tension tool is inserted into the core of the lock and turned slightly in the direction that the lock opens. This tension is maintained throughout the picking operation. As the pins are raised to their shear line the tension you are exerting will prevent them from falling back down into the core.

Locks that use regular, smooth pins are the easiest to pick, and are the best to learn with. Modern Yale, Corbin, etc., are usually equipped with special pins to make picking a more exacting operation. It is quite essential that one learn to pick on a smooth pinned lock before attempting the challenge of an anti-pick lock. So . . . try and choose a cheaper, older lock to begin with.

Place the end of your tension tool into the keyway in such a fashion that it does not block your access to the pins. Most locks will take the tension tool at the bottom of the keyway best; however it makes little difference to the lock, or for that matter, to me, where you place the tool.

Exert a medium tension on the tool in the direction you suspect the lock turns, as shown.

Take your curved pick and insert it into the lock directly under the first pin. Now, while maintaining the tension, push the pin up into the lock.

While still maintaining your tension, remove the pick. If the pin is picked the top (or driver) pin will remain up in the lock itself, freeing the shear line. The bottom pin may fall back down into the lock, but if done correctly, the top pin will wedge against the edge of the core (because you are turning it slightly with the tension tool) and remain up.

Now move on to the second pin and while maintaining tension (so the first pin will stay caught) carefully move the second pin up into the lock; of course, you are being careful not to dislodge the first pin by a clumsy motion. You are being careful, aren't you?

Good.

Now about this time you may discover that some of the pins slide right back down without binding as you've come to expect from my clever instructions. You must realize that some of the pins will be thicker than others (either on purpose or due to uneven wear factors). This means that the thin (ner) pins will slide back into the core while the thicker pins remain picked.

To overcome this little problem one simply picks all the thick pins first and then goes back and attempts the thin ones. As each pin is picked, the core turns a bit more and as it turns the thinner pins will bind against the edge. Soooo ..... go through the lock, picking all that will, and then go back and work on the more difficult buggers.

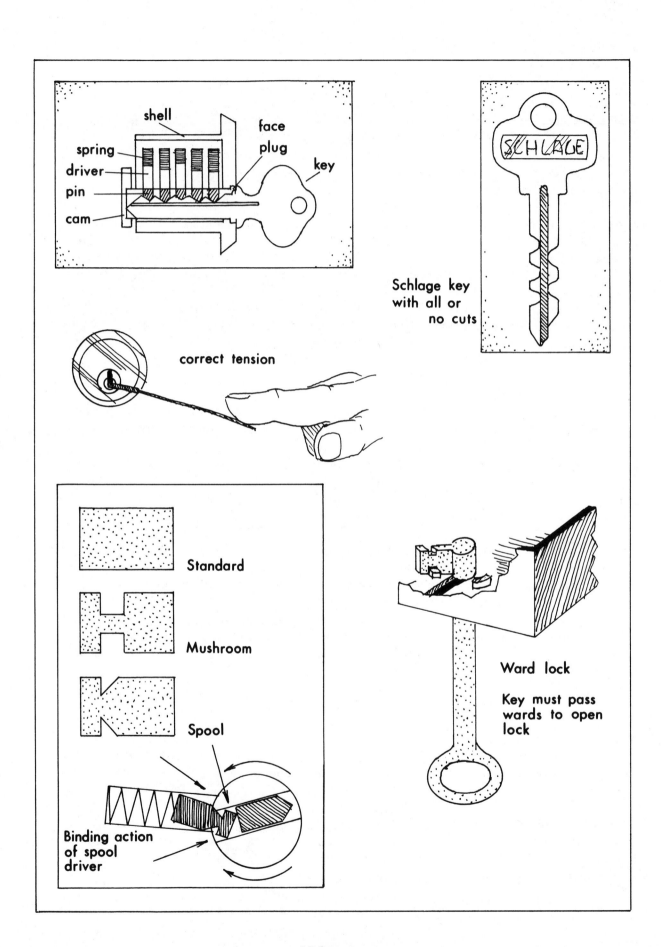

shell

spring
driver
pin
cam

face
plug

key

Schlage key
with all or
no cuts

correct tension

Standard

Mushroom

Spool

Binding action
of spool
driver

Ward lock

Key must pass
wards to open
lock

HOMEMADE PICKS. . .

The most common way to obtain lock "tools", is to have a friendly locksmith order them for you. As much as I hate to say it, many people "become" locksmiths themselves and order the goodies on a letterhead. Some suppliers DO check to see if they are legit, some do not.

If you choose to skip all this worry and make your own pick set simply follow these easy to remember rules:

Get some clock spring, or even shim stock from an auto supply house. You want the thin type, sold in strips, not the sheets.

A good range of pick thicknesses is from .025-.035; too thin will slip the pins out of alignment, and too thick will bind in the keyway. The most useful pick is probably the curved variety, although a straight and a rake or two also have their uses...

Cut the metal on a grinding wheel, dipping it in water quite often. Take care not to burn the metal. For the curved variety you want a slight upward curve in the end of the pick. Do not make a gradual upswing, rather a slight, sudden upward curve directly at the end of the tool.

Your other important tool is the tension tool. This is in every way as important as the pick (s) and must fit the job or it too will bind.

Tension bars can be constructed from the same clock/spring steel. Bend the tool into the classic "L" shape near the end as shown. Also make several sizes and thicknesses of tension tools.

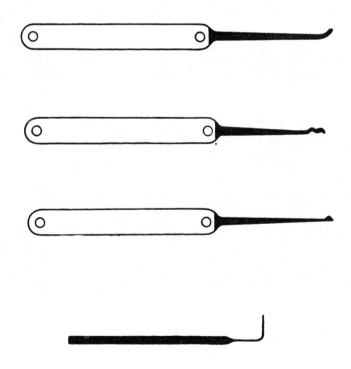

Curved, Rake and Diamond picks and tension tool.

114

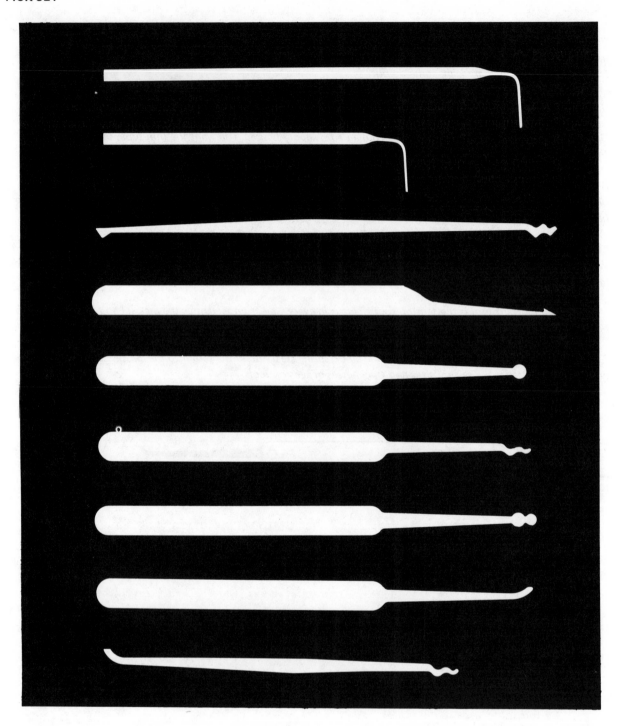

Actual size/shape of a small, but adequate, pick set.

It really makes no difference if you pick from front to back or skip around, choose the method that best matches your personality. An agent should be at harmony with himself at all times.

As you push a pin up into the lock and it falls back down, you must decide if gravity is the cause or if the pin is being pushed by the spring. If the latter is the case, it is, of course, not picked.

Fat pins will be harder to push up, but they will stay picked. Thin pins go up easily and come back down easily. One may have to pick thin pins several times before success shines its bleary eye on you.

RAKING

Once you have mastered the art of picking you are ready for bigger and better things. This next method is especially nice if you're in a hurry, or say, you've picked up this little fox in the local singles bar and you've brought her along on this big secret mission to impress her.

Now she's got this low-cut thing on and you're a bit nervous, right? Maybe you don't trust your hands too well, so you decide to try the rake.

Rake, I said rake. Get your mind out of the gutter.

Insert the tension tool as before and hold the necessary tension on the core. Now select your pick (I prefer the rake pick, but the circle, triangle or even curved, will suffice) and push it into the lock as far as possible (so it is resting under ALL the pins at one time.)

Now bring the pick up until you feel it start to push up the pins, and then draw it towards you rapidly, watching to see that it comes into contact with every pin on the way out.

Always keep your tension on the core, and repeat this maneuver several times in quick succession. You may have to adjust the height of the pick as well as the turning tension as you work. Start with a medium pressure on the tension wrench, then try light, then hard.

If the lock fails to open in 10 rakes, release the tension and start again.

In raking you are still performing the same function as in individual picking - i.e. you are raising the pins to their shear line. Of course, you are doing it faster than you could with each separate pin.

As you rake the lock the tight pins will pick first and then the loose pins as the core turns ever so little, just as in single picking. With any luck at all you should be able to open the lock in 5 or 6 rakes.

This method will open many locks in a matter of seconds.

MUSHROOM PINS

Sooner or later in most every agent's career, he encounters a lock which appears to pick nicely, but when the plug starts to turn it suddenly stops and will go no further for man nor beast.

Oh unhappy day! One can be reasonably sure one has encountered a lock with one or more special pins known as mushroom pins. These pins (see the clever little diagram I have included) are cut skinny in the middle and wide at the base. When they are picked they turn a fraction with the core and then the base binds, preventing the lock from opening. Mushroom pins are normally only employed as top (driver) pins, so it is impossible to be as certain whether a lock employs them by sight alone.

When one finds a mushroom pinned lock one must decide upon a course of action, take the bird by the tail, as it were. If one holds the tension, the mushroom pins will continue to bind, if one relaxes the tension, any straight pins (there are usually a mixture of both kinds in a mushroom lock) will fall back down into the core.

There are a couple of avenues of approach for this problem. The most popular method is to pick the tight pins as normal. Now the core has turned ever so slightly and is binding against the mushroom pins. Then push the mushroom pins up with the pick, exerting quite a lot of force. At the same time lighten the tuning tension just a hair, but not enough to let the straight pins fall back into their respective holes.

This will (hopefully) cause the mushroom pins to pop upward into the lock which, of course, will turn a hair more, causing the pin to bind at the shear line rather than falling back down.

This performance takes a certain, developed touch. Practice.

RAKING MUSHROOMS

Raking works well with mushrooms. First rake to pick the straight pins, then relax the tension the same hair (see above) and re-rake hard, continue relaxing the tension mite by mite, and raking harder until the mushroom pins have snapped upward.

After 12 or 13 rakes (assuming the lock has not opened, of course) relax the tension and start over.

UPSIDE DOWN PICKING

There is still another method for attacking mushroom tumbler locks: WITHOUT using the tension wrench place your pick under ALL the pins and raise them up as high as possible.

Now, take your tension wrench from your tension wrench holder and insert it into the key way and apply HARD tension. Remove the pick. At this point, you will notice that all the pins, top, bottom, mushroom and regular are stuck up in the lock mechanism.

Now, slowly relax the tension somewhat and lower the pick, letting ALL pins gently back down into the core. The core will still be turned slightly from your tension and the driver pins should stop at the shear line, and voila! the lock will open.

However, you may find that the loose (er) pins will slide back down into the core along with the bottom pins.

Now the solution to this current stalemate is to let the tight pins pick first, then re-pick the loose pins, using a different pick each time. (Rake picks with different cuts to provide new levels each time are best.)

Gradually the lock will pick open.

ACE LOCKS

ACE manufactures a tubular pin tumbler lock as seen on vending machines and other special application locks. It is basically the same as a normal pin tumbler except that the pins are arranged in a circle around the core.

It is possible to pick with conventional picks if one uses a special tension tool to grip the core, but it is much easier to pick with special picks (as shown) made for this purpose.

Seldom should a good agent ever be called on to pick a vending machine lock ....

AUTOMATIC PICKS

There are several "automatic" picks on the market. Probably the best one of these is the Lockaid gun.

This "gun" employs a thin, straight pick which is mounted on a flat steel spring. When one pulls the trigger a hammer strikes the spring, causing the pick to jump sharply upward.

To use the Lockaid, one places the pick under ALL of the pins and pulls the trigger. This causes the pins to jump upward, of course you are applying tension in the usual manner, so the pins will lodge at the shear line.

It normally takes several shots to pick all the pins (as the tight ones go first, then the next, etc.) but your author has opened several locks on the first pull of the trigger .....

Another method of employing the automatic pick is to use the thin pick (.025) making sure it does not bind against the keyway. Placing it under all the pins as before (but not quite touching the back of the lock) we raise it a fraction until the pins just start to rise and then pull the trigger KEEPING THE PICK STRAIGHT AND LEVEL.

Now, at the same time, you are using a light turning tension and holding the pick low enough so the bottom pins can bounce back down into place.

As the bottom pins are suddenly jarred into contact with the top pins, a strange, Newtony, phenomenon occurs; the top pins bounce upward and the bottom pins bounce back down. With any luck at all, this separation leaves a neat little space at the shear line, and your lock will suddenly spring open.

When employing this system, use a light tension and then a bit more, and then relax back to light again. Often, the lock will open as you return to light tension.

LOCK PICKING EQUIPMENT

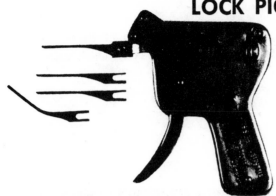

POLICE LOCK RELEASE GUN

A scientific tool for all police investigators

This tool opens every type of pin tumbler lock—mushroom, spool or regular—even pick-proof locks.

One tool fits all keyways!—Shoot it like a gun—just pull a trigger to open any pin tumbler lock!

Simple and easy to use—throws all pins into position at one time! Never damages or harms lock mechanisms!

SOLD ONLY TO LAW ENFORCEMENT BODIES

Cat. No. 100-553 . . . . $29.00

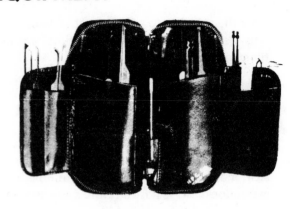

LOCK PICKING SETS

Professional—improved sets. Contains picks, tension tools and key pullers. Best steel tempered picks. All sets supplied in zippered leather case.

Set No. 1, containing 60 Picks, Tension Tools and Key Pullers $24.00
Set No. 2, containing 32 Picks, Tension Tools and Key Pullers 18.00
Set No. 3, containing 16 Picks, Tension Tools and Key Pullers 14.00
Set No. 4, containing 11 Picks, Tension Tools and Key Pullers 12.00

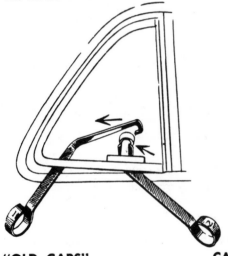

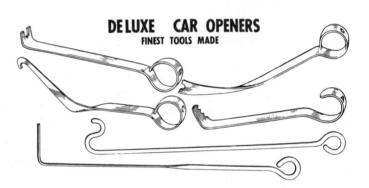

DELUXE CAR OPENERS
FINEST TOOLS MADE

"OLD CARS" CAR WINDOW OPENING TOOLS "NEW CARS"

These tools will open a car which is supposedly "locked tight" by inserting them in and under the rubber moulding around the front wind wing windows. The window itself can be opened easily. Inexpensive, simple and efficient.

Car Window Opening Tools, per set, Cat. No. 100-554 . . . . $14.75

FORD MASTER KEYS

ALL FORD PRODUCTS

F-1—IGNITION & DOOR—All Models from 1967 to Current Cars . . $29.50
F-2—TRUNK & COMPARTMENT—All Models, 1967 to Current Cars. $29.50
F-3—IGNITION & DOOR—All Models from 1936 to 1966 . . . . $19.50
F-4—TRUNK & COMPARTMENT—All Models from 1936 to 1966 . . $19.50

CHRYSLER MASTER KEYS

ALL CHRYSLER PRODUCTS

C-1—IGNITION & DOOR—All Models Current Cars $29.50
C-2—TRUNK & COMPARTMENT—All Models Current Cars $29.50
C-3—IGNITION & DOOR—All Models 1969 . . . . $29.50
C-4—TRUNK & COMPARTMENT—All Models 1969 . . . . $29.50
C-5—IGNITION & DOOR—All Models 1968 . . . . $29.50
C-6—TRUNK & COMPARTMENT—All Models 1968 . . . . $29.50

GENERAL MOTORS MASTER KEYS

ALL GENERAL MOTORS PRODUCTS

GM-1—IGNITION & DOOR—All Models Current Cars $29.50
GM-2—TRUNK & COMPARTMENT—All Models Current Cars $29.50
GM-3—IGNITION & DOOR—All Models 1969 . . . . $29.50
GM-4—TRUNK & COMPARTMENT—All Models 1969 . . . . $29.50
GM-5—IGNITION & DOOR—All Models 1968 . . . . $29.50
GM-6—TRUNK & COMPARTMENT—All Models 1968 . . . . $29.50
GM-7—IGNITION & DOOR—All Models 1967 . . . . $29.50
GM-8—TRUNK & COMPARTMENT—All Models 1967 . . . . $29.50
GM-9—IGNITION, DOOR, TRUNK & COMPARTMENT—

All Models from 1936 to 1966 . . . . $19.50

There is another tool called the "Snapper" which works on the same principle. It is shaped much like a diaper pin for the Jolly Green Giant. One pushes the works together and releases them producing a bounce in the pick-end much as the Lockaid gun.

The techniques presented for the Lockaid gun work nearly as well with the Snapper.

WRONG WAY PICKING

Many locks will pick in either direction, but open in only one. Due in part to the law of defeating averages, most seem to pick much easier in the wrong direction.

When this happens, we have a situation commonly known as "crying agent". However, you, hopefully, are always prepared for any eventuality.

The problem is to spin the core back past the keyway fast enough so the pins do not have a chance to fall back down. This is possible through the grace of a device known as a plug spinner.

This is a coiled piece of spring steel constructed to have one end pushed in under the pins and the other end twisted (while you hold it). When you let go the tension will spin the core rapidly in the other direction, bypassing the keyway.

HARD TO PICK LOCKS

Some dastardly types utilize locks which are designed to frustrate the picker by some sort of device which will grab the pins if a turning pressure is applied to the core.

Should you encounter this situation an extremely light turning tension is in order, or try the upside down method detailed earlier. However, often the best method for this situation is what we fondly refer to as the crowbar picking method.

NON-PICK METHODS

There are a variety of alternate methods for opening many forms of locks and locking devices. These techniques often make up in speed what they lack in finesse:

Drilling -

Pin tumbler locks can be drilled in a couple of different manners. One is to take a high speed, large (say ½" bit) and simply drill the core completely out of the lock.

The other is to use an eight-inch bit and drill through the lock just barely above the core in a direct line with the tumblers. When you have drilled through all the tumblers, you will have created another shear line with the new drivers above and the new tumblers below. The core will now turn.

DOOR LOCKS

On some doors a strong bent wire can be forced through the crack in the door and into the bolt locking lever; it is turned and the lock will retract.

If a lock cylinder collar does not have a high security guard ring, it can be often ripped out of the door with a pair of sturdy tongs.

One can often break or cut a piece of a window and reach in and unlock the door.

The metal or wood jamb can often be peeled away with a heavy screwdriver to gain access to the bolt. Sometimes a pair of heavy screwdrivers can be placed in the door and pried apart, forcing the door and the jamb apart enough to let the bolt slip out of the bolt hole.

Hacksawing through the bolt is a good means of entry and most bolts can be hammered, by placing a heavy metal bar over the bolt and hammering downward.

Night latch type door locks, where the locking bolt is held in place by spring pressure can often be forced by slipping a thin piece of metal or plastic (credit cards work very nicely, thank you) in the crack of the door and pushing back the locking bolt.

Some small locks such as cheap padlocks and filing cabinet locks can be opened by inserting a long, skinny pick through the lock keyhole, bypassing the pins until the pick touches the locking bolt at the rear of the lock. Now simply jam the pick into the locking bolt, move it backward and release the lock.

WAFER CHEATING

A Yale key cut to Yale code 4H225 will act as a marvelous rake, opening many of the filing cabinet and drawer wafer locks. One inserts the key into the lock and then runs it back to and fro, applying a light tension.

IMPRESSIONING

Impressioning is a method of opening locks without mangling or picking. One distinct advantage of this method is, besides opening the lock, you can produce a key which will open the lock again and again with no further hassle.

To impression one selects the proper blank to fit the lock. It is always best to have a supply of blanks on hand, but a suitable one may be purchased from your friendly locksmith.

Take your blank and hold it SECURELY in a pair of vise grips or heavy pliers. Now, coat the blank by one of several methods: Hold it over the flame of a candle, thereby depositing a coat of soot on it, use airplane dope, boot black, carbon black, or a specially purchased agent.

Now insert the key into the lock and turn it from side to side. Remove the key and notice the markings. Wherever the key has rubbed against a tumbler the impressioning agent will have been rubbed off.

Take a number 4 American Swiss rattail file and file the places where the rubbings occur. Re-insert the key and re-twist. Now file again. Repeat the procedure until no more marks occur on the key. The lock will now open.

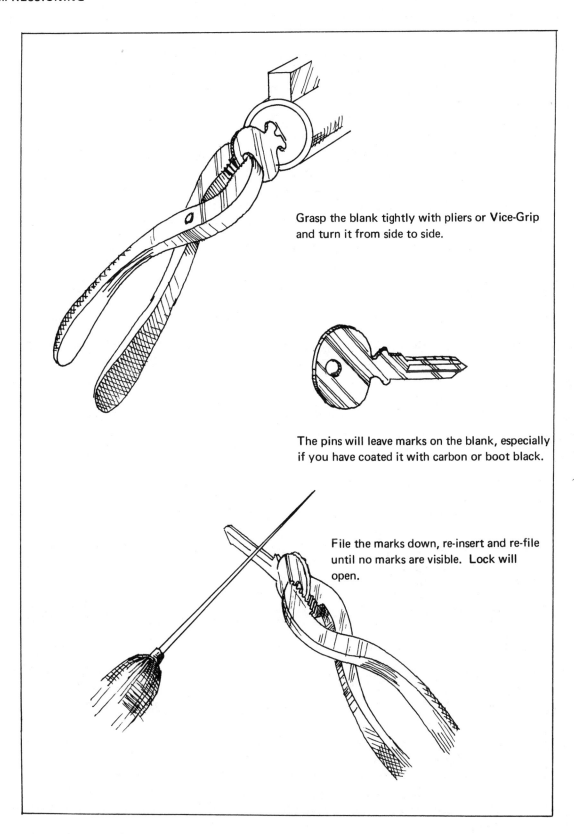

Grasp the blank tightly with pliers or Vice-Grip
and turn it from side to side.

The pins will leave marks on the blank, especially
if you have coated it with carbon or boot black.

File the marks down, re-insert and re-file
until no marks are visible. Lock will
open.

Locks that are master or cross-keyed are usually easier to impression. Besides, which you may inadvertently end up with a master key when your impressioning is done.

Mushroom pins make no difference in this technique.

WARDED LOCKS

Warded locks are impressioned much the same as pin tumblers. Coat the key, insert and give several sharp twists. Use a flat file to file down the indicated spots. Be sure and notice BOTH sides of the key in warded locks; if rub marks appear on both sides, file both sides.

After impressioning clean the key with steel wool to remove all burrs.

WAFER LOCKS

A bit harder to impression, but still possible, insert the key and remove to decide just where the tumblers are. Now make SMALL indentations where the tumblers are with the rattail file.

Reinsert the key and apply a hard, slow forward pressure at the same time the key is turned. Withdraw the key and file the marks straight down in SMALL steps until the key functions.

On wafer locks the marks will be quite faint and care must be employed.

SCHLAGE

This type of lock lends itself to the impression technique. There are only two types of cuts in a Schlage lock - full or not at all.

Insert the key into the lock and push hard. Withdraw and notice the END of the key. File this part until the key can be completely fitted into the lock (bypassing the end tumbler). Now insert and turn. Withdraw and notice the location of the tumblers.

Reinsert the key and turn as well as move up and down. Withdraw and cut all NEW marks down to the center of the key.

Sometimes a maker will design his locks with a restricted keyway, made to accept only certain blanks. Often these blanks are not available except by direct order from the manufacturer. When this sort of problem is encountered, some sort of picking method, rather than an impressioning method will offer more chance of success.

Many keys are cut by codes (often seen stamped on the key itself). These codes are either direct, i.e. they correspond directly to the depth of each cut on the key, so a 4 cut would be twice as deep as a 2 cut, or they may be indirect. If the codes are indirect they must be looked up in a special code book put out by the lock manufacturers and various publishers. A good locksmith will have the most common code books.

If you see the code and manufacturer of the lock you want to open, the key can be made, sight unseen, by a good, but not too careful locksmith. The keys can also be cut by the clever agent who purchases (or has his locksmith purchase it for him) a set of depth keys that show the correct cuts for each manufacturer's keys and a set of special punches made to cut keys.

OTHER TYPES

HANDCUFF LOCKS

There really is no reason for me to be showing you this ..... a good agent should not have to worry about having to open handcuff locks, right? Alas, there will be a few of you who will only read the good spots in this book, go out and attack some embassy or another and wind up handcuffed to a squad car door handle. So ......

Handcuffs are made of two locking arms that are mounted on a pivot. One has back cut teeth which are pivoted into the other arm and stopped from reversing by the locking mechanism. Cheap handcuffs can be opened by placing two screwdrivers INSIDE the open arm, right at the pivot point and spreading the arm apart, to allow the mechanism to slide by.

Assuming you are in no position to ask for two screwdrivers, there are other ways. The normal key is a warded key with a hollow stem. The stem fits over a little pin in the cuff lock and the key revolves around the pin. The key's end is a small projection which engages and unlocks the pivot arm.

A metal ball point pen cartridge will fit over the pin quite nicely, thank you, and if a small metal burr is bent outward from the end, it will open most handcuff locks.

A paper clip can be straightened out and poked inside the mechanism as shown, and used to pry the lock open. A thin metal shim may be passed OVER the teeth of the locking arm, but UNDER the ratchet and the arm opened.

Better handcuffs will have guards against shims and locks which are a bit more difficult to open, but hardly impossible for the determined (or scared) agent.

LEVER LOCKS

Lever locks are based on a number of levers which project against the fence, (a small metal pin mounted on the bolt which stops it from unlocking). All the levers are held in place with spring tension and must be raised to the spot where each lever's gate (or slot) is in direct line with the fence, allowing the bolt to retract.

Lever keys are generally nickel silver, have square cuts of varying depths, and resemble safe deposit box keys. Lever locks are found on post boxes, safe deposit boxes, telephones, and other specialty applications. (One should note here, that the telephone company uses special blanks which are not generally available and has many of its boxes mounted with such interesting devices as key keepers which grab and hold the key, or alarms which indicate when the box is being opened; something to think about).

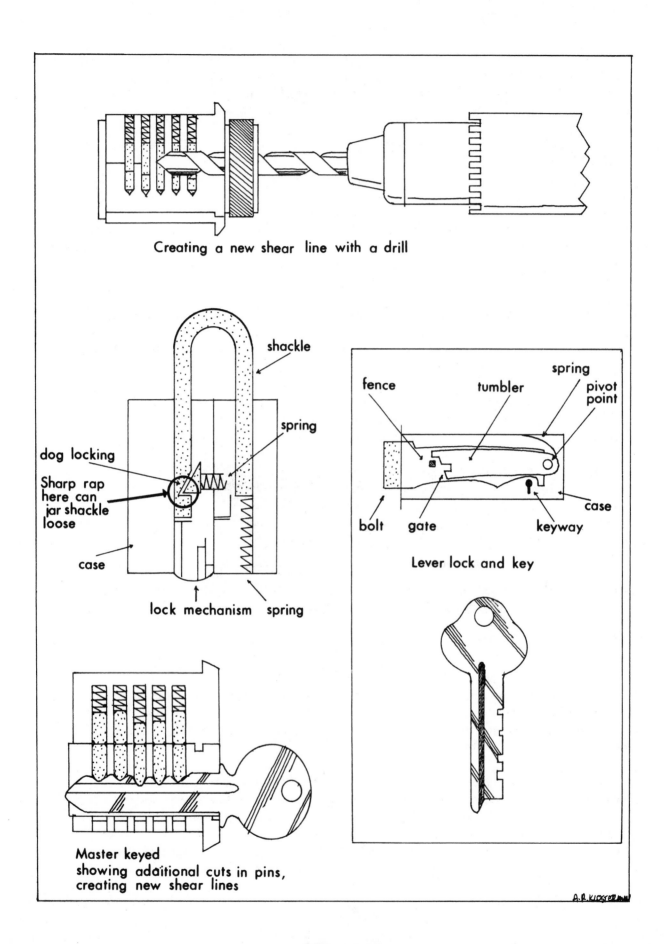

Creating a new shear line with a drill

shackle

spring

dog locking

Sharp rap here can jar shackle loose

case

lock mechanism   spring

fence   tumbler   spring   pivot point

bolt   gate   keyway   case

Lever lock and key

Master keyed
showing additional cuts in pins,
creating new shear lines

A.R. KLOSTERMAN

Lever locks are susceptible to impressioning, but BE SURE to use a file no thicker than the lever or too big of a hole will be made, allowing more than one lever to be moved by each cut.

WAFER LOCKS

A medium security device used in some cars, drawers, coin boxes, luggage, cash registers, etc. The wafer lock uses metal wafers as tumblers. These wafers are held in place (or out of place, actually) by springs and attached to the lock core which will not move until all wafers are brought into alignment at its shear line.

Schlage is probably the biggest manufacturer of wafer locks, and their locks are often found in doorways as well as lesser applications. The Schlage lock has a total of 14 wafers, making a possible 600 different key combinations. (Wafer keys are all cut to the same depth).

This fact, that all depths are the same, makes the wafer lock easily attacked by impressioning, or reproducing from a drawing or clay-wax impression.

There are two different types of tumblers in a wafer lock series and combinations. The series tumbler requires a no cut on the key to line it up and the combination tumbler requires a full cut.

If you are attempting to duplicate a key for a large system that is master keyed (such as a missle plant or military building) one can often compare several individual door keys to get the position of the series tumblers and make a master for the entire system by cutting the opposite places ....

PADLOCKS

Basically the attack points of your average padlock are thusly: The lock mechanism, the shackle lock mechanism, and the shackle itself.

The lock may be picked or drilled as formerly described, the shackle may be defeated by the use of shims which wedge themselves between the shackle and the locking dog (a wedge shaped metal bar which fits into the corresponding indentation on the shackle itself) and forces the shackle out. On some locks, primarily older ones, an ice pick can be forced through the keyway until it reaches the shackle locking mechanism and worked to release it.

The shackle may be cut, if of poor quality, or rapped loose as described below.

RAPPING

Many locks which are not securely mounted in something, such as padlocks, can be quickly opened by inserting the tension wrench and applying the usual pressure and then hitting the lock directly OVER and on top of the pins with a mallet, screwdriver handle or hammer handle.

It may take several sharp, quick raps to line up all the pins, but this system can work quite well.

PADLOCK BYPASS

Many padlocks can be opened by turning them upside down and pulling HARD (this is assuming the shackle is locked on something - if not, tie a rope through it and tie on to something sturdy) now, maintaining the pull, hit the bottom of the shackle (not the lock itself) right before it enters the lock case with your hammer handle/mallet.

Hit it several short, hard little raps and the shackle will more than likely bounce out of the locking bolt and open.

All these methods will work, but a good agent uses a surreptitious method that leaves no trace of his coming or going whenever possible. Many operations, such as the planting of a listening device, or the photographing of information will be voided if the person knows someone has been there.

WARDED LOCKS

Warded locks are the types used in old houses, cheap padlocks, and some drawers. The principle of the lock is simple; various obstacles, or wards, are placed between the keyway and the opening bolt, the key simply has cuts made to pass these wards. One turns the key, it passes the wards and the end of it opens the lock.

Warded locks are hardly for high security. A few pass keys will open most warded locks, and they are quite easily picked.

Warded lock keys are easily recognized by their square cuts, usually of uniform depth. The key does not have to be cut well; as long as the cut is not too small, it will pass the ward, there is no way of being too wide...........

Impressioning works well with warded locks.

A set of skeleton keys for warded doorway locks is easily purchased in most old-fashioned hardware stores and will open most of these locks.

DUDLEYS

While the average dudley has two sets of pins running horizontally down its little ol' keyhole, one must open only ONE side to get the core to turn. This can be done with a normal pick, but more than likely, a good rake or two will do the job with minimum hassle.

BEST

Best locks are six tumbler locks and fairly hard to pick. They have access to two combinations, one for changing the mechanism and one for opening the lock. If you pick the change combination the entire core will come out in your astonished little hands, but no matter, one simply inserts a screwdriver into the now vacant hole and activates the bolt.

SARGENT KELSO

Three rows of locking pin tumblers. Rough. Designed to hang you up long enough to be found. Best to drill.

MAGNETIC

Pin tumblers combined with a set of magnets which correspond to other magnets in the key are made by a couple of devious manufacturers. Would take a set of blanks with the magnets mounted, plus a lot of impressioning to open. Drill it.

WARDED PICKING

Most warded locks are held fast by a piece of flat spring steel which wedges the shackle in place. To pick, simply insert the pick, (usually a curved type) into the lock until the retaining spring is located. Then it is simply forced outward by twisting the pick.

Cabinet locks (warded that is) can be defeated by inserting a pick and turning around the center pin. If the wards are effectively by-passed, the pick will open the bolt.

LEVER LOCKS

To pick a lever lock, one must line all the little slots up directly under the fence. A special tension tool is needed. This tool is inserted completely through the keyway until the smaller "L" is resting into the locking slot of the bolt. Now a turning tension is applied and the levers are picked into place with a regular pick. This is best accomplished by going under the levers, holding the pick point upward, and raising each one until it stops at the gate.

When all is well and done, the tool will turn clockwise and release the lock.

WAFER

A normal, everyday, wafer lock will pick to the right. One inserts the tension wrench into the keyway at the bottom, and takes a curved pick into the lock above the tension tool.

The wafers are then raised, one at a time, to the shear line, where, if your tension is correct, they will remain. As each succeeding wafer is brought into alignment, one can feel the core slip a bit more. This action makes the next wafer easier to pick.

If the lock does not pick in several tries, release the tension and start over with a different tension level.

The wafer is accessible to a good rake artist. Use the curved pick, or a special rake pick. Start with a very light tension, and increase it in stages until the wafers hang up at the shear line. Start at the back of the lock, angle the pick slightly and bring it forward with much dispatch. BE SURE to hit each tumbler as you bring it forward with much dispatch.

Often you will open a lock in a few seconds with this technique.

MASTER KEYING

Master keying refers to the situation where one key will open more than one lock. Pin tumblers are the commonest master keyed locks and they are master keyed thusly: In one or more of the tumblers (sometimes in all of them) a SECOND split is made. This means you have, in reality, TWO driver pins above the master keyed tumbler.

Now the regular key lines up the normal tumblers, and the master key lines up some of the normal tumblers (meaning the keys are cut the same in these spots) and the master tumblers. The lock will open.

Locks can be keyed up through master, grand master, great grand master, super, ad infinitum, by adding more pins to create more opening combinations.

AUTOMOBILE

GM uses a modified wafer system with a side bar to prevent picking. It is indeed difficult to pick a GM lock, but a set of 64 tryout keys which will open all GM locks is available through locksmith suppliers or through the mail.

In fact, you used to see these very same keys advertised in comic books; yes, comic books. "In case you lock yourself out of your car". This was one of the few home study courses ever advertised in comic books that actually did make quite a bit of money for the student.

Ford, Chrysler, and American Motors use a pin tumbler lock. This type can be impressioned, picked, or tryout keys are available.

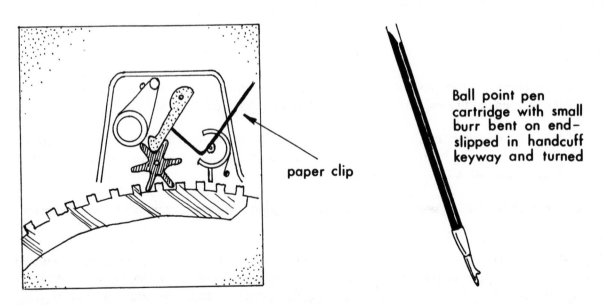

paper clip

Ball point pen cartridge with small burr bent on end— slipped in handcuff keyway and turned

Two methods of handcuff defeating. Either system will work on most cuffs.

PREMISE
AND
SAFE ATTACK

During the Watergate trials it was announced that attorney Tom Huston had anticipated some "nit-picking" about the term surreptitious entry, which some might call burglary. He did admit that it was illegal but stated, "it is also the most fruitful tool and can produce the type of intelligence which cannot be obtained in any other fashion."

"Tom has a gift for making everything concise," said his wife.

PREMISE

Many times a situation will arise wherein the agent discovers the information he needs access to has been thoughtlessly locked within a building, or room, that he does not have access to.

In the unfortunate situation, the agent must assess the posibilities: is the time, a time or pretense by which he can gain authorized entry?

Should this appear improbable, the agent's line of attack may be what is referred to in the trade as, surreptitious entry. Outside the trade, it is often referred to as burglary.

This sort of thing should only be attempted by those who are prepared for any eventuality: alarm systems, guards, locks, safes, prison, etc.

In any illegal activity there is always the chance for error, or plain bad luck to come into play. However, this possibility can be minimized through careful planning and a few simple precautions.

No matter how easy the job looks, avoid being overconfident. For a crystalline example of what I mean, we once again turn to the Watergate thing wherein a 19-year, ex-CIA man (Haldeman) allowed his crew to tape a door latch open after picking the lock because he "thought the guard had been taken care of"........

PREMISE ATTACK

Most good buildings rely on three basic keys to avoid unauthorized entry: Denial, detection and deterrence. Denial is found in high fences, thick doors, guards, safes, etc. This is designed to deter the amateur and delay the pro long enough to be apprehended.

Detection, usually, is in the form of burglar alarm systems and other warning devices.

Deterrence is a psychological factor tied in with denial. High fences, well-lighted areas, etc., all contribute to put the "entryer" on the defense, making him nervous and likely to be caught.

Remember, the good agent has the initiative. You can decide where the system's weak points are, when the attack is right. DO NOT allow yourself to be put on the defensive. If at all possible, check the situation out well in advance. PLAN!

You also have the advantage of surprise. IF the security system has not been recently violated, the security may be lax. ACT like you belong there! Self confidence is a must. One should realize that the average security guard is some kid or retired cop being paid $2 - $3 an hour, who often knows little about the security systems, or wants to know. Many guards steal themselves, and only wish to avoid work.

This is especially true when an outside agency is hired to do the guarding, rather than a member of the organization you are trying to violate. Many times these "special police" will stick some kid on the job without any instructions other than to stay awake.

If a foray is planned shortly after a new guard has been put on the job, a good bluff will carry one through an amazing proportion of the time.

Part of your planning is to appear to fit in the picture. If it is a large organization, a janitor's suit, or even a guard's uniform can be invaluable. If surprised, a "I belong here", or even a "it's my first night on the job and I'm lost, please help me out" sort of attitude will pull one through.

The author knows of an actual operation where the agent was surprised in the act by an armed guard and managed to pull it out by convincing the guard (with the help of a $5.00 badge and a phony ID card purchased in advance) that he was a higher-up checking on the guard. A few compliments about his work and an offer for coffee allowed the agent to go back and complete the job . . . .

Use the layout to your advantage. Often the physical layout will be set up as to afford a great deal of protection from unauthorized entry by CONVENTIONAL methods. This is often true of a cheap, hollow, wooden door with a ultra-modern, pick-proof lock on it. Needless to say, don't waste your time on the lock.

Walls are often another weak point, and can be chopped through in far less time than is necessary to defeat a good lock.

PREMISES SECURITY

An alarm is designed to tell an outside party when a certain condition is occuring within a given area. There are many types of alarms, some can only be found and avoided.

There are four main phases to any alarm system: 1. alarm sensing mechanism, 2. transmission of signal to, 3. receiving and/or signalling equipment, 4. action point.

Some alarms will allow themselves to be voided at one stage, some are weak at a number of spots.

SENSING

Usually one of six varieties: Contact, audio, vibration, photoelectric, capacitance, or motion.

Contact devices are the simplest and oldest form of alarm. The sensing devices are basically switches that break or connect an electric circuit. The tearable magnetic foil found on store windows, coupled with door and window switches is a good example of this type.

The commonest form of trip device is a magnetic switch. This is a two-part switch with a set of magnets that hold the circuit in one position. When one side is moved a couple of three inches, the other side closes or opens, setting off the alarm. Often found on doors and windows.

These devices may be studied and if they are found to be open devices, the circuit may be wedged opened, if they are closing devices, the circuit may be circumvented by running a piece of wire from one side to the other, or a magnetic field may be introduced to duplicate the existing one.

All these methods are a little risky as some of the better circuits have a system to detect changes in impedance (i.e. tampering) and it is easy to mess-up trying to duplicate a magnetic field.

Probably the best thing about these systems, is that they are usually visible and can be defeated on that basis alone. Chopping through a door will not set off a magnetic switch, cutting the glass out of a window and then lifting it out with a glazier's suction device or gaffers tape and crawling through the hole will not set off tear tape IF DONE CAREFULLY AND SLOWLY.

Floor mats are often switches in this type of system and the areas in front of door/windows should be avoided. Micro switches are sometimes placed in drawers to go off upon opening as are mercury switches that trigger when they are lifted or turned upside down. A good agent will find the wires leading to these little devils and avoid them or short them out IF THE CIRCUIT IS ALREADY FIGURED OUT.

AUDIO DETECTION

Audio sensors react to a noise in the area. They are a microphone, contact mic, or other type of transducer which converts the sound into electrical energy and are coupled to an amplifier and triggering device. Some are extremely narrow bands and react to sounds like the breaking of glass, and some are wide band, reacting to all sounds.

Some are set to only react after a certain number of triggering pulses, so if you muck up and make one noise and don't get caught DO NOT think you are okay and continue. Audio alarms are often used along with other types of sensors.

LIGHT

Light activated alarms are photoelectric cells and light sources. When the beam of light is broken, the alarm is triggered. The cells are placed at heights where the intruder is likely to break them and at access points to rooms, stairs, etc. The light can be bounced with small mirrors, or can be in a direct line with the sensoring cell.

Some units use normal everyday white light, but the better ones often use ultraviolet or infra red light. Either type can be seen with the naked eye IF YOU LOOK VERY CLOSELY, but neither the UV or IR can be detected from any distance.

Some good agents carry UV and IR filters that enable them to see the beams with greater clarity. Such filters can be purchased from good scientific suppliers.

Occasionally we will hear of an agent (often of the TV variety) defeating a light alarm by substituting one of his own sources in the beam and stepping through the original. This is not usually possible as the beams in better systems are modulated and the receiver recognizes its own frequency.

By careful observation, an agent can often defeat photo alarms by simply avoiding them. Remember, the alarm can not be utilized in an area where equipment is in the way of the beam.

MOTION DETECTION

There are a couple of types of motion detectors, but they work in the same fashion: when anything moves in the coverage area, the waves produced by the alarm transmitter are disrupted and the alarm is set off.

Some are ultrasonic, or just above the human hearing spectrum. These types were thought to be very unreliable because telephones, radios, trolleys, and a host of other items also produce UV noise, often enough to trigger the machine. Ultrasonic systems operate with one master transmitter, and a number of receivers. The receivers signal is compared with the transmitted one (as in radar; it uses the doppler effect) and the alarm triggered or not triggered.

Modern ultrasonic systems are limited to crucial areas, such as doorways, over safes, hallways, etc. to reduce the chances of accidental tripping. They are narrow beam units.

UV units can be detected with a converter that brings the 19,000 or 20,000 cycles per second down to a frequency that can be heard by the human ear.

Microwave systems operate in the same manner, but utilize the much higher frequency microwave (say 10 BILLION cycles per second) and are narrow beam.

Microwave systems are generally more stable, cover a smaller area and will penetrate walls and floors. This makes them impossible in some applications, where people are moving about in other nearby rooms.

PROXIMITY DETECTORS

This is a device that senses the capacitance change in a certain area. It requires a metal "antenna". This can be a metal plate or can be part of the actual thing it is guarding, such as a metal filing cabinet, safe, etc. Anything coming within a couple of feet of the antenna will set it off.

TRANSMISSION AND ALARM

Some alarms are local, that is, they ring a bell or siren in the area they are located. This is designed to scare away the intruder, as well as alert outsiders that help is needed. If it is located in a non-populated area, or too unobtrusive of a signal, it becomes less effective.

Some are silent, signalling to someone outside the area that the alarm is triggering. There are a couple of methods used to accomplish this:

Often the phone company provides loops, or special circuits which go to an answering service, or an alarm office (as in ADT systems) or directly to the police station. The phone loop can be a continuous signal that triggers at any break or a open signal that needs a triggering pulse to set it off.

If the agent can decide which it is, the phone line can be cut or shorted out. If the wrong move is made, the alarm will trip right then and there.

Central alarm systems such as ADT maintain a 24-hour station which monitors all their lines and constantly tests them to maintain the system. They can analyze any problem remotely, and decide to notify the police or not.

Some cheapies use a dialer that automatically dials the telephone to the police and gives a recorded message. Some cities do not allow these machines. If you suspect one is in use, cut the phone line.

Analyze the system. Can it be successfully avoided by careful maneuvering? Can you by-pass it by not opening, but going through windows, doors, etc.? Can the triggering device (bell, sirens, etc.) be defeated first? Can you gain access to the wires, use a VOM and determine if they should be shorted or opened?

One final word, most alarms above the $69 variety have their own power source which goes into play automatically if the outside power is shut off . . . .

Also, most alarm companies ALWAYS include the restroom in their alarm patterns.

MISCELLANEOUS

Here are a couple of quickies that can be employed in an emergency if you think you know what sort of alarm is in effect in your target area.

RADAR: These types will NOT penetrate metal objects. Sometimes it is possible to construct a path to your goal by utilizing file cabinets, desks, etc. that are already in place. REMEMBER, don't move any metal object or you're in trouble.

ULTRASONIC: Often set with motion time-trip to avoid false alarms. If you move VERY SLOWLY, like one slight move every couple of seconds, you may not trip this override and ring the chimes.

LIGHT BEAMS: It is often possible (very simply, but still there) ultraviolet beams in a dark room. Much easier if you are equipped with a conversation filter made for viewing ultraviolet light . . . . . .

AUDIO: Obviously, be as quiet as your fragile little body can be.

135

PLANNING

Before the good agent attempts any job, no matter how trivial, he makes out a plan of attack. This includes the area needed to penetrate to obtain the necessary information, the physical layout of the building, the type of alarm system (if known), and a complete plan of operation, which includes such factors as your first and second choices of attack (can the locks probably be picked? Will the door require some special tools to break through?), as well as a first and second choice of escape routes, and a cover story with the necessary credentials (cards, badges, uniforms, panel trucks, etc.) to back it up.

Remember, the person who catches you probably has never seen a phone company ID card, or a special police badge. If it and you appear official and composed, it will often work.

A complete case of the joint, to coin a phrase, is essential whenever possible. Go during daytime hours and study your necessary points, take photos if at all possible, for later use.

WRITE down your complete attack plan in advance (although never carry it with you) and memorize it. Notice whether a necessary safe can be seen through an open window and if you can move it to a less risky spot. Figure out what you are going to need to carry with you to accomplish the job and NEVER carry any extras. It's damn hard to explain a crowbar at times.

An accomplice who you can trust is an invaluable asset, but ONLY if he/she has been briefed beforehand on the job, where you'll be, the escape routes, the cover story, where to hide, etc. A nervous accomplice is bad news.

It is often possible to leave him at or near your main danger point with a radio to give you plenty of advance warning in case of trouble. Another possibility is to have a phone number printed on your fake ID card and a friend who has the sense to answer it with the company name and will be your "boss" if needed.

It's amazing how many otherwise sane people will believe an anonymous, official sounding voice, on the telephone.

Remember:

Plan
Case
Have a ready escape and cover

A system is only as good as its weakest link, so find it, use it.

There is NO unpickable lock, unclimbable fence, or unbreakable safe. Planning, patience and persistence have it.

SAFES

Once the determined agent gains successful entry to the premises, he may find that some no good son-of-a-bitch has not only placed the necessary target in a locked and alarmed building, but has also employed a safe to help insure the virginity of the target materials.

A good agent will be prepared for such an eventuality by being armed with one or more possible opening methods, and necessary implements.

Success often depends on the degree of security offered, coupled with the age and make of the safe.

Safes come in a wide variety of sizes and applications. One can encounter wall, floor, or vault models of varying thickness and offering a wide variety of resistance to the determined agent.

Most safes have at least one combination mechanism. The combination is preferred as there are no keys to lose or have copied, and the number of possible combinations varies from over 1 million to 1 billion, thus making it a bit time consuming to open one randomly.

The dial is marked with a reference point and a series of numbers. The dial is connected to the spindle which appears as a skinny metal bar and to the tumblers (which are connected to leg bone, leg bone connected........).

The spindle transmits the motion of the dial to the tumblers, which appear as metal wheels with a cut in one spot. The tumblers are all packed together.

When the spindle turns the tumblers, they first all turn together (as each has a small metal post which hooks the next one). As the dial is stopped at the first number, that tumbler remains in the position. The one turns the dial to the other direction moving all but that tumbler, the next number, and so on.

When all the correct numbers are dialed in the slots will be all lined up directly under the "fence" which falls into the slots allowing the bolt to be retracted.

SOUND OPENING

Some safes can be opened by sound, much as in the movies, but most that were manufactured, after the mid 60's are not susceptible to the following method:

A high gain amplifier is used. A small, direct-coupled amplifier can be purchased for about 5 dollars from the various electronic supply houses. A contact microphone (i.e. one that "hears" vibrations rather than actual sound) should be employed. BE SURE to use a matching transformer if the impedances do not match; and in a pinch, a crystal phone cartridge can be employed as a contact microphone.

The spike mic amplifier shown in the electronic surveillance section makes an ideal tool for opening safes.

Place the contact mic on the safe, near the dial. Now, turn the dial 5 times to the left to clear it. Now, turn back towards the right. On the first revolution, you should hear a distinct click as the cam and lever engage. Read the number. This will be the opening number, or the last number dialed to open the safe.

Continue turning to the right. You will hear an additional click during the next 4 or 5 turns. This indicates how many tumblers you are actually dealing with. Most safes will have 3, but some will have 4 or 5.

While you are determining the number of tumblers, disregard the drop-in click that occurs at the opening number on each turn.

Our turning the dial to the right 5 times also performs another duty; it clears the mechanism. This means that the dial has picked up all the tumblers and is moving them in rotation with the dial.

After our five turns to the right, we move the dial about 10 points BEYOND the opening number. If the opening number is 15, we would move to 25 and stop. Now we move back the exact opening number.

This procedure puts the opening lever and cam in position to open the safe (although the tumblers are not lined up so it will not open) now at this point, you can rock the safe dial back and forth without actually turning it.

This rocking motion causes the lever to click against the tumblers (through the lever slot). This clicking can be heard by the manipulater in his ear phones. The whole secret here is the fact that the noise will vary depending on the number of tumblers the lever is clicking against. (Much like the difference in hitting three notes on the piano at the same time, or just hitting one.)

Should we have happened to line one of the tumbler slots under the lever, the sound will be that of the lever clicking only two tumblers (as the lever will fit into the slot of the lined up tumbler, creating no sound).

Each time we rock the dial to make the lever-tumbler combination click we (assuming that there was NO difference in the sound) move the dial back to the right where it picks up the tumblers and then we move it about 2 digits past the last number. Now one moves the dial back to the opening number to realign the lever-cam slot, and repeats the rocking motion.

When you hear a sound difference, (indicating that the tumbler slot is lined up) you turn the dial back to the right until the click indicating the cam has picked up the tumblers. Now immediately stop and read the number that is lined up when you hear this click.

This is one of the combination numbers.

Now continue to the right 2 digits past the last try and move the dial back to the opening number and repeat the procedure. Do this until you have all the combination numbers.

Now, we know the opening number is the final number, but we don't know what order the combination numbers are arranged, so you will have to try all 9 (assuming 3 combinations and one opening number) possible variations. One will open the safe.

Sometimes you will have to move the dial a couple of points beyond the opening number to get the cam to retract the bolt and open the lock.

Some locks open to the right, i.e.   R four turns   22
                                      L three turns 18
                                      R two turns   46
                                      L to opening   15

Some will be the opposite (L-R-L-R).

Most locks will open no matter which way it is turned, however, a rough guideline is:

Sargent-right
Diebold right
Yale - left
Mosler - left

This sort of technique will not work on high quality modern safes as they employ nylon tumblers, sound baffles, and devices to prevent the lever from touching the tumblers until ready to open. Because of this, the good agent will have a couple of alternate methods in his repertoire.

DRILLING

A good way to tell where to drill is to place your MICROPHONE against the safe about half way between the handle and the dial.   Now shake the handle violently.

This should make the tail piece hit the bolt. Keep it up until you can locate the point where the noise is loudest, i.e., where the tail piece and bolt come into actual contact. Drill here.

It makes little difference whether you drill off the tail piece or the bolt; either will open the safe.

It is safer to use a large bit, say one inch, on a powerful drill. This may require more than one person pushing on the drill . . . . .

Use special hardened carbide or diamond points, and always carry 4 or 5 with you.

Some safes have hardened plates covering the vital areas to discourage those who would use this method. When you encounter such an area, press very hard on the drill and DO NOT ease up, even for a moment, as this will cause the bit to burn up.

You may have to take your torch (you did bring a torch, didn't you?) and heat the plate quite hot, let it cool, or throw water on it, drill some more, re-heat, cool, drill, etc. Most hard plates are fairly thin. . . .

PUNCHING

In this case, we are not referring to what the frustrated agent often resorts to when the safe fails to open, but rather, a quick method of forced entry. The agent knocks the dial off with some heavy instrument and punches the spindle with a center punch and hammer. With a bit of luck, the safe can often be opened.

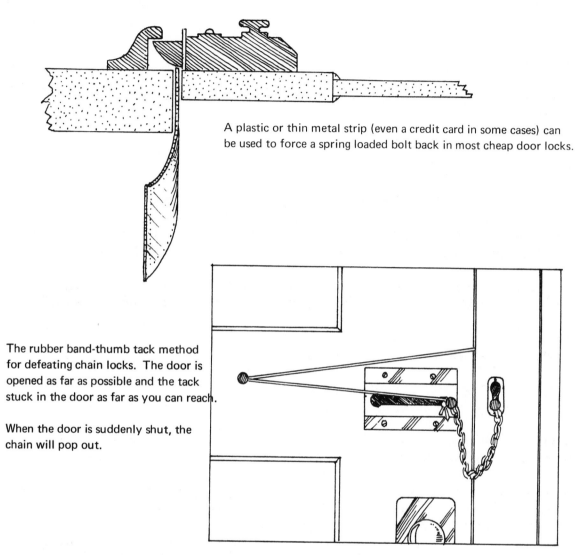

A plastic or thin metal strip (even a credit card in some cases) can be used to force a spring loaded bolt back in most cheap door locks.

The rubber band-thumb tack method for defeating chain locks. The door is opened as far as possible and the tack stuck in the door as far as you can reach.

When the door is suddenly shut, the chain will pop out.

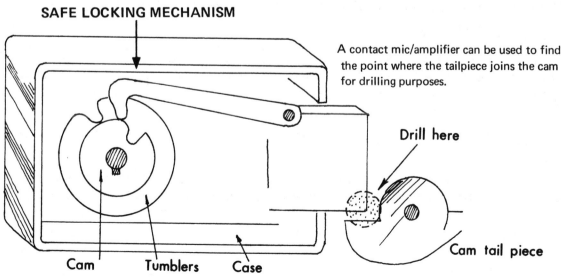

SAFE LOCKING MECHANISM

A contact mic/amplifier can be used to find the point where the tailpiece joins the cam for drilling purposes.

Drill here

Cam   Tumblers   Case

Cam tail piece

140

However, on many high quality safes, any punching attempt will shatter the spindle, or cause the bolt to dead-lock. Some safes have a surprise in the form of tear gas which will be released when punched or burned.

GRINDING

A high speed electric grinder with a carbide wheel may be employed to cut away the safe wall around the lock mechanism.

BURNING

One of the most popular methods over the years has been the burn job.

This is accomplished with a acy-oxy, or acetylene torch. The protecting wall in front of the dial mechanism is cut away revealing the tumblers which are manipulated to open the door.

Many modern safes are laminated steel connected to something like copper, which conducts heat rapidly away from the burning area. Also one must consider the possibility of tear gas releasing at about 130 degrees.

Paper can withstand temperatures up to about 350 degrees . . . . .

OTHER

Many people feel they must go in via the door as that is the conventional way, when, in real life, the door may be the protected part of the safe.

Often, turning a safe on its top and attacking the bottom with a sledge or heavy duty axe may yield opening results. However, this method does lack a bit in the finesse department.

Peeling is another possibility: Here one drills a hole in the corner of the door (thereby missing the anti-drill plate) and inserts a crowbar and peels back the first layer of the door. This will usually expose the locking mechanism.

One can also drill from the rear, look into the safe, decide if it is worth opening. As an added bonus, most safes can be opened by turning the dial while watching the mechanism from the rear and visually aligning the tumblers.

THERMIC LANCE

A thermic lance, or burning bar, will cut through most safes with no noise, minimum hassle, and have the added advantage of being small and concealable and simple to operate.

WEAPONRY

SMITH & WESSON MODEL 76 — 9 mm. SUB-MACHINE GUN
(Available only to authorized Municipal, State and Federal Agencies)

No. 26-6200

The Smith & Wesson 9 mm. sub-machine gun is a straight blowback, magazine-fed weapon of unusual reliability and rugged construction. It was specifically designed to meet the need of Law Enforcement Officers requiring a light and compact weapon with great fire power—approximately 720 rounds per minute. It can be fired both semi-automatic and full automatic. Minimum recoil insures greater fire power without loss of control.

SPECIFICATIONS

CARTRIDGE — 9 mm. Parabellum
LENGTH OVERALL — Stock folded, 20¼"; extended, 30½"
BARREL LENGTH — 8"
MAGAZINE CAPACITY — 36 rounds
WEIGHT — Unloaded, 7¼ lbs.; Loaded, 8¾ lbs.

		POLICE PRICE	
		W/O Exc. Tax	With Exc. Tax
No. 26-6200	Model 76	$73.44	$79.50
No. 26-6209	Magazine for Model 76	$11.00	

WEAPONS

A private agent rarely needs to rely on any sort of physical violence to accomplish his objectives. Contrary to TV, many private detectives do not even carry a gun (Hal Lipset remarked that his permit had expired five years ago, and he simply forgot to renew it. . .).

On the other hand, the various government spy agencies (FBI, CIA, Internal Revenue Service, etc.), not to mention the police, take a great stock in pride of their veritable arsenals.

Besides satisfying your insatiable curiosity, a working knowledge of the alternatives available, as well as those you are likely to run into in the course of your daily activities, would be helpful.

UNARMED

The various martial arts offer the best possibilities for unarmed self defense/attack, although, none are foolproof. Any finely honed fighting skill, be it Tai Chi, Thai boxing, or the Marquis of Queensbury boxing, must be considered a martial art. There is no one "great" art which overshadows all the rest, any fighting skill is only as good as the person utilizing it, (there is a saying in tournament karate, "there is no great style, only great people"). Although some "martial arts" are more sport than street fight.

If you are planning on participating in a martial art, there are a few things to keep in mind; the first and most important is the fact that it's really impressive to go into a dojo (studio) and see some dude toss another guy onto the floor and mash his larynx with a heel stomp, and think "I wanna do that". The obvious mistake to forget is that for the first two years, you're going to be the guy on the floor. . .

The only even vaguely practical advice I can lend as to unarmed combat situations is to think un-American and do the unexpected. Any one who plays "fair" in a street situation is likely to be the most respected patient in his entire ward. The no-hitting-below-the-belt rule is strictly for times when the referee is looking.

There is a real shock element in the surprise of an elbow to the face or a knee to the groin, which may jar a good boxer right to his roots.

Even a verbal red herring may get the person off his guard enough to allow you the first punch. I once witnessed a situation between a small gentleman of Puerto Rican ancestery and a large (I mean LARGE) gentleman of some undetermined ancestery, or lineage, as the case may have been.

The large guy was attempting to provoke some action by various hostile movements and insults. The Puerto Rican retreated while maintaining "I don't want to fight, man — no trouble, brother", etc. The big dude began getting a bit more confident and overbearing to the point of laughing.

Right near the beginning of the laughing part, the smaller guy looked upward at his 6'2" adversary, and spit directly into his open mouth. The guy's look of pure horror was accompanied by a quick bending over and gagging whereupon, the Puerto Rican gentleman delivered a coup de gras, in the form of a rapidly rising knee to the other's face. . .

I have no idea what martial art encourages the use of precise spitting, but I have nothing but respect for it.

Failure to utilize anything at hand is sheer masochism. A bottle, chair, broken off car antenna, mother-in-law, etc, will all render the best fighter unconscious, if applied to the correct areas with the necessary force.

Target areas should be those which will do the most damage with the least effort. The throat, temple, eye will all do nicely. Another good shot is the leg area, BUT, if you are not a practiced kicker, it may be unwise to square off with someone who may or may not be. If you do use feet, keep them low; high kicks are less effective and easier to stop. A good kick should go no higher than necessary, i.e., the groin.

Other good foot moves include a hard mash kick to the knee (a very small pressure will dislocate or break the knee, ending any confrontation) or a hard down smash on the ankle/shin.

Most of this is a moot point, because you just ain't, contrary to the comic books, going to learn any martial art from a book, and in the field of fighting, the expression, a little knowledge is a dangerous thing, is quite applicable. It is far better to have a healthy adrenalin/fear rush and fast feet, for protection than six months of karate.

MINOR WEAPONS

Any weapon is a definite DISadvantage to the wielder, UNLESS, he has working knowledge of the device, as well as a good feel for it. This feel can come from instruction and/or simple practice.

There are a number of weapons which can be legal, or at worst, quasi-legal, and still do a hell of a lot of damage. The most common is the good old knife. This primitive device still cuts and kills a horrifying number of people each year, and can be used to scare the Holy shit out of anybody with the sense to be frightened, BUT, if the guy is A. Not frightened; B. Adrenalined to the breaking point; C. Crazy, you damn well better know what to do with that blade. . .If the opponent is a skilled fighter, and you have never drawn blood, save cleaning fish, the knife can become an un-natural extension, making you too aware of that direction and not aware enough of the weak side.

NUNCHAKU

My personal, perennial favorite is a modified Okinawan grain thresher, known as Nunchaku. This simple device (two heavy wooden sticks about 14 inches long, joined by a short cord/chain) can be used with deadly force and accuracy. Generally, one stick is grasped, and the other whipped in a short arc to block/brake/dismember. The end of the propelled stick may reach a force of 1,600 pounds at its whip point. Eight pounds is required to break a bone. . .

Like the others, this weapon requires a bit of instruction/practice, but is effective against anything short of a 45. . .

Some karate studios will teach the use of the Nunchaku, and it is still commercially available at the time of this writing, BUT, the Nunchaku is gaining rapid popularity with the police departments, and following Ray's Rule (anything that the police utilize, will soon be outlawed to the general population) has already caused the Nunchaku to be declared illegal in California, and may soon outlaw its use elsewhere.

The ancient Asian (Japanese, Okinawan, etc.) warriors had a number of other highly refined weapons which can (and sometimes do) find good application in today's paranoid world. Shuriken, or Ninja darts were (are) small, flat metal darts in the shape of many pointed stars, or squares with sharpened corners, or swastikas. They are grasped between the forefinger and thumb and thrown at the folks with a spinning motion. With a bit of practice, they are quite accurate, and while not deadly, will often distract the enemy to the point of stopping the attack.

The darts are occasionally found commercially, and can be made with little trouble.

Brass knuckles are an old favorite, and although a bit crude, still quite effective. They are an instant bust if found, and difficult to get commercially.

The police use a much more refined method of hand-hardening: gloves with lead inserted to "help subdue unruly suspects". These "subduable" gloves are impossible to distinguish from ordinary gloves and allow the cop to bash heads without the stigma attached to a billy club.

Mace is sold commercially in several varieties and is quite effective if the subject is hit properly. However, distance, high winds, or uncooperative subjects may cause a miss, or not deliver enough to stop the charge.

Some states, again notably California, have outlawed the civilian use of tear gar or mace. California lawmakers outlaw any weapon which can be used primarily for defense purposes, for some twisted reason known only to themselves, which creates an ideal situation for the would be mugger (leave the dreary streets of New York, come to sunny California. . .)

Hairpins (long hairpins) have been used for espionage execution since times long past. Their use has been restricted pretty much to women agents, but with today's long hair styles, they are applicable to many male agents also. The long pin is not really outstanding for defense, but poked into an ear (i.e. brain), spinal column, heart, etc., it will noiselessly kill the victim.

HAND CONDITIONING

It is possible to condition one's extremities to a degree approaching brass knuckles with a bit of patient training. There are possible drawbacks to this sort of training, and if you plan on doing any intricate work with your hands in the future (such as typing), I would not attempt this sort of thing.

Karate people condition their hands by concentrating on the first two knuckles of each hand. Hard striking into a padded board known as a makawara, coupled with push-ups on the first two knuckles on a wooden floor, will harden these two knuckles and enlarge them to a frightening degree. The problem here is that you must hit ONLY with those two knuckles, as the latter two will not be able to take the same pressure.

Chinese boxers (or "Kung Fu" artists) harden the entire hand by striking into a bag filled with sand or gravel.

145

MARTIAL ARTS

Due to the instant popularity of the various martial arts movies and tv shows, the number of practitioners (and teachers) has taken a dramatic upswing in America. There are several things to consider before you succumb to one or more of the various choices.

Do you want to study primarily for physical fitness, for sport, or for self defense? The various arts differ widely in their applications and involvement needed for success. It is wise to judge your wants and desires and your physical make up before making any decisions.

A good way to get a taste of any particular art is to look in the nearest "free" university for a 6 weeks or so beginning course. Barring this, you can often take advantage of special "introductory" rates at accredited martial arts schools, or perhaps find a club at the nearest straight college.

The average price for any martial arts course ranges between $10 — $25 per month (depending on number of classes, size of classes, use of facilities above and beyond classes, etc.). It is generally unwise to pay any more than this. Besides, the monthly fee you will probably need to spend another $15 on a gi (pronounced ghee) to wear when practicing (although the gi seems very appropriate for this sort of thing, it is actually a copy of a Japanese peasant's farming uniform. It is very loose fitting and affords maximum freedom of movement).

A horrible number of perople have taken advantage of the self defense craze and have started schools when they have no real right or talent to do so. How can you tell between the bogus and the real?

First off, you can ask to see the instructor's rank certificate; he should be at least 2nd or 3rd dan (degrees of black belt) and the certificate should be from a recognized style. Avoid schools that promise to make you a deadly weapon in three months and make you sign things about not killing innocent bystanders with your new-found power. Avoid schools that make you sign contracts for any number of months (most schools will ask you to sign a waiver of responsibility; this is necessary and some schools will offer you a price break to sign for three months at a time. This is generally done because it is hard to see any improvement or feel any confidence in your learning for about three months. . .but avoid mandatory contracts). Most schools will let you make up missed lessons, especially if you are out for a week or more.

TYPES OF ARTS

Kung Fu (or Gung Fu)

This art is a real paradox, primarily in that it doesn't exist. Kung fu is an Americanized word used to describe various types of Chinese martial arts. Most of these arts are more rightly known as Chinese boxing or Wu Shu (although they bear little resemblance to the Marquis of Queensberry).

Chinese martial arts began hundreds, perhaps thousands, of years ago. The most famous practitioners of Chinese boxing were the monks of the Shaolin temple who studied day and night to perfect their fighting styles. The monks watched animals fight and incorporated the movements they observed into their own styles. Gradually, the monks broke off and formed their own styles such as Praying Mantis, Tiger, Dragon, White Crane, Leopard, Snake, Monkey, etc. These styles still exist and actually still retain many of the original animal-based moves (Praying Mantis, uses long arm techniques, Tiger uses rips to tear muscles, Monkey hops around and uses short punches, White Crane uses winglike blocks and beak-shaped hand strikes, etc.).

A Chinese emperor became quite interested in the arts and gathered together 100 slaves. He then stuck the slaves with long golden pins in various parts of their bodies (this may have been the forerunner of acupuncture). If the slaves died, he marked the spots on a chart and incorporated them into his fighting style as a striking point. These points still survive as "nerve centers" in kung fu and karate.

The intense popularity of "kung fu" tv shows and movies has caused many karate instructors to suddenly become kung fu instructors overnight (a good instructor will have studied for AT LEAST seven years). This causes much phony kung fu to be taught. Real kung fu has very few kicks and usually incorporates one or more of the animal styles. For many years, this sort of thing was not taught to non-Chinese, but these barriers have come down in the name of commercialism to a great degree.

Most Chinese styles are fun to learn, graceful, and probably not as effective as karate as pure self defense. This is not true as the Chinese stylist progresses into a couple of three year's worth of learning. Then it becomes quite effective, but for the first year or two, it is generally not as self defense oriented. Generally, Chinese styles are self oriented with little fighting each other for sport and few injuries to practitioners. Chinese stylists often wear street clothes, including shoes, and place little or no emphasis on rank.

There are several good non-animal styles also such as Wing Chun, Pau Kau, etc. These forms are more for fighting and are quite effective, but is very difficult to find a real teacher of these arts outside of San Francisco or New York.

Tai Chi Chaun

Tai Chi is a "sport" practiced by more people in the world than any other, including football, soccer, baseball, etc. This is primarily because every Red Chinese practices it faithfully.

Tai Chi is a set of slow motion exercises. The entire set can be performed in just a few minutes. It looks like a ballet routine done at ¼ speed. Tai Chi was developed as the only exercise a sick person could do. It is said to be extremely good for your body, especially your heart and is designed to bring your "chi" (or Ki) in harmonious flow.

Oddly enough, when mastered completely (say in 20 years of very hard work) it is the foremost fighting art in the world. Unfortunately, for the first five or so years, it is fairly useless in combat.

Judo and Jiu Jitsu

Jiu Jitsu is the forerunner of judo. Both are arts which deal with throwing your opponent, and although Jiu Jitsu uses some punching, neither has much other action in the form of punching or kicking.

Judo, advertisements notwithstanding, is primarily a sport, much like wrestling. There are situations where it would be useful for self defense, but it is primarily a good way to get in shape, learn to fall without getting hurt, and learn balance and poise.

Aikido

A blending of judo principles and a bit of other arts thrown in, Aikido is probably the only pure self defense art there is. Every Aikido principle is based on your reacting to aggression, rather than your punching or kicking your opponent. Aikido uses the centering technique of the body to make the opponent's strength and movements work against him. It is quite frustrating to fight someone who is proficient in Aikido.

Karate

Karate was "invented" in Okinawa in the early part of the 20th Century. Several Okinawans learned some Chinese boxing and began incorporating their own movements into it.

At the time karate was being formed, the Okinawan government had forbidden the people any weapons and the police and soldiers wore armor and carried swords. To fight this oppression, the karate enthusiasts developed their knuckles into huge callouses that could penetrate armor. They demonstrated their prowess by breaking boards. As few people actually wear armor today, many karate styles have de-emphasized this hand conditioning and board breaking (it is a wise idea to ease up on hand conditioning if you plan on using your hands for delicate things like typing).

Karate is a combination of kicks and punches which are designed to maim or kill an opponent. They are directed with the body's entire power rather than just the arm or hand and are usually aimed at joints or other sensitive areas of the body.

Some karate schools stress self defense, some stress sport. In karate "sport" refers to fighting other students in a controlled situation known as kumite. In theory, everyone stops their punches and kicks just short of doing any damage when fighting other students, but in a full force, fast moving, fight situation, this is often impossible.

This means, if you are into karate as a sport, sooner or later, you are going to get hurt. This is just a fact you have to realize and accept.

Karate encourages the use of rank (shown by the color of the belt) and kata, or forms. A black belt (usually two — six years in the making) means you are a "first grader", or ready to start learning the real essence of karate. Karate stresses non-aggression and builds confidence, but it is a sport which can be, and is readily used for aggression.

Types of Karate:

Japanese: Equal combinations of kicks and punches. Probably the most popular styles in the world. Major schools are Goju, Kyokushinkai, Shotokan, etc.

Okinawan: Again kicks and punches. Very aggressive format. Major schools are Uechi Ryu and Shorin Ryu.

Korean: Primarily kicks, very little hand work. Much emphasis on spinning and flying kicks. Major schools are Tae Kwon Do, and Tang Soo Do.

Kempo

A sort of combination of karate and kung fu. Quite aggressive.

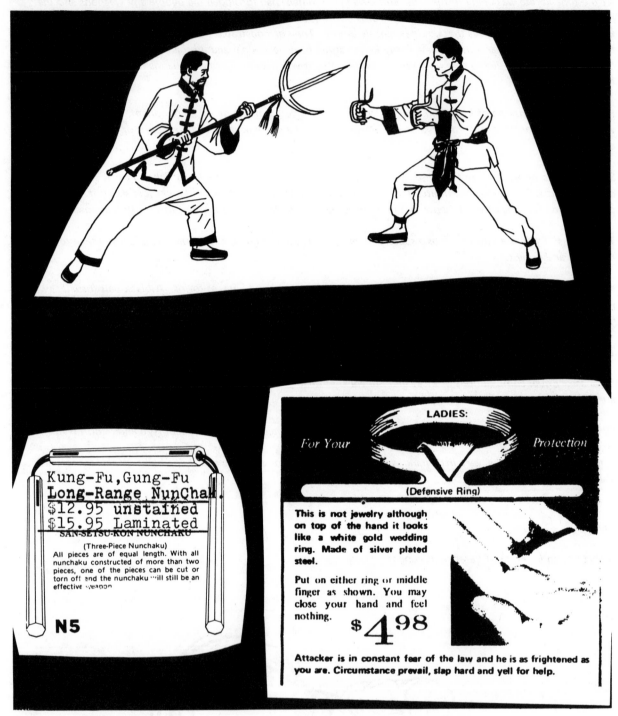

Kung-Fu, Gung-Fu
Long-Range NunChak
$12.95 unstained
$15.95 Laminated
SAN-SETSU-KON NUNCHAKU

(Three-Piece Nunchaku)
All pieces are of equal length. With all nunchaku constructed of more than two pieces, one of the pieces can be cut or torn off and the nunchaku will still be an effective weapon

N5

LADIES:

For Your   *Protection*

(Defensive Ring)

This is not jewelry although on top of the hand it looks like a white gold wedding ring. Made of silver plated steel.

Put on either ring or middle finger as shown. You may close your hand and feel nothing. **$4⁹⁸**

Attacker is in constant fear of the law and he is as frightened as you are. Circumstance prevail, slap hard and yell for help.

An unusual and fun catalog featuring numerous "kung-fu", karate, and judo supplies along with assorted oriental and not quite so oriental weapons including the Ninja darts, chains, sticks of one sort or another, and even a couple of "defense rings", that look like plain, run-of-the-mill rings, but seem to contain some sort of weapon on the underside. I suspect they would also be good for opening beer cans...The instructions are to slap your attacker with the magic ring and then yell for help.

By this point you would probably be joining your attacker, and the combined screaming should bring some sort of help.

This latter procedure can also be used on elbows, side of the hand, etc.

GUNS

Carrying a gun is a dangerous act in itself, and should be avoided unless really necessary. Besides, the obvious bust, it gives the wearer an inflated sense of security, which is quite misplaced unless you actually intend to use the gun at the slightest provocation and can do so with a good chance of success.

Guns employed by agents are usually of medium size, say around a .32. This is a compromise between the mini's (.22, .25) and the cannon-sized .357 and .44.

The mini's just don't have the necessary stopping power, and the cannons are quite bulky and unbearably noisy.

You should realize the real range on a handgun, especially in a crisis situation, is about 15 or 20 feet. Using a Walther .765 at a block distant target is good for James Bond, but few others. . .

On the other end of things, you should know of the true power of a gun. A .22 will penetrate 7 inches or so of a soft wood, a .44 will go through a car LENGTHWISE, including the block. . .so the hiding-behind-the-wooden-table-ploy is really not that effective. . .

GUN DEFENSE

The best all-around defense against an assailant armed with a gun is generally to raise your hands slowly above your head, keeping a wary eye on which hand he holds the gun in. Once you have assumed this position, you should talk, if only to distract him. The best thing you can say is something like, "yes sir,", or "what can I do for you?"

The second best defense, at least against handguns, may be some form of body armor. Up until a year or so ago, this meant a more or less conventional bullet proof vest (or other clothing part. . .). This device was usually made from some sort of metal/fabric mixture that weighed somewhere between 8 - 30 pounds, or, more recently, a fiberglass and boron carbide mixture that is considerably less cumbersome and a bit more resistant.

Then, lo and behold, a company developed a tightly woven fabric which was used by duPont (and others) as a long wearing replacement for the steel usually used in radial tires. Then some smart son-of-a-bitch in the Justice Department heard about the fabric and decided that it might have a better use. He appears to be dead on center. . .

The fabric, called Kelvar, can be woven into a vest, shirt, underwear, etc., adding less than 2 pounds to the weight of the garmet. It can stop a bullet, at fairly close range, from 90% of the handguns in use today. Now, there is still some shock involved when a chunk of hot lead slams into your fragile rib cage at 2,200 feet per second, but it does not penetrate the fabric, causing far less damage to the wearer.

Kelvar is being manufactured into garments by several companies, at the time of this writing. The most widely known one is an outfit called J. Capps and Sons. As I sit here typing this very page, it is not known if the sale of Kelvar clothing will be restricted to law enforcement types, political figures, etc., for a few years, or if the powers that be will find it in their hearts to classify Kelvar as strictly a defense "weapon", and let the general, paranoid public have a crack at it.

SILENCERS

Silencers are illegal in virtually all countries, something that should give you pause, right off the bat. They are pretty hard to purchase, and give varying degrees of success, at best.

The smaller calibers can be silenced fairly easily, but any large or fast bullet that travels over the speed of sound (1,180 feet per second) will also produce a sonic "boom" which is impossible to silence, except by reducing the bullet's speed to sub-sonic levels.

A low caliber bullet that has been effectively silenced will produce about the same level of sound as a BB gun. Any revolver with an open breach cannot be silenced.

Temporary silencers are often constructed in the following manners:

Window screen can be wrapped around a dowel, or wooden pencil to approximate the outside barrel diameter of the gun in question for a length of 6 inches or so. This tube of screen is then placed even with, and extending from the front of the barrel and additional screen is wrapped about the tube and back a couple of inches onto the barrel. The whole thing is then wrapped in adhesive tape.

A series of 20 or so pop bottle caps with holes punched in them (with a church key, folding the triangular flanges backwards) or a series of washers, can be forced into an aluminum tube or piece of electrical conduit. The tube is then taped onto the gun barrel. It is of extreme import to line the holes up so the bullet does not strike any of the baffles. . .

One shot silencers can be made from a balloon, or better yet, baby bottle nipple which has been stretched to cover the end of the barrel. The old shot-through-the-pillow, is also a good standby.

Commercial silencers are made from tubes filled with pourous material. Holes in the walls of the tube allow the gas (which produces the noise) to escape slowly. It is also possible to drill a series of holes (small holes) in the barrel of a pistol, such as a luger-type .22, near the breach. This will help silence the gun, and, as all silencers do, slow the bullet down making it less powerful.

POISONS

There are many, many poisons available to the crafty agent, but I refuse to get too involved here, for the simple reason that I am generally optimistic and feel the divorce laws in this country are changing for the better.

Needless to say, the real, honest to Uncle Sam, secret agents have a variety of poisons to draw on, which leave no trace to the curious coronor. One of the FBI's favorite places for such poisons is

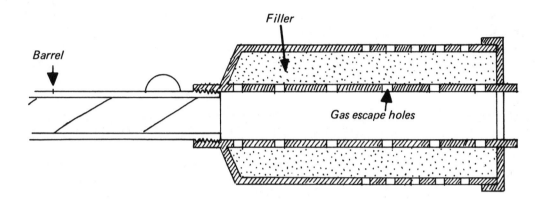

Pipe-type silencer.

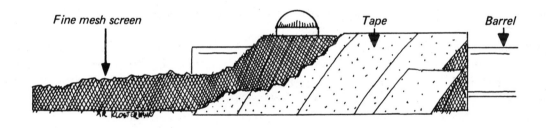

Window screen/friction tape silencer.

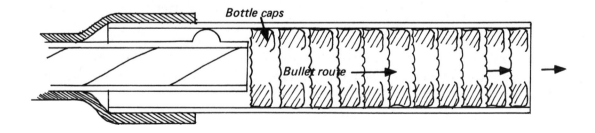

Bottle cap silencer.

reported to be in the subject's toothpaste. . .This is especially disheartening when you realize that most of the hippie drugs (LSD, STP, etc.) were actually developed by or for the military or other government agencies.

One particularly scary drug is Di-methyl Sulf Oxide or DMSO. This wonderful little chemical has the unusual characteristic of passing through tissue at an alarming rate. If you place some lemon juice mixed with DMSO on your hand, in a span of seconds, you will taste the lemon on your tongue. . .If it were mixed with poison, or mind bending substances and painted on railings, door knobs, in after shave lotions. . .well, no need to be graphic.

DMSO used to be fairly hard to get, which of course, limited its use to people with connections, or the government. Recently, the government cleared the use of DMSO in horse linaments, to help get the medicine inside the colt's coat. . .

There can be little doubt that the government employs exotic poisons whenever it deems it best to do so, but the civilian use of such things is also astounding. A recent drug testing center in California (set up to test street drugs, such as LSD, grass, smack, etc., for purity and content) reported a huge number of people who felt they were being poisoned by someone. About 50% were correct. . .

One gentleman brought in a bowl of cereal to be analyzed, which turned out to contain more arsenic than sugar. . .his wife had been feeding him a progressively larger dosage for some time. . .

Probably the most creative poison was employed by a branch of the Japanese "secret service". It consisted of small slivers of bamboo that were bent double and tied with fine cord. These slivers were mixed in with some ambiguous oriental dish and eaten (who knows, maybe relished. . .) along with the other small objects. Once in the digestive tract, the cords dissolved and the splinters unfolded to puncture the stomach and intestine. Quite painfully, I should expect.

This particular form of torture is still occasionally employed against small tippers in certain Chinese restaurants.

Prussic acid has always been a favorite of mine. This lovely stuff was used on a seemingly regular basis by the KGB to knock off enemy (uh, in this case, us) agents. It was stored in small glass capsules and simply sprayed into the agent's face from the inside of a rolled-up newspaper. Upon entry into the lungs, it causes an immediate, and fatal, heart attack. The agent swallows pill-sized amounts of soidum hypothisoluate (photographer's hypo) for several days previous to the big day. This procedure renders the heart fairly impervious to the prussic acid.

The fact that an alarmingly high number of CIA agents were keeling over in their tracks with heart attacks must have worried the State Department no end, until tiny slivers of glass were detected on the collar of one such casualty. . .

BOWS AND SUCH

Whether 'tis better to suffer the slings and arrows of. . .The bow is an ideal execution weapon, due to its fairly long range, good accuracy, and silent firing condition. The main drawbacks are size and skill involved, but these can be overcome with today's folding bows and, if necessary, crossbows, which are fired much like a rifle.

153

WEIRD THINGS

The Russians have apparently been experimenting and using (they were busted several years ago aiming a crude version at an American embassy. . .) a device which is about the size of a transistor radio and produces RF energy at a frequency of about 388 mc. This little "black box" will cause anyone nearby to become very confused, lose his memory (including to the point of not remembering his own name) and may cause permanent insanity after a prolonged exposure. These devices are fairly simple to put together and the plans are commercially available, so it is fairly safe to assume that the CIA has done some research into this field also.

The CIA reportedly has a drop-in phone device which will fry the brain of the person who answers the phone in about 5 seconds. It is very possible that this device also operates in the dangerous 384-388 MHz area, and is pulsed at about 11 CPS.

Just imagine the possibilities; a "phone repairman" comes in to check the unit, spends a minute or two and leaves, giving you the "all clear". The phone rings a minute later, you answer, and WHAMMO! Your wife is collecting. (My insurance company, why New England Life. Why?)

Even more exotic research is going on about the possibility of brain control (much on the order of a heart pacer) by electronic stimulation. This stimulation can be either through wires or radio signals. . .(Sort of an updated Manchurian Candidate. . .)

DEATH RAYS

Of course, we all know about the laser, the magical light beam which can drill a hole in an armor plated tank at a several mile range, or knock the eye out of an orbiting satellite from a ground control point, but lasers have their bad sides also. A really powerful model, one that will cut glass or steel, is EXPENSIVE, bulky, and requires your own little PG &E sub-station for power.

However, even a small laser can blind a person from a considerable distance, and the ever-continuing march of science is producing smaller and smaller power models.

About the only good defense against a laser is to reflect or disperse the beam. A conventional mirror will do the trick, SOMETIMES, but a good heavy-duty laser will drill right through the mirror, not to mention the person holding it. Brausch and Lomb have developed a shield which reflects about 90% of the light, rendering the beam harmless.

Another real possibility for a Buck Rodgers ray, lies in the area of sound. A couple of recent approaches have rekindled the interest in sound as a weapon. It has been known since the WWII days that very low frequencies, i.e., in the range of 7 CPS can be amplified and aimed at various items with devastating effects, including making buildings literally crumble, and human organs to rupture. A good 400 watt rock and roll special hi-fi amp will produce enough drive to initiate the process. . . (The movie "Earthquake" used low frequency [around 20 cycles] to shake the movie theatres during the movie).

Any sound projected at 2,000 watts will make all verbal communication impossible and produce high pain levels in everyone in the area. Much thought has been given to simply cranking up 5 - 400 watt amplifiers and turning them loose on any "disruptive" crowd. Chances are quite good that they will immediately search for another, more hospitable area.

The only problem here is that sound is not linear — the police would suffer as much as the crowd. However, a good ear protector, such as those used by airline employees, will protect the friendly side. This method leaves no injuries, no mess, no tear gas, and is quite portable.

Many peace keeping forces have often wondered about the feasibility of using sound as a weapon; several have gone beyond the musing stage.

The French police are supposedly using a device which consists of a high frequency sound generator (about 25 - 35 KHz) coupled to high efficiency tweeters and some concentrating baffles. The device vaguely resembles a hand held bull horn and is used for "crowd control". When subjected to the beam, one develops a sudden urge, or more correctly, set of urges, to: A. Vomit. 2. Go to the bathroom. 3. Hurt 4. Get the hell out of there. The one drawback is the fact that it can cause permanent brain damage if used too close/too long, but that is a small price to pay for disrupting a crowd of militant pickets or other criminal group, right? Police in the U.S. are reportedly testing the concept.

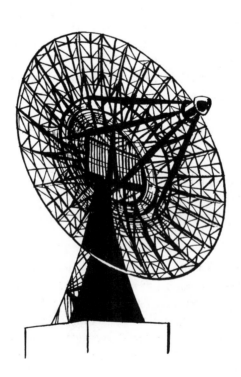

SOLDIER OF FORTUNE
Omega Group Limited
Box 582
Arvada, Colorado 80001

Charter Subscription — $7.00

There are a number of publications, publishing houses, and suppliers for people who like war, espionage, weapons, and other unusual hobbies. SOF is a TIME-formatted magazine for the mercenary. Well, they like to read, too, right?

Anyway, you can find such articles as "Underwater Knife Fighting Techniques", "The 223 Galil Assault Rifle", and even things with titles sounding like, "My First 900 Yard Kill". This magazine tells where the various mercenary armies are being formed, what the pay and conditions are, evaluates weapons from all over the world and shows you how to kill, maim and torture with the best of them.

An interesting idea.

NORMOUNT PUBLICATIONS
Drawer N-2
Wickenburg, Arizona 85358

A publishing house which publishes their own books, reprints other people's (notably the government's), and even stocks some of the best of their competition's works. One of their best books is entitled, "THE PLUMBER'S KITCHEN", and shows, in graphic detail, many of the weapons and devices used by various government agencies such as the CIA. This book sells for $12.95.

Nice, thumb-through reading. . .They also stock many other books about silencers, bombs, guns, and having fun.

PALLADIN PRESS
Box 1307
Boulder, Colorado 80302

Palladin is one of my favorites. They used to be called PANTHER PRESS, but, when the Black Panthers became popular, they felt a change in style might be a good idea. A wise move, as they are on the opposite end of the political spectrum from the Panthers, or from almost anyone else in the world.

Palladin reprints many, many government manuals such as: BOOBYTRAPS, INCENDIARIES, IMPROVISED MUNITIONS HANDBOOK, SILENCERS, and other old army favorites. They also stock fake sub-machine guns, other books on making secret inks, shooting people, sticking people with hairpins, getting a seat on the bus, etc.

Palladin has been in business for a number of years and is quite well respected in this, ah, field. . .

OPTICS

A NEW AND EFFECTIVE DEVICE FOR LAW ENFORCEMENT AGENCIES

*Can Be
Viewed Using
Both Eyes*

*Ideal for
Long-Term
Surveillance*

No. 50-9500   MK 505A with camera attachment

OPTICS

The field of optics has jumped as far ahead as any other surveillance related field; maybe further. Many of the devices and techniques available to the amateur or professional (i.e. government) spy are around thanks to the wonderful folks in the armed forces, particularly those nice people who brought you that old, but unforgettable war in Viet Nam.

In fact, the field of optics is getting so far ahead of what us consumer oriented fools are often told, that it is actually putting many real spies out of business, thereby creating more competition in the amateur field.

It all started with Gary Powers, you remember, the U-2, the plane that shocked the world (by the way, an interesting fact to throw into the conversation at your next cocktail party is the fact that Gary is now directing traffic reports from a helicopter for a Los Angeles radio station) by flying high, high over enemy turf and taking photographs of the activity on the ground below.

Well, the sneaky Russians developed a rocket that could go as high as Gary's neat plane, and on the next trip, instant surprise! So, we pretty much stopped flying over enemy territory, at least those enemies who bought rockets from the Russians.

Then, came the first satellite. . .A whole new world opened up to the people with enough money and enough interest in other people's business. The first few satellites were just for the fun of the idea, mice, little transmitters, letters home, that sort of thing.

Then, we (and one must presume the Russians) started launching "weather" satellites and "scientific observation satellites". True, some were actually used for observing the weather and some observed things of a scientific nature (such as the series that learned to "see" what minerals lay under the ground in what countries, so we knew who to support/make friends with/take over), but along with the honest weatherman's friend, came the spy moons.

The first generation must have been pretty crude, just spotting ships, new factories, mass troop movements, etc. Then came the second generation, which were a little better, and then the third, which were. . .now, my friends, we have satellites which can circle the earth, or remain stationary over any point, and which can take and transmit high resolution pictures of any point on the earth. How detailed? The current speculation is whether or not we can read the lips of the people on the ground. This is no joke. We can recognize single people, maybe we can read their lips. . .Who needs a heavy spy force to find out the enemy's strengths, new defense installations, or personnel deployment, when you can stay at home and watch the whole show on TV? This is causing a reduction in our foreign spy force, possibly increasing unemployment and hurting the economy.

Besides actual photos, our little spy-in-the-sky (s) can find plant "signatures" (usually infrared traces), which is a handy fact, if you're looking for fields of certain plants, say poppies or marijuana, or minerals in the soil). They can monitor all sorts of energy expenditures from camp fires to nuclear explosions, and perform other such routine chores.

What about here on earth? Well, the amateur spy, thief, crook, pervert, introvert, or city person usually feels quite safe, secure, and innocuous in the dark. He shouldn't. . .

You remember the snooper scopes that were around in WW II (the big one. . .)? They used a light source which had an infrared filter to convert most of the light to invisible infrared, and then a special photo tube to convert it back to some sort of recognizable visual display. They were usually mounted on a rifle, and worked, sort of.

Then, in Viet Nam, a new toy came into play. Some smart scientist, who is still probably collecting a military pension, realized there was light out there in the night; light from the stars, moons, street lamps, luminous bushes and animals, all light, just too low level to be of much help. Why not, he reasoned, (just read the damn stuff, don't worry about my writing style) take this available light and amplify it much as one would a normal stream of electrons. This would be a passive device, requiring no light source.

The device came out under their trade name of Star Tron. The first generation viewers amplified the light about 50,000 times, enough to turn any night time scene, except the very, very blackest, into instant daylight. Besides which, there was no infrared source which could lead an enemy right back to the good guy's side. ,

For several years, the Star Trons were restricted to military, then the police bagan to get them. And, now, folks, even you, can buy a second generation Star Tron viewer (a two stage amplification of about 85,000 times), assuming you have $2,500 to throw around on such things.

This device can be hooked to various lenses to make your new-found daylight scene come close, or even be mounted to a gun or TV camera to record, or kill your new-found daylight scene. In fact, several companies offer special, very low light, CCTV Porta-Pack type units, which can let you make your own home movies, in total darkness. . .

Best believe, every police force in any town larger than Spotted Horse, Wyoming, has at least one such night-into-day device. . .Now you understand the old saying, "the night has a thousand eyes. . ."

Infrared is another field that is just coming into its own. It is possible to purchase special films for most cameras which react to infrared light, rather than visible light. Since infrared light is near the heat end of the energy spectrum, it is possible to take passive photographs, with no light source present.

Of course, you can't get Kodak detail, but any living body, or other heat source, will give off its own "signature". It is even possible to take an infrared picture of something AFTER it has left by recognizing its residual heat signs.

If you purchase special infrared flash bulbs, or use a filter over a conventional bulb, quite good photos are possible without any visible light on the scene.

These films require special developing and handling, but they are available in most commercial formats.

Speaking of cameras, by god, what sort of a camera does the private spy utilize? Well, a good 35 mm, single reflex is always handy, expecially with a long lense or two close by. Many people will also invest in one or more of the mini-cameras. . .

There are a number of such cameras to choose from; the Minox line is one of the most popular. The C (around $200) is a nice model with built in electronics that can set the exposure automatically, or give you a warning light when you need 1/30th of a second or more (meaning you better have a tripod. . .). The Minox line uses an 8 mm format, similar to the movie film. The film comes loaded in a drop-in cartridge.

In any of the Minoxes, you advance the film by pulling the camera body apart and then back together again. Shutter release in the B and C is by a conventional shutter button. These cameras come with many handy accessories including an adapter for hooking directly up to binoculars and a special carrying chain. This chain is knotted at 8″, 10″, 12″, 18″ and 24″. This precise knotting system is used for taking close ups, and corresponds to the distance settings on the focus dial.

The 18″ length is perfect for a full page shot of an 8½″ x 11″ page, which will come out in nice detail when blown up to 8 x 10. . .Almost if they had made it for taking shots of printed pages. . .

There are a number of other minis which can also be used; Yashica Actoron is another 8 mm camera at about $115. Minolta makes several models using a 16 mm format (which is, in theory, at least, a bit easier to blow up and gets a bit more detail) ranging in price from $30 - $90. They lack the flexibility of the more expensive cameras, although the top Minolta, the 16 MG does have a special lens for close-ups (as all the Minoltas have fixed focus).

Rollei makes a 16S, which uses the 16 mm format, costs about the same as the Minox C and does about the same things as the Minox.

All these cameras are handy, can be hidden and take reasonable photographs. They are not portrait cameras. On anything past the length of the Minox's measuring chain, you must estimate range (although most, including the Minox, have a universal setting good for about 6 feet to infinity). They are handy, and can be used for copying written pages. . .

What else is new and exciting? Binoculars are a good all around surveillance device, although their low magnification makes them better for close work, or for use in "spotting"; wherein a higher powered telescope takes over after the subject has been located.

Gyroscopically stabilized binoculars are now available from the various police and criminal suppliers. These devices automatically compensate for any movement of you or your position, making it possible to follow a moving subject FROM A MOVING VEHICLE. They are a trifle expensive, but can be hooked to cameras to record the action.

COUNTERMEASURES

How do you counter optic surveillance? If someone is using a telescope or binoculars to watch you, when you do not feel like being watched, you can direct a bright light (the best is to use a hunk of mirror and redirect the sun) at the person. This will stop anyone. . .There is the possibility of damaging the other person's sight, if the light is bright enough. . .

These techniques will also work well against any sort of TV cameras, including closed circuit surveillance cameras. A bright light directed at the lens will cause the entire scene to immediately "wash out". If bright enough, it can damage the photo tube (especially on low-light cameras).

The ultimate defense against any sort of optical spying is the laser. . .A quick laser shot will stop all optical viewing; as well as the person's eyes doing the viewing. . .

To counter a camera, you can try a couple of different things: If you can get within range, a quick shot of spray paint, or even a dab of vaseline on the lens will stop any camera. Sudden defenses include holding your hands in front of your face (if you don't mind looking like a convicted mass murderer), or giving some obscene gesture which cannot be used wherever the photos are heading for.

What can we expect in the future? You will be happy to know that your government is working to finish a device started in Viet Nam. You see, the enemy soldiers used to hide behind various kinds of covering foilage, so the government developed a secret device that could effectively "see" through foilage.

They are now trying to get the device to the point where it can "see" through brick walls. . .And, in fact, may have done just that as you read this article.

Now, the ultimate is going to be when they equip satellites with Star Tron viewers, stabilized long lenses, and devices to see through walls. Oh, what fun!

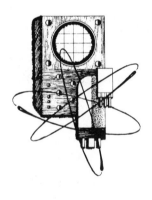

STAR-TRON™ BRAND — PASSIVE NIGHT VISION SYSTEM

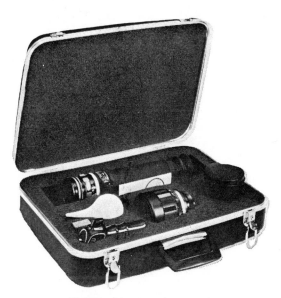

No. 50-9100
MK 202A with 135 mm. f1.8 lens and Biocular Viewer

MK 202A with case and accessories

TWO MODELS — MK 202A and MK 505A

Eyes that can turn night into day . . .
Eyes to see but not to be seen!

Image or light intensifying systems, originally developed for the military, are the most advanced type "night vision" instruments available today. These electro-optical devices are unique in that they require no light sources or bulky battery packs for operation. They are completely passive, allowing for covert observation, eliminating the risk of detection.

In areas of apparent total darkness, there is actually a considerable amount of low intensity light (starlight, atmospheric backscatter, etc.) that cannot be perceived by the unaided eye. In the simplest terms—light intensifying night vision equipment electro-optically amplifies the available light and displays an image analogous to a high resolution television picture.

The great advantage of the STAR-TRON™ BRAND family of devices is that they remove one of the policeman's major handicaps—his inability to see in the dark. Now it is possible for patrol officers to inspect alleyways, in between houses, parks, or other areas where the ability to see is hampered by the lack of adequate lighting. The device gives the significant advantage of being able to make inspections covertly without attracting attention through the use of flashlights or spotlights. Detective and surveillance squads will also find wide applications for the STAR-TRON™ BRAND since it allows them to carefully observe night-time activities without causing a change in behavior. Cameras may be coupled to the device enabling detailed photos to be taken unobtrusively.

The MK 202A is a compact hand-held unit that can be mounted on a tripod or rifle. Although slightly larger than a rifle scope it is completely portable and designed for use by one man. The detachable pistol grip allows the unit to be held in one hand, keeping the other free for access to a sidearm or other equipment. A Light Shade Field Control Iris is optional. It is powered by one small 2.75-volt battery located in the housing. A variety of lenses may be attached to the housing by a canon breech lock mount thereby providing great versatility. Particularly impressive is the fact that the MK 202A not only will operate in conditions of near total darkness, but in high light levels of city viewing as well.

FILES, FILES, AND GETTING TO THEM

The Los Angeles Times reported that the IRS has investigated thousands of taxpayers because they opposed the war in Viet Nam. These names were supplied by the Justice Department at about the same time they were given to the CIA.

A Philadelphia newspaper reported that a division of the IRS, known as the IGR (Intelligence Gathering and Research Unit) had collected strictly personal data on politicians, celebrities, and citizens. This information included such facts as their drinking and sexual habits as well as their friends and members of their families.

FILES, FILES, FILES . . . . . AND GETTING TO THEM

Let's take a quick stroll down the downy path of Ozdom . . . exactly who does keep files on whom and for what, (not to mention where, or how . . .). Let's start with the biggest, the FBI.

The Federal Bureau of Investigation has one large division called the Identification Division, which has the job of keeping tabs (via fingerprints, primarily) on some 190 million Americans. This includes anyone ever arrested, or having been in the armed forces.

They also have a couple of other divisions such as the Counterintelligence Program (for commies, pinkos, and other subversives), and Political Intelligence Files, etc. They also maintain the NCIC; National Crime Information Center, a computerized agency which disseminates information to law enforcement agencies via radio and telephone, within a matter of minutes, or even seconds. The info in the NCIC is not as complete as the other departments, but much quicker; aimed at getting the data to the cop while he is still talking to the suspect. They deal with about 100,000 requests per day.

The FBI is quite good at getting arrest records, as all state and local authorities forward such data on to them with the diligence of Hercules cleaning the Aegean stables. . . . In return the Bureau sends the info, all correlated, back upon request. The problem is they are not so hot about recording dispositions or expungements. . . . .

However, things are looking up a bit. The FBI will still give all arrest data out with disposition, but since 1974, they will not forward arrest minus disposition UNLESS THE RECORDS ARE LESS THAN ONE YEAR OLD.

The FBI has admitted it feels one of its prime functions is to supply information to prospective employers and credit checkers, to keep hazardous people from gaining employment in sensitive areas.

Let's go back to the beginning . . . . . . All public schools keep records of their "children". These little devils are "tracked" according to the way the teacher feels they should be categorized from first grade on. These reports decide what classes are open to said child, etc., etc.

Also . . . . . The LEAA gave around 60 million dollars to start and maintain programs known under several different names, notably VISA (Volunteers Influencing Student Achievement) which fingerprint KINDERGARTEN children and track them from then on to help identify POTENTIAL lawbreakers and troublemakers. Teachers and other administrators make entries into this 1984 file . . . . and follow the child throughout his educational career.

Until the Freedom of Information Act, these records were not available to the parent(s).

Juvenile records, such as arrest records are supposed to be expunged at a certain age, but, in fact, they end up with the FBI, Traveler's Aid Bureaus, Civil Service Commissions, Red Cross, Public Welfare Department, etc. Anytime you sign a release (and many times you do not) these records can be gotten to.

The Army has data files on 25 million Americans, MANY OF THEM CIVILIANS. They also keep records on their "own". In fact, most vets realize discharge papers carry their own stigma, i.e. SPN codes. Any good employer has access to these numerical codes, which indicate such things as bed

In 1966, under the leadership of none the less than Lyndon B. Johnson, you will be happy to know, an act known as the *Freedom Of Information Act* was signed into existence. This act was designed to free-up all sorts of government held information. If you as a tax avoiding citizen, wanted any particular piece of government info, except that having to due with national defense, you simply had to request it from the proper agency? Great, right?

Well, well, there was only one little problem, see there were no teeth in the law; no punishment for anyone who did not answer or comply with your request. Needless to say, many requests were not granted. A number of writers, editors, lawyers and such attempted to get various government reports and studies and, quite simply, failed.

Even I, your tried and true author, attempted to convince the Customs Department to loan me a copy of their field manual on drugs for a drug book I was writing. I got the bureaucratic shuffle, which ended up in my attorney requesting the manual, pointing out the law as it stood. . .I didn't get it. . .

Well, lo-and-will-such-things-never-cease, in 1975, a scant 9 years later the amended *Freedom Of Information Act* was passed. Under this new version if you request a specific piece of information and it does not concern the national defense, unless enforcement proceedings are in progress, or you having that piece of info would prejudice someone's right to a fair trial, or invades the privacy of someone or makes the government admit to an illegal procedure (i.e. wiretapping), the info is yours. . .

What good is this to you? Well, many agencies like the SEC will be coughing up things about corporate transactions some people might like to know, and in fact, you may even want to know what sort of things the government has on little old you. Sounds like fun, right?

Okay, to get a copy of your FBI file you need to: Supply the FBI with a set of your fingerprints on an approved fingerprint card (this can be gotten at some official fingerprinters [look in the Yellow Pages] or you can write the FBI or the government printing office and ask for card number 1973-524-273), supply your birthdate and social security number and sign your name. Now add a certified check or money order payable to the Federal Bureau of Investigation for $5.00 and mail all of the above to:

United States Department of Justice
Federal Bureau of Investigation
Washington, D.C. 20537

By the way, if a government official does not reply to your request within 10 days with the info or a good reason why not (and in the latter case they have an additional 20 days to decide an appeal request), he is suspended without pay for sixty days.....

When your file arrives, if you feel it is wrong, you will be happy to know that the FBI will be happy to discuss the changes with you if you again refer to them by your fingerprints, name, etc., and the arrest or case, or whatever number (which you now have from the file).

Does this work?

A copy of my file is on the following page.......Oh yes, I have deleted bits here and there that are none of your damn business............

UNITED STATES DEPARTMENT OF JUSTICE

FEDERAL BUREAU OF INVESTIGATION

WASHINGTON, D.C. 20535

March 26, 1975

Mr. Scott French
Post Office Box 6820
San Francisco, California 94101

Dear Mr. French:

In reply to your communication received on
March 18th, based on the data you furnished, we could
not identify any information in our central files concerning you. I am, however, enclosing a copy of our
identification record on you.

Sincerely yours,

Clarence M. Kelley
Director

Enclosure

UNITED STATES DEPARTMENT OF JUSTICE
FEDERAL BUREAU OF INVESTIGATION
WASHINGTON, D.C.   20537

The following FBI record, NUMBER 770 074 G   , is furnished FOR OFFICIAL USE ONLY.
Information shown on this Identification Record represents data furnished FBI by fingerprint contributors. WHERE FINAL DISPOSITION IS NOT SHOWN OR FURTHER EXPLANATION OF CHARGE IS DESIRED, COMMUNICATE WITH AGENCY CONTRIBUTING THOSE FINGERPRINTS.

CONTRIBUTOR OF FINGERPRINTS	NAME AND NUMBER	ARRESTED OR RECEIVED	CHARGE	DISPOSITION

This FBI identification record is furnished
to Scott Robert French
pursuant to Departmental Order 556-73.

Notations indicated by * are NOT based on fingerprints in FBI files but are listed only as investigative leads as being possibly identical with subject of this record.

IDENTIFICATION DIVISION

FREEDOM OF INFORMATION SAMPLER

To request a file, or information, under the Freedom of Information Act you should remember a few things:

Firstly, direct your request to the agency having the records, its general counsel, or the agency having the responsibility of FOI matters. You must "reasonably describe" the records you want; you do not need the formal name or number of the document in question, but give all the details you can.

The government has the right to charge "reasonable and standard charges for document search and duplication." You can set a limit on such fees in advance.

The agency in question has 10 days with which to answer your first request (working days). If some, or all, of the information is withheld, you must be told of your right to appeal and given the name of the person who will decide your appeal. They will have 20 days to act on your appeal.

If you lose the appeal, or get no response within the lawful time periods, you can file suit in federal court. The government must then answer within 30 days.

There are nine legal reasons for not granting your request: 1. If a document has a "Secret" classification given in the interest of national defense. 2. Documents that have to do solely to "the internal personnel rules and practices of an agency," and do not affect the public. 3. Things that fall under federal law such as patent applications, income tax returns, etc. 4. Commercial trade secrets that were furnished on a confidential basis. 5. Inter-agency communications which may contain recommendations of officials on establishing policy, or legal matters. 6. Other peoples personnel files which would constitute a clear invasion of privacy. 7. Investigative files which would comprise someone's right to a fair trial, disclose illegal investigative procedures, disclose the identity of a "confidential" source, or endanger a law enforcement person. 8. Reports to or from agencies responsible for supervision of financial institutions. 9. Geological data, including maps and other information gotten from private firms.

If you still have problems with an agency you can contact: Freedom of Information Clearinghouse, Box 19367, Washington, D.C. 20036; this is a Nader-run agency to help people secure their rights under the FOI act, or Project on Freedom of Information and the National Security, 122 Maryland Ave, N.E., Washington, D.C. 20002.

Here is a sample request—

XXXXXXXXX
XXXXXXXXX

Dear XXXX,

Under the Freedom of Information Act, 5 U.S.C. 552, I now request access to, or a copy of (put your best description of the documents you want here), together with all appendices and other attachments to this document.

I am enclosing the sum of $5.00 to help cover any expenses incurred in fufilling this request; should there be any additional fees required, please inform me in advance for my approval.

I would like any portions of this document that do fall under the act's provisions; should a portion of said document be labeled exempt from release, please provide me with the remainder. I do, however, reserve my right to appeal any such decision on your part.

Sincerely,

XXXXXXXX

wetting to "involuntary commissioned officer under sentence of dismissal, and warrant officer under a sentence of discharge waiting review."

At least one million vets have bad SPN codes. The department stopped giving them out in '74 and if you look yours up and see it is not good, you can write the Defense Department requesting a copy of your discharge papers minus the codes.

However, the department keeps its own records, and will release them if someone asks for them. Meaning, if you sign a blank release for a job search, an employer or credit bureau can write and get your code anyway.

If you ended up with anything less than honorable on the discharge end (such as general) you cannot legally fight it unless you had 8 or more years of active service.

Life insurance firms keep a cross-file known as Medical Information Bureau. Each time you get a physical for a job, or license, or have an accident/disease etc., that is insurance connected, it gets entered into this medical credit bureau. About 13 million Americans are already there. . . . . These records are available to all insurance companies.

Mental hospitals are pretty lax about their entries and will give them out to insurance companies, police, etc. Credit bureaus cannot always get the full details of why you went there (maybe you were just curious, right?), but best believe they will find out you were in a mental hospital . . . . . Most states also allow access to any sort of narcotic treatment programs.

OKAY, OKAY, you say, so what! Well using what you know and what I am about to tell you about the FOI act, let's try to see who has your files that you might be interested in getting your sweaty little palms on:

FBI, any division you might have been involved with, including wanted person's and check passer's divisions
US Attorneys Office
NCIC
Army Data Bank
Local Law Enforcement agencies
DEA (Drug Enforcement Agency)
Welfare Department
Aid to Dependent Children
Public School(s)
Veteran's Administration
Selective Service
Civil Service Commission
Office of Economic Opportunity
Department of Health, Education and Welfare
Justice Department
CIA
Passport Office
House Internal Security Committee
Army's Automated Military Police Operations and Information System
Department of Housing and Urban Development's Debarred Bidders List
The Federal Communication Commission

Securities and Exchange Commission Name and Relationship System
State Department Passport "lookout" list
Department of Transportation National Driver Register
Civil Disobedience file (Department of Justice)
Organized Crime Intelligence System (Department of Justice)
Law Enforcement Assistance Administration files on Wanted Persons
TECS system (Customs Department)
IRS - Intelligence files, Special Service Staff Files and Secret Service Files
Federal Deposit Insurance Corporations files
Small Business Administrations Investigative Applicant checks, etc. etc. etc.

In fact, at least 55 Federal agencies have over 850 data banks on you, Mr. American. Many of the banks operate without any sort of legal authority. The day is surely drawing nearer when all the banks will become computer interfaced without any human help. At this point, God forbid, anything and everything will be available to anyone - anywhere, anytime; if the system has a few built-in safeguards to prevent misuses and mistakes as now. Well, I would suggest buying that little cabin cruiser you've always wanted, NOW . . . . . .

WHERE'S ANYBODY WHEN WE NEED THEM?

Much of our national BBA (Big Brother Activity) emerges from the huge National Security Complex at Meade, Maryland. It is behind this set of hallowed (or was it hollowed?) walls that our real, dyed-in-the-wool, spies are trained. Here also, hundreds of people spend their time listening to damn near every word uttered over just about any airwave anywhere in the world.

Some of our most complex, if not our most complex, computers are also in residence at Meade where they are used to break codes and unscramble messages intercepted by agents.

One of the National Security Administration's top computer experts and behaviorial scientists, one John Meyer, has come up with a plan to solve most of our national problems which must rival anything George Orwell could've done in his prime

Mr. Meyer suggests we attach mini-transmitters to about 25,000,000 (count 'em), Americans. These little transmitters would be connected to a huge computer network which would keep track of the wearer's whereabouts at any time.

In theory, these devices would be attached to every criminal, parolee, political subversive and possibly alien, in the country. These undesirables would then be tracked and arrested if they went anywhere they were not supposed to go, or associated with anyone they were not supposed to associate with...

Taking off your little albatross would be a felony. The entire program could be paid for, Mr. Meyer suggests, by simply leasing the devices to the people wearing them at some small, say $5.00 a week, fee....

I mean this is America, you know? Land of the financial genius......One can only wonder how long it would take them to getting around to making democrats wear little transmitters.....

In the same light vein, the director of the US Passport Office, Francis Knight has suggested that all US citizens be required to carry national ID cards, she feels that, "the US government owes each citizen a true national identity."

Such internal passports are common fare in most communist countries and several Latin American lands. In Peru you cannot get any sort of transportation without your little card, in Bolivia you must show your card when you register at a hotel, and then this data is transmitted to the police, in Cuba the cards are used to keep track of the population by the secret police.

In all fairness it should be noted that this act would probably save millions of tax dollars now spent in helping one agency or another delve into the private lives of US citizens........

CREDIT:
THE GOOD,
THE BAD,
AND THE RE-NEWED

From remarks made before the senate:
"I have received information from a former Army intelligence agent that during the course of its surveillance of domestic political activities, the Army was not merely concerned with fringe groups which may have demonstrated a predilection for violence or illegal conduct. The individuals who were targeted for surveillance-spying-include a member of this body, a former governor of Illinois, a member of the House, state and local officals, plus well known contributors to both political parties, newspaper reporters, religious figures, lawyers and local and national political figures. These are only a few of the reportedly 800 individuals who were the targets of military intelligence operations in only one state, Illinois."

CREDIT

The credit field is one area where big brother tactics, man's best friend - the computer, can literally run/ruin a person's life. Good credit is a real necessity to survive in today's buy-today-pay-tomorrow society. Unfortunately, credit is extended on the Catch-22 basis of those who have money; i.e. don't really need credit, can easily get it, while those who have the potential of making money, but little on hand, well . . . . .

Another problem with the credit game is the elephant's memory factor; credit people do not forget; one little slip away from the fold, one mistake, and ka-pow. A scientist can fail twenty times before he messes up with the successful answer and be a raving success, but let a man slip once in the credit field, either by missing payments, getting something repossessed, or even something as lamb-innocent as refusing to pay for defective merchandise which is eventually returned, but goes on record as missed payments, and that's all she wrote . . . .

An interesting sidelight is the fact that a person who pays with cash, never goes in debt, makes a fair amount of money and lives sensibly, is NOT a good credit risk . . . See, you've got to have gone in debt at some time or another to be a good credit risk. Makes sense, right?

Well, anyway, credit is a game. As some unknown, but should have been famous, person once said, "the best way to borrow money is to act like you don't need it . . . "

When you apply for credit, let's say at a bank, the banker (who generally enjoys his power trip of playing the great credit god) looks for a number of determining factors. To each particular determining factor he/his bank assigns a certain point rating. These factors can consist of as many items as: Married, 1; Single, 2, Dependents, none, 0, 1 or 2, 2; three or more, 1; Years at present address, up to 5 years, 1; over five years, 2; years at present job, less than one year, 1; 2 or three years, 2, four or five, 3; etc. Monthly bills, less than $25, 2; over $250, 1; Monthly income, XXXX XXXX XXXX; loan background, at the bank you are applying for, 5; others, 3; Account at the bank you are applying for, 2, etc. Some may count a telephone in your name as 2 points, several years in the vicinity as 2 points etc. The bank loan officer adds up your numbers to see if you reach a certain minimum (around 17 or 18, usually) he will probably also check with a credit rating bureau in the area. Some credit is of course, easier to get than others. The determining factor being how much the bank is going to make off the loan, Master Charge and other such huge (18%) percentage loans are quite easy to get and may only require six or so categories (salary, married, residence, dependents, bills, length of time at job, spouse employed). While other, such as personal loans of hard cash, require much more of a reason for the bank to cough up the bread.

It should also be pointed out that banks have a certain "ideal" percentage of loans that are in each category, such as auto, home, personal, etc., and if your particular bank is down on the type of loan you are requesting, it may slip the requirements a hair or two to grant you the loan. By the same token, if they are filled to the brim on your type of loan, you may not get it - no matter how good your credit is rated. It pays to shop around when getting a loan (not to mention the fact that rates will differ several percentage points for each type of loan at any particular bank).

Now, the name of the game for a bank credit situation is stability. You are trying to look secure, stable, and all around American in your living situation. If you can come up with 5 or so years (always shoot for a trifle higher than the reality, you can't be expected to remember the exact day), on the job and living in the same place for several years, not to mention a wife, well, you're halfway home!

If you can get your boss or WHOMEVER ANSWERS THE PHONE IN YOUR PLACE OF EMPLOYMENT to fudge a bit on your length of employment and salary, no one is going to write the IRS to verify it. This little "favor" costs the company nothing and many employers will often give a bit to help a valued employee build up a decent credit rating.

The same with landlords. Most banks won't even bother to verify length of residence, BUT THEY MIGHT if it is easy to reach your landlord. Of course, if the voice on the phone at the number you gave them SAYS he's the landlord, well, it's surprising how many people will take this at face value. Remember, if you don't own your home, it is much better to be renting on a lease basis AND ON AN UNFURNISHED DEAL. If the bank thinks you own your furniture it's a bonus in your direction. (They need not know your wife is Japanese and you eat on rice mats on the floor. . .)

Another must is a listed telephone in your name. Everyone has a telephone in the U.S. There are more telephones than people. You're ODD without one. There's something wrong with you, little children will point in the streets if it becomes public knowledge, dogs will bite at your heels, the bank won't loan you money . . . . .

If you are without this modern convenience, convince a friend to list his phone in your name also. You can pay the phone company about $.50 a month for this privilege and no one is the wiser. Bear in mind when you go for credit you should look the part; do not expect the bank to jump for joy when you apply for a loan if you are: self-employed, an actor, waitress, cook, taxi driver, telephone operator, nurse, bartender or other social dropout.

Once you have established a semi-acceptable job, you can always claim you pull in an additional $50 - $100 a month in your spare time (I don't know, maybe you raise orchids, or you're one of the marvelous few who made the comic book dream come true and you raise earthworms in your garage, or you do odd jobs in your spare time . . . . whatever).

There is one, almost never miss; sure-fire system for revamping a bad credit rating, (or simply establishing a new one). This system will give one top line rated credit in a 1 - 2 month period, and costs very little.

First of all, you need some money. (Remember, I told you it takes to get . . . .) About $500 or $600 should do the trick. Now, this wad is not going to be spent, it is simply an investment, of which you will get almost all of it back.

First of all, take your hot little bankroll down to some friendly local bank (preferably a large one) and open a savings account with the entire bankroll. The bank will be quite happy to see you do this, they like savings accounts, they make money from savings accounts . . . Wait a few days (a week if you can afford the luxury) and re-visit your friendly bank. This trip talk to a loan officer and ask for a loan for the same amount you have in your account. PUT UP YOUR SAVINGS ACCOUNT FOR SECURITY. This means your savings account money is now locked tight somewhere in the great interior of the bank and you cannot withdraw most of it until you have paid off your loan. The good part is, simply, the bank will be happy to loan you the money without a credit check, because you have given them FULL SECURITY on their loan. If you suddenly decide to take up residence in Santiago, Chile, the bank is not out any money (except a small amount of interest) as they simply confiscate your savings account.

Now, this means you have a loan at X% interest (say 9%) and you have the same amount of money in a savings account drawing X% interest (say 5½%). This means you are only liable for the difference in interest, and assuming no pre-payment penality, if you pay it off sooner, you lose even that debt. It is best to get about a year loan on one of this size, monthly payments should be around $40 odd dollars on $500.

Okay? Get the picture? Now, go to another bank, deposit your borrowed $500 in that bank's savings account, wait a few days, go back and do the loan bit again. ("I've got these pressing debts, they're about to break my legs for not paying, at a higher rate of interest!) So, you again pledge your deposit and get a loan.

Next week do it again at a third bank. Re-deposit, re-pledge, wait and get loan. Make all loans for about one year. Now take your $500 or $500, whatever, a go open a checking account at one of your banks, preferably the larger one. Now EVERY WEEK make a full payment - one EACH loan, so you are paying your $40 or $50 bucks to each loan EACH WEEK, ahead of time, after three or four payments (Remember, made each week, not each month when they are actually due) you will have established a credit rating showing you are prepaid four months ahead of time on three loans and you pay on a regular basis. Needless to say, DON'T SPEND ANY OF YOUR REPAY MONEY, JUST REPAY THE LOANS.

Another neat feature of this system is the fact that banks do not report exact amounts of loans, they simply rate them with rating numbers, if you put $500 or $600 in these accounts, it could appear like you have 3 savings accounts with $1500 to $3000 or so (depending on the rating system used) and three loans which you have prepaid several months in advance (your first payment will not actually be due for 30 days or so).

Now start hitting up small credit cards, gas stations, jewelry stores, department stores, other such things. Most of these people will look at the references you list, ask the local credit bureau for an non-investigative credit rating (as this is much cheaper) and the credit bureau will look to see if you have these loans, and hopefully not look too much further.

Then start with BankAmericard, Master Charge, etc. At least one of your helping banks will have one of these cards. Avoid Diner's Club and American Express, as they check a bit more and have more stringent requirements. Remember, if you pay off your bank cards within their "free" period, usually 14 to 30 days, there is NO interest rate or charge, if not, you pay through the nose (18%) generally.

Lastly, do not tell bank two and three about bank one - or each other, just use your pocket cash and your application. Avoid finance companies if at all possible, they charge higher rates than the banks do, they will also enter and keep a record of ONE late or missed payment, and they cooperate with each other like a den of thieves. NEVER list a finance company loan as a reference if you have violated one of these rules . . . . .

CREDIT BUREAUS

Virtually every American has a file of some sort or another on himself and his comings and goings in the financial world recorded in a credit bureau. These bureaus keep financial records, and in some cases, personal data, on people and then sell this information to subscribers.

The idea started out to protect banks, credit card companies and the like; giving them instant access to a person's past financial history. They have expanded into much more. In fact, only about 20%

of the credit bureau's reports have to do with credit applications. The majority are bought by licensing agencies, employers about to hire someone, insurance agencies, private detectives, etc.

Retail Credit Inc. (Credit Bureau Inc.) is the largest such agency in the world. They hold files on millions and millions of Americans. Now, Retail Credit not only keeps track of your record, they also are what's known as an investigative agency; meaning they investigate you. . . . .

They do this by employing some 5,000 field reps who work from 1,500 offices. These reps interview victims, as well as their neighbors and friends. They inquire into such things as if you are a good housekeeper, known to fight with your wife, seem to drink, have a bad driving record, criminal background, hang around with disreputable types, gamble, etc., etc.

These "field reps" average about 25-30 such reports PER DAY. One can surmise some of the reports are less than totally accurate . . . . .

TRW Credit is the second largest data bank. They do not use "investigative" tactics, but stick to reported facts. They only have 35 million Americans on file and are used primarily by banks, oil companies, loan companies and other credit lenders.

There are also 2,000 local credit bureaus around the country keeping tabs on another 100 million Americans. Most belong to the Associated Credit Bureau and interface information. They will perform both collection and gossip collecting functions for the right fee.

Where do these agencies get all their info? Well, from your entries at loan and finance companies, bank records, aforementioned "investigative techniques", and, oh, yes, the FBI supplies information to credit agencies and other such agencies (insurance, licensing, etc.) at the rate of thousands, perhaps hundreds of thousands of requests per day. In return, credit agencies supply the FBI with fingerprints and other garnered data.

Once, in 1971, a law was entered into Congress to make it illegal for the FBI to give out any information; except to law enforcement agencies and for legit purposes. It failed to pass.

When you apply for a job or loan or some such, and sign anything to the effect of you giving the prospective employer the right to check your credits or statements, you can bet they will do so, probably with the big gossip monger in the sky - Retail Credit Inc. If the job requires bonding, THEY WILL CHECK.

Some low-paying jobs do not check, some medium to high level jobs do not until you are being considered for a higher spot within the organization. . . . . Collection agencies are an offshoot of credit bureaus; sooner or later almost every red-blooded, God-fearing American will come in contact with collection agencies or, at the very least, their methods. Should this occur to you, there are several factors to bear in mind.

A. It costs for a merchant to use a collection agency. A fee of somewhere between 25-50% of the total monies collected will go to the agency. The merchant realizes this and may settle for a flat settlement of about the same amount from the debtor.

For small debts, they will NOT go to court. Small claims court often has a minimum, takes a small registration fee, takes a summons service fee ($6 - $20) and takes up half a day's time for someone to go down and sit through court.

Your credit will not go to hell for non-payment of a small bill (in fact, the only way it will seriously affect your credit rating is a large default and preferably a loss in court). Every collection agency, or other persons employing the tried and true collection methods will first send a number of vaguely threatening letters. These will talk about lawyers, courts, credit ratings and other such trivia. If you are not going to pay the bill, it is best to ignore the letters completely . . . . . Often these letters (especially the last few; they are often sent in groups of five, with the last few being much harsher sounding than the first few) may come on a lawyer's stationary, or in a telegram, night-letter format, OR PHONY TELEGRAMMEY LOOKING ENVELOPE. All this means absolutely nothing. You have not lost any case, nor been summoned until you are served in person by a server or sign for a registered letter CONTAINING A SUMMONS. No amount of three-hour deadlines before legal action, is at all relevant.

In fact, it is a dead give away that the creditor is desperate and probably down to last ditch efforts when you start getting hour type deadlines. If he is going to actually sue, he will probably inform you as such, calmly, and then go ahead and do it, no two-hours-til-serious-legal-action crap.

The first thing a non-payer should do is grasp the fundamental psychology of the collection bureau. They are trying to get you to admit your debt, hopefully in writing. Any sort of "I'll pay as soon as I can afford it" nonsense is an admission of the debt. They will come on soft and ask for a small payment. If you pay anything at ALL this will: a. Admit you owe the debt. b. Extends the debt so the statue of limitations has no effect at that time.

A good collector may come on soft, win your confidence and then ascertain the facts he needs. Your address, place of employment, where your bank account is, etc. He should also make you see you should pay this particular bill before any others or else he will file suit, call you at work, etc., etc.

BEATING THE COLLECTOR

The usual run of debtor tricks are simply to ignore small bills by marking the envelope(s) deceased, moved, or even cross out address and write in a phony forwarding address. The usual thing is simply to stall, hoping the debtor will go away, which he will on small debts, or even try to hide/stall long enough to beat the bill of limitations on debts in your state.

Stall tactics include claiming merchandise was not up to par, or was returned, bill was already paid, etc. If a debtor feels he is going to be sued, he will often hide his assets, which includes not working, or getting an exemption from wage-garnishment, or even out and out SKIP.

Remember, a collection agency IS NOT allowed to threaten you, subject you to public humiliation, libel or slander you, send dunning POSTCARDS which threaten lawsuits, send letters with "collection agency, bad debt," or some such embarrassing thing on the outside, harass employers, neighbors, etc., and generally use any public means of shock or embarrassment to force you into paying. If he does, you can countersue, and usually win.

If you do receive a summons, either by registered mail, or in person (you do not have to sign for it, just have it set down within a certain radius of you while the server tells you it is a summons), you will be sued in court. If you lose in court, you will be ordered to pay. If you do not comply, the agent can attach your wages ALTHOUGH A NEW RULING ALLOWS ONLY A 25% ATTACHMENT FROM EACH CHECK, order you to appear in court and testify under oath as to your financial position and holdings, such as bank accounts, etc., which can be seized by the court, put a lien against you or your property. If a lien is put on, you will find that the court takes a certain portion of your property either when you sell it, or, if they wish, by seizing and selling it themselves, to cover the debt. Even if you own no property at the time the lien is applied, it lies there, dormant, until you do get some. Then a title search will turn up said lien.

You can often convince the judge to give you exemptions from wage attachments because you must support your wife and sick mother, etc., but these will be periodically reviewed and you must continue to produce evidence that you are in desperate need of such exemption.

You will not go to jail UNLESS you are caught perpetrating a fraud, or the agent can prove you are about to skip the state.

In major debts, you can always threaten bankruptcy. If you do go bankrupt, the court sells your assets (except a certain amount, which varies from state to state, some let you keep a car up to a certain value, a house up to a certain value, cash). The court charges a couple hundred bucks to do this, then pays off your creditors on a pro-rated basis, wherein they receive a few cents on the dollar (normally). Because of this they do not want to see you go bankrupt. If they feel you are serious about this, they may relax a bit, or settle.

You can go bankrupt once every 6 years.

If the situation is bad enough to consider bankruptcy, think about a couple of other actions first. You can go to a financial counselor, who will charge you a flat fee of about 10% - 18% off the top of your debts to consolidate your debts, contact your creditors and make arrangements to pay them off at some extended rate. This leaves you enough to live on, BUT creditors do not have to agree to this, can still sue, and you do have to pay the counselor, no matter what.

The other alternative is to go Chapter 13 . . . . . . Under Chapter 13 of the Bankruptcy Act, there exists a beast known as the Voluntary Wage Earners Plan. Herein you go to the courts, who charges you an under $50 filing fee and appoints a trustee for your account who gets 10%. Now you come up with a plan to pay off your creditors wherein you remain viable, keep enough money to live on, but still pay off your debts.

When the court accepts your plan, it pays the creditors each month from the payments you make. The creditors CANNOT sue, your personal property is protected, you pay directly (employers don't even need to know about this little matter), and if you suddenly inherit money or property you do not have to sell it off to help pay.

If a majority of creditors accept your plan, the courts will force the rest to follow suit. All interest charges are suspended for the length of the plan, and you take up to 3 years to pay off all the debts.

Credit agencies and collection bureaus are often called upon to track down a skipper, or when located, find any real property he/she/it may own. Unless the account is very large, a private detective will not be used, rather the bureau will try a few cheap shots of its own. Some of the practices which are occassionally used by the less ethical of these animals are less than legal, however, they often get results.

A good credit or collection agency will employ almost all the tricks described earlier, i.e., using the city directory, all the city hall records, phone book, insurance company cross files, etc. Most will also have quasi-legal, or damn illegal access to utility company billing lists, unlisted phone number lists, bank accounts, etc.

If the agency cannot find the deadbeat, they will often go to his last place of residence or employment. Here a variety of ruses can be employed (it is illegal to say the victim owes money). A common one is the "need to find him for an inheritance" bit, or a package from some fairly nice store that needs to be delivered, possibly even the old friend from out of town routine may find its shoddy way into this application.

If the "researcher" can find any bit(s) of information, the "Expansion" method can be applied. For instance, if you think the skipper may work or have worked at a certain company, and you know he is from Denver, originally, a quick call from "Denver" through a phony operator, and a story about having to locate his cousins, long lost next door neighbor's mother who is in San Francisco too, because he/she/it is about die in the hospital and IT IS IMPERATIVE THEY GET IN TOUCH WITH DEAR OLD Johnny ASAP. If they think dear old Johnny still works there they may call in off hours and try to convince whomever answers the phone, that it is a real emergency and give out his home address.

If he has moved out of a town, a person-to-person call is the easiest, even if he refuses the call, he is dead-centered located. If they have a suspicious address, a registered letter (or certified) will be sent, disguised with as little return address information as they can get a hold of, so you will accept the correspondence.

REA will help these sort of people out by allowing a slight draft to be taken out in the name of the skipee, for a $.50 charge they will go to the last known address of same, and ask around from the manager, neighbors, etc., who will often turn the driver on the the next known address, thinking he has a package for said skipee. If this does transpire, the driver will file a report, which ends up back in the hands of the investigating party.

Other standard American ploys are checking the tax rolls, voter registrations, the local schools (if skipee has a school-aged child), clever tracers may call the last place of employment asking for a reference, or wanting to hire skipee, but can't find him at address given on his old resume, etc.

BANKS

Big brother is in evidence at your friendly bank to a certain degree also. A short time ago a law was quietly passed, making it mandatory for banks to photograph ALL transactions and turn them over to the Federal government. The law was in effect for some time before enough people discovered it and managed to exert the necessary pressure to get it withdrawn. Banks still photograph and record for the various agencies, all transactions over $2,000 in amount, and will do a much more complete job at the request of the Tax people, FBI, etc. It is generally believed that the FBI keeps a close watch on the accounts of "radicals", democrats, and other subversives.

In at least one case, a statement and photograph was mistakenly sent to the account owner instead of the FBI. The person in question happened to be a slight "radical". The bank admitted it had been turning all his financial records over to the authorities for some time. The person sued the bank for a hefty amount . . . . . .

FAIR CREDIT REPORTING ACT

Under a law passed in 1971 you now have several rights with regard to credit agencies; If you have been denied a loan, credit, or employment on the basis of a credit report you have the right to be told the nature and sources (except for investigative type sources) of the information held about you.

You can do this by visiting the credit agency in person bringing anyone you wish along with you and asking for the information. If your request stems from a denial within the last 30 days this information shall be furnished to you free of charge HOWEVER, YOU DO NOT HAVE THE RIGHT TO PHYSICALLY HANDLE YOUR FILE, NOR REQUEST A REPORT ON YOURSELF FROM THE AGENCY. If you have not had a denial within the last 30 days, you can be charged a "reasonable fee", (usually around $5.00) for this information.

You also have the rights to be told who received a report on you in the last 6 months, the right to have incorrect information re-investigated (at their expense) and if found inaccurate, removed from the file as well as having the people who have already received a report containing these inaccuracies told of the new findings. If you and the agency do not agree on the findings of the new investigation, you can request that your version of the story be placed in your file and given to all new requests, or, if you pay for it, that your version be sent to previous report takers.

You can demand that all detrimental information over 7 years old (except for bankruptcy, which remains active for 14 years) be removed from the files. You can demand the right to be notified that a company is doing an investigative report on you.

You can try and sue a credit reporting agency BUT you must prove that any false information given by them (or by a source to them) was done so with malice or willful intent to injure. Needless to say, not many such suits are won...

If you want to conduct such a fact-finding tour you should call the credit agency within business hours and arrange for an interview for that purpose. If you feel they have violated this act you should contact the nearest office of the Federal Trade Commission.

The main problem within this fine act is that you can be turned down for a job or some such, and never be told that this happened because of a negative credit report. You were simply turned down because "someone else was better qualified".

Because of this you should probably go down and set up an interview with a couple of credit agencies from time to time just to keep up to date on your "credit fingerprint".

Of course, the alternative is to ask someone who owns a store, or otherwise belongs to a credit reporting agency to run a report on you and show you the results. Do not mention this fact was a favor when you go down to complain...

As I have mentioned before, Credit Bureaus wield a lot of power that can be used against you, or by the same token, if you join or use someone else's membership, these organizations can give you alot of "free" investigative information on damn near anyone...

If you need access to a person's bank balance, there are a couple of methods. Banks still normally tell you if the person in question has an account there, but will never divulge the amount of cash present. If you are suing the person, this information can be subpoenaed into court, and/or the whole account "attached" by the sheriff to cover the amount of the court loss. This "attaching" procedure is often used by collection agencies.

A quick estimate can be gotten by calling the bank saying you are such and such car dealer, and the person in question has just written you a check for XXXXXX dollars. Banks will usually tell you if the check is good, BUT will often want to know the person's account number at the same time.

Banks will often cooperate with one type of credit agency or another as to facts and figures.

TRYING TO GET THE EXACT AMOUNT OVER THE PHONE BY PRETENDING YOU ARE THE PERSON IN QUESTION SELDOM WORKS. SOME BANKS WILL SIMPLY REFUSE, SOME WILL WANT TO KNOW SOME WEIRD LITTLE FACT THEY HAVE REQUESTED FROM THE PERSON WHEN HE/SHE OPENED THE ACCOUNT. OFTEN THIS IS THE MAIDEN NAME OF THE ACCOUNT HOLDER'S MOTHER.

Banks still keep microfilm records of all checks they CASH for 6 months. If a government agency wants to see your account, after your bank has cleared it by sending you the statement containing the cashed checks, they can go back to each bank that originally took in each check (this is recorded) for the last 6 months and request a microfilm record.

After 6 months, this information is supposed to be destroyed.

"I don't know," said the Ethiopian, "but it ought to be the aboriginal Flora. I can smell Giraffe, and I can hear Giraffe, but I can't see Giraffe . . . . . "

(Thank you, Rudyard Kipling!)

Many people have beaten the computer watchdog effort in America by "disappearing" and then, lo and behold, re-surfacing under a completely different name and lifestyle.

The most prominent group of disappearers must surely be criminals of one sort or another, who have been arrested and suddenly decided they have better things to do than reporting to prison. However, many others disappear, or at least maintain complete ID in at least one other name; veterans with bad discharges, draft deserters, those with heavy arrest records or prison records, and even people who just become fed up with their spouse(s) and decide to fade into the woodwork.

It is unfortunate that large numbers of people have to take this route, but in a country that continues to punish its black sheep by refusing jobs, and/or civil rights to people who have made a mistake and have paid in full, many are left with little choice (this is particularly true in the case of the millions of veterans who have bad (less than honorable) discharges, or honorable releases with a bureaucratic, seemingly looking, SPN code).

Many who decide to establish an alternate life have no idea how to begin. A common mistake is the purchase, and attempted use of the "blank" birth certificates, driver's licenses, etc., offered in most magazines that carry classified advertising. These are little better than useless, maybe they will fool an employer or your next door neighbor, but do not try to use them on any person who might have a working knowledge of the real document - they won't pass. The very worst example of this is the phony birth certificate. Remember, REAL copies must have the county seal on them, not a blank, fancy, King 100 gold seal, but a real, embossed, official seal.

A few people stumble on the "correct", or best way to change identities by trial and error, or else by word of mouth.

The most important item in the journey to oblivion is the birth certificate. A real birth certificate will open just about every door you need opened, and they are fairly easy to procure. By far and away the best way to get one is to let the government do it for you, after all, you pay taxes, don't you?

There are a couple of methods to get a birth certificate. They all entail you "borrowing" the ID of someone who doesn't need it anymore, i.e. a dead person. The simplest, but riskiest way to do this is simply to read the obituary column of a newspaper, preferably one outside your area. When you locate a dead person of approximately your own age, race, sex and general disposition, you write a note to the funeral parlor that handled the persons after-thoughts and say you read of Dear Joe Jones demise and wonder if that is the same Jones that you knew and loved during the war (or any other likely story) and could they send you information as to where he was born, home town etc.

With this information you drop a note to the county clerk of the county where Jones was born. Enclose $2.00 and request a copy of "your" birth certificate . . . . .

The problem with this idea is that dear old Mr. Jones may have left you any number of warrants, traffic tickets, debts, wives and children, or other such undesirable inheritances. A safer method of establishing your ID is to go to the local library of any metropolitan area, or the newspaper morgue (either will have microfilmed records or newspapers from years and years ago), or better yet, go right to the county clerk's office and look through the death certificate records (public records which anyone has access to). You are searching to find a child that died somewhere around the time you were between 2 and 6 years of age. The child would have been your race, sex, eye color.

If you locate the child in the obituary column of the microfilmed newspaper, you must write the county in which he died, hoping that he was also born therein (unless, of course, it tells where he was born, as many will do when several members of the family all die in an accident or some similar tragedy), requesting a copy of "your" birth certificate. If you find the person you want to use in the death certificate book, it will probably tell where he/she/it was born and if it is in the same county, you can go in person and apply for the birth certificate . . . . . .

If you are having it mailed, it is a nice touch to bring it to a post office box, or a letter service. You can get a box in someone elses name by having a friend apply for it and adding your name to be able to receive mail, or applying in a fake name and staying with a friend who is about to move for a few days while they verify the fact that you do indeed, get mail at that address.

Once you have "your" birth certificate, you are practically home free. A drivers license and/or a state ID can be gotten from your friendly drivers license office by presenting your birth certificate (and, of course, taking the drivers test if you applying for a DL), explaining that your old license was from out of state and you lost it . . . You will be issued your temporary, and the permanent one, with the nice photo (in most states) will be mailed some time later. It is possible to use a post box for an address in most states.

Social Security is the next one. You can get a form to fill out at any SS office, and mail it back in with the completed data. They will also mail the card to you BUT, remember, if you are using a birth certificate of someone who kicked off as an adult, he probably already has a SS number and you must state you are applying for a DUPLICATE. If you are getting a "firstie", ESPECIALLY if you go down to pick up the card in person, you should have some little story ready about why a 36-year old man never had to work. Good possibilities are the fact that you have been in school a long time, lived with your dear, bless their collective hearts, parents overseas, worked on a commission basis (which doesn't require a SS card), suffered amnesia all your life and were unable to work, married rich at 16, and so on.

Additional nice looking ID's can be easily picked up in the form of passports (you need $12.00, a certified birth certificate, one piece of ID with a photo on it). Your passport will be issued in about 10 days unless you pay an additional, small fee to have it expedited down to a couple of days. An "international" drivers license will be issued by AAA if you already hold a valid US facsimile, (with no test yet!) hunting and fishing licenses are nice, and fairly cheap, etc. etc.

All this disappearing is made possible by a couple of glaring inconsistencies in our security-happy government: Namely, nobody keeps a cross record of births and deaths, NOWHERE, NO ONE. Your birth certificate is never "cancelled", if you were born, that's all it takes. Social Security numbers will not be cancelled or held, unless someone notifies them (such as the wife), a complaint is filed, or the FBI wanted the person whose name you borrowed.

Drivers license bureaus will take a thumb print, or some such token, but they will not cross check to make sure it is really "you".

It is also possible to use any of the fingerprint fouling methods described elsewhere in this viable publication, but remember that the clerk may notice it is not coming out A-OK and make you wash, or repeat it until it does . . . . .

SUPPLIERS

From John Dean's testimony during the Watergate hearings:

Q. "I will ask you if the Americans who were to be the subject of these information or intelligence gathering operations were designated by such terms as 'subversive elements' without further definition."

A. "It was very broad, that is correct."

Q. "And second, 'selected targets of internal security interests?'"

A. "Yes sir, again that was a very broad description."

Q. "Now was there anything in the documents that told who was going to do the selecting? These selected targets of internal security interests? And that was left up, by the document, to the imagination or interpretation of anybody engaged in the intelligence work?"

A. "That is correct sir."

Q. "And, I will ask you as a lawyer, if you do not think that surreptitious entry, or burglary and the electronic surveillance and penetration constituted a violation of the Fourth Amendment?"

A. "Yes sir, I do."

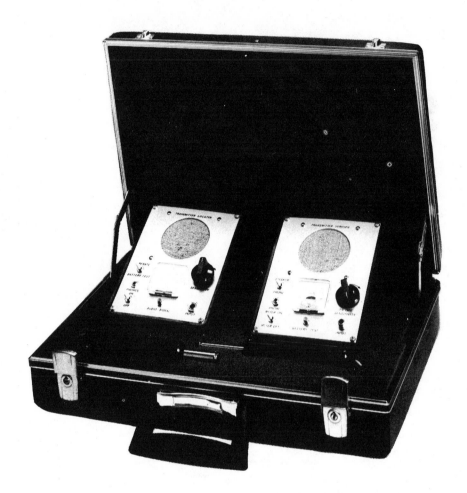

The CCC MicroWave TRANSMITTER DETECTOR KIT
is an invaluable aid in the **detection of unauthorized
transmission.** There are two complementary pieces of
equipment: Model C, which seeks out any signal being
transmitted; and Model A, which verifies the results of
Model C. Together they are an unbeatable combination
providing flexibility, accuracy and consistently high
performance. All CCC products have been engineered
for operation by persons who have not been schooled
in the use of sophisticated electronic equipment.
Both Model C and Model A are available individually.

CCC offers a number of nice anti-surveillance devices including a complex RF detector (actually a pair of units),
the good ol' Mark III, CCC III, etc., wiretap defeat system, and a number of "tap-proof" phones in various styles, or
they will even modify your phone upon request.

COMMUNICATION CONTROL CORP

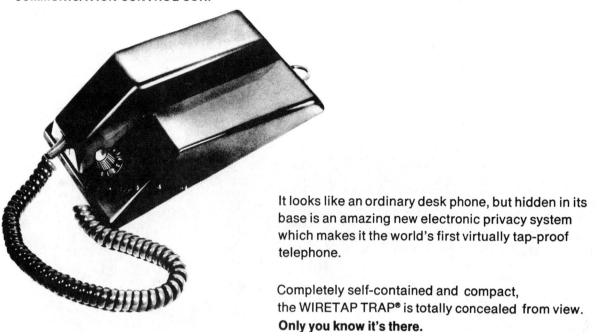

It looks like an ordinary desk phone, but hidden in its base is an amazing new electronic privacy system which makes it the world's first virtually tap-proof telephone.

Completely self-contained and compact, the WIRETAP TRAP® is totally concealed from view. **Only you know it's there.**

The revolutionary new CCC "Tap-Proof Phone" is the only telephone unit on the market that has its own built-in wiretap defeat system.

- Automatically cancels out illegal wiretaps now on your phone or lines ... or which may be added later.
- Knocks out any telephone operated room "bugs."
- Prevents clandestine tape recordings of your phone conversations by automatic devices or human eavesdroppers.
- Knocks out virtually any telephone wiretap transmitter.
- Lets you know if someone is trying to eavesdrop illegally on your conversations.
- Fools the "bugger" and allows you to feed misinformation with the switch "off" ... or speak in security with the switch "on."

SABER (Fargo Police Equipment), 1162 Bryant Street, San Francisco, California 94107

Defense Against Clandestine Eavesdropping Devices

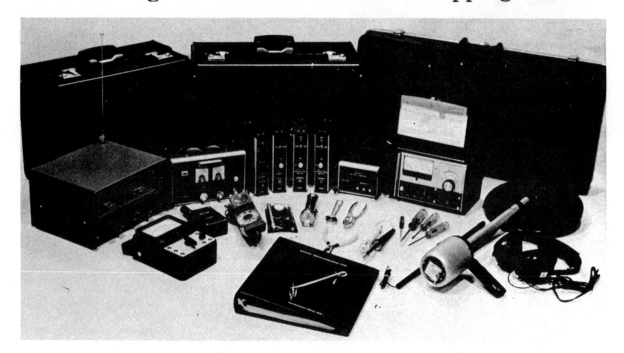

The Saber system is one of the more complete, albeit one of the more manual, countermeasures systems on the market. Saber seems to believe the operator, with a bit of practice, can make more accurate tests than an automatic device can.

The Saber CM-300 includes: High gain modular amplifier for activating carbon mics and listening for audio leaks, an RF detector, metal detector for checking walls and furnishings, presumably for the possibility of spike mics and such, a sweep generator for making hidden mics "squeal", induction probe for tracing weird wires, a telephone analyzer, RF receiver capable of detecting AM/FM/SSB over a wide range of frequencies, a control device for checking the various detectors, a wide band AM/FM receiver for double checking various signals, a physical inspection kit which includes all the screwdrivers and such one needs and lastly, but not leastly, a manual giving complete instructions in operating all your new gear.

This is a wide band system, used for all sorts of sweeping from telephone to room to line tracing and does include just about everything one could want to perform state-of-the-art protection.

Oh yes, the CM-300 is $5000, FOB San Francisco............

The unique GRETAG Speech Scrambler SC 101 has been designed to protect your voice messages transmitted over radio or regular telephone channels from unauthorized listeners. The GRETAG SC 101 will be used by military, police or other government agencies.

Unauthorized and specially trained persons are not capable to understand the confidential information even when repeatedly listening to a recorded tape. Cracking the message with computers and other sophisticated methods is made very difficult due to the fast and continous change of scrambling parameters.

The scrambled message may be transmitted over regular telephone or radio circuits since the bandwidth of the transmitted signal is not increased by the scrambling process.

On the other hand the intelligibility bandwidth of the original clear signal is not reduced by the scrambling and is equivalent to the bandwidth of a typical telephone channel. Operating the SC 101 is as easy as operating an ordinary radio hand-set. High reliability, easy trouble shooting and state-of-the-art technology are only some of the outstanding features of the GRETAG SC 101.

Saber (Fargo) also offers several voice and data scramblers. The model shown is a portable voice encoder that allows the operator to select a number of codes.

The Mark IV (not shown) is a more complex, briefcase sized device for enciphering large amounts of data onto tape and then sent out over teletype, radio or mail in the encoded form. The device offers 10 to the 38th power separate programs to choose from......

Mason TT3 Telephone Test Set

Tests Performed:
1. Line voltage off hook (each active line)
2. Line voltage on hook (each active line)
3. Tone Sweep (automatic) on line (each active line)
4. Line listen on hook, on line (each active line)
5. All wire listen, on hook, on line (all wires)
6. All wire listen, on hook, off line (all wires)
7. High voltage pulsing, on hook, off line (each active line)

F.G. Mason Engineering
1700 Post Road
Fairfield, Connecticut 06430

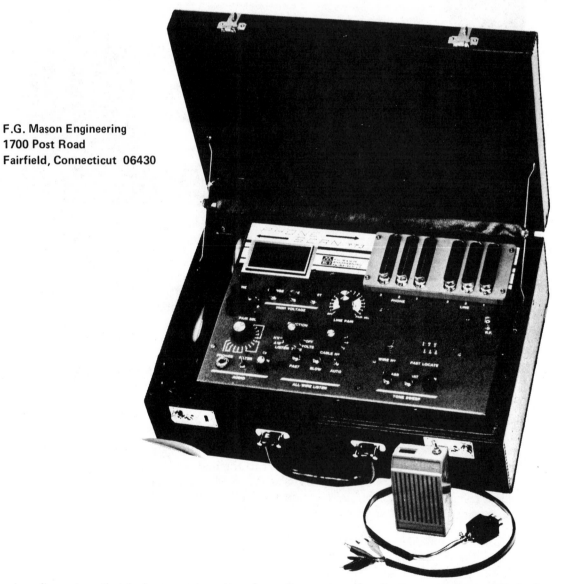

Mason carries a fine automatic telephone anaylzer. It performs the necessary functions on a semi-automatic basis and retails for $3650. They also feature a spectrum analyzing receiver system which will detect RF signals from 2 Kz thru 2000 Mc and display it on a mini-scope as well as provide audio verification. The receiver uses plug-in modules for maximum sensitivity and has an automatic scanning system; around $7000.

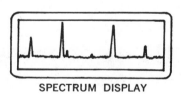

SPECTRUM DISPLAY

The Mason wideband surveillance receiver system. Plug in modules offer a range of better than a million-to-one for all AM/FM/SSB transmitters. The system offers both audible and visual ouputs; the visual end of things is displayed on a small spectrum display unit. This sort of indication allows one to tell the exact strength of the signal, place on the band, and even type of signal (the spike indicates a signal—up and down movement indicates AM, side to side means FM, and stable shows it's a CE signal). The only sacrifice is a bit of sensitivity.......very, very weak signals may slip by...............

MICRO ELECTRONIC, 2000 Hamburg 13, Badestrasse 36, GERMANY

Ah, the wonders of the German mind; from the wonderful people who brought you WW II......here is a full range, no schlock company devoted strictly to spy goodies. The best part may be the fact that they don't bother to put up a "law enforcement" or "electronic babysitter" facade. Their only warning advice is something to the effect that the purchaser must ascertain if he can get/use such devices, and that all risk (except those covered by post insurance, if you pay for it, of course), falls directly into the ill-prepared lap of said purchaser once the package has been delivered to the post office.

Their catalog is a regular Christmas Playboy for those into such things; every type of microphone and transmitter your evil little heart could desire is right here between its blue covers. . .prices are low and design exceptional.

Fer instance.....how about a device "not much bigger than a matchbook", that has twice the range of audio pick-up of the human ear, a transmitting range of 150 meters, and will transmit on self-contained batteries for 6 MONTHS! Price for this little gem, only 160 DM....cheap even at today's exchange rate.

Or wait, a drop in transmitter for 240 DM, or a little marvel that picks up voices "whispered in a large room" and transmits them 250 meters, yet is the size of a postage stamp. . .Or a contact mic/transmitter with suction cup "feet" that allow instant installation on a window where it faithfully reproduces all vibrations back into audio and then transmits them for 1000 METERS!....

Wait, wait, there's more, gosh I'm so excited, fountain pen transmitters, ashtray transmitters, (a rather mundane looking ashtray actually, but one can't have everything), contact mics, shotgun mics, scramblers, remote control transmitters, a very sophisticated tailing system, and even a couple of Star-Tron type night vision systems........

Very, very nice, needless to say, much of this stuff cannot legally be shipped into the USA.....Now, one would just presume they mark their cartons "radio parts" (the standard markings for this sort of thing) and that some of it does get into the country as customs cannot possibly establish the purpose of every piece of electronic gear brought into the country, BUT a couple of people have been arrested for attempting to bring bugging gear in via the mails at this time.

One friend of the author's ordered several items and had them sent to a rent-a-box-mail-forwarder in Canada and then drove over and picked them up with no trouble at all....

Oh yes, the Catalog costs, I think 5 DM, plus one should send a couple of bucks for air post unless you are in NO hurry.........

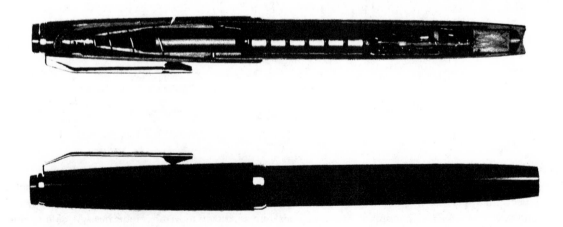

191

Electronic Stethoscope Transmitter

TRM 104 S

This new development fills a genuine gap in this particular field of special devices.

Voices or other noises produce vibrations on flat surfaces (window panes, doors etc.) which are picked up by the highly sensitive built-in microphone and subsequently reconverted into language or noise again.

The built-in sender will transmit these sounds over a distance of 1000 metres. Sounds and voices thus received are as clear and audible as in origin.

Apparatus of this kind are easily and quickly attached to doors and windows by their suction head.

Operating period:
20 working hours with three button cells of 1.5 V each
80 working hours with three button cells MALLORY RM 625 with 1.4 V each

Frequency: Adjustable between 85 and 110 M.c.p.s. with trimming screw

May be received on every VHF (FM) radio

Plug-in aerial

All of the components are cast in silicon rubber and thus rendered proof to vibrations and tropical climates.

Case: Polystyrene — black — impact resistant

Dimensions: 58 × 38 × 18 mm (without suction head)

Weight (less battery and suction head) approx. 50 grams

Wireless Telephone and Space Monitoring Apparatus

TRM 103

This new apparatus will not only monitor all telephone conversations but also the room in which the telephone is installed — and that simultaneously.

Localisation is reduced respectively made altogether impossible as an integral power souree prevents the measuring of current drops. Telephone conversations are thus clearly and audibly transmitted.

Operation period: 1500 hrs
Range: Approx. 100 metres
Battery: Mallory MN 1500
Frequency: Adjustable between 85 and 110 M.c.p.s. with trimming screw
May be received on every VHF (FM) radio

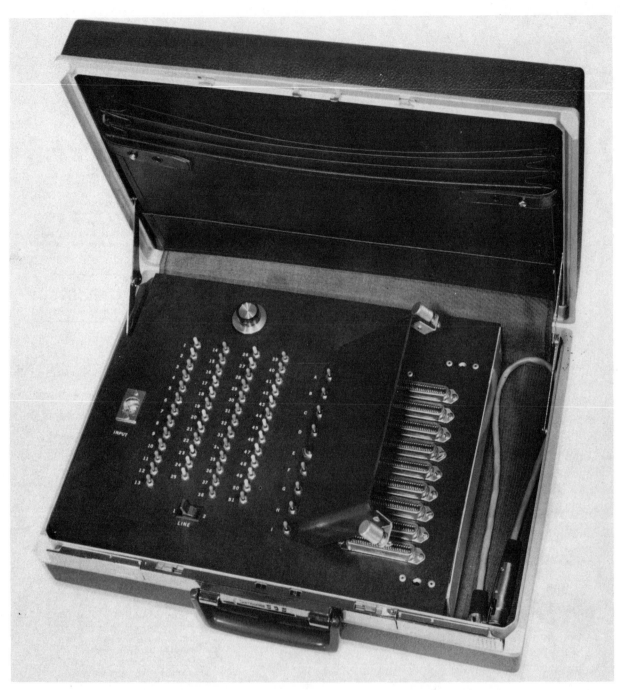

DEKTOR COUNTERINTELLIGENCE AND SECURITY INC, 5508 Port Royal Rd, Springfield, Va 22151.
Dektor makes some of the most advanced countermeasures equipment available to man or beast. Their telephone analyzer is broken down from an ultra-sophisticated, all-in-one package which does all the usual tests up to and including some performed by no other equipment on the market at this time, such as audio checking on techniques splitting the connector pair between separate connectors or even using the cover as a connector with conductive paint. The unit is digital logic based and is quite simple to use. If 5,200 ($) is a bit over your budget, they also sell units which perform most of the tests, or require some external components (meters and such) for less outlay. They also feature a anti-tap phone that is the best we've seen and would actually stop 99.9% of all bugging attempts. The entire line is professional in design, but still easy enough to use that a non-pro could easily perform the necessary tests.

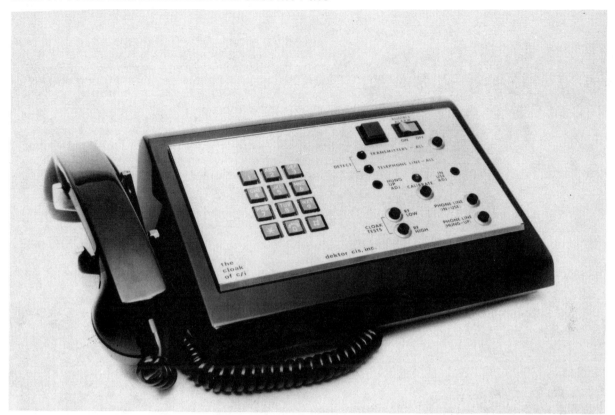

The DEKTOR CLOAK is a "loaded" phone which detects RF signals (radio bugs) between 100 Khz and 1000 Mhz, most all powered bugs, infinity transmitters and even provides automatic internal **separation** of functions to avoid all types of diode, neon bulb, and other "mic defeat" taps.

DEKTOR SPECTRUM ANAYLZER (or monitor) is a device which detects all types of RF radiation including SSB, or those with the carrier removed (very top level bugs use this technique to avoid detection by carrier detection systems). Even pulse width transmissions are picked up by this device. Extreme sensitivity is claimed as well as band coverage from one end to the other. $1,650.

Model LEA 1000

SPECIFICATIONS

The unit is rugged and versatile, designed for such diverse applications as remote night surveillance, night or in-the-dark photography and TV camera pick-up, marine and air navigation, astronomy, medicine, biology, agriculture, metallurgy, fire detection, HV corona detection, thermal process monitoring, solid state research, pollution control, etc. . . . As specific examples, the hand-held or tripod mounted Starlight Viewer can be used from a darkened vantage point or a patrol car for surveillance by law enforcement agencies, or from ships and aircrafts to view dim navigational aids, approach paths, landmarks, ect.; other applications derive from the Starlight Viewer capability of detecting infrared radiation up to 900 nm, corona discharges, hot, but non-visible bodies, etc.

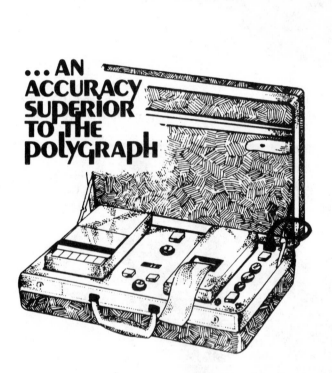

MC-2, "world's smallest tape recorder"; 2½ hour cassette, condenser mic, actual size.........$800....

LEA is a general law enforcement supplier; i.e., they stock latent fingerprint kits, handcuffs, etc. They also carry a fairly nice selection of anti-bugging stuff, as well as a few automatic telephone taps, body transmitters, one room jammer, as well as a Star-Tron type night viewer (Starlight Viewer) that appears to be a second generation type with an amplification factor of about 50,000 (retails at $3000) as well as easy coupling for connection to TV cameras, telescopes, etc. They also stock both models of the Mark II voice analyzer.................some nice stuff........

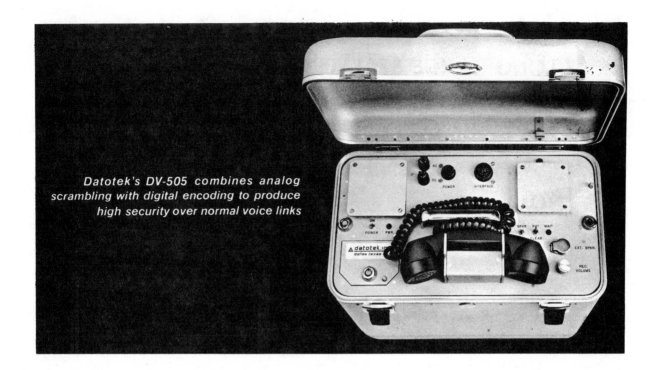

Datotek's DV-505 combines analog scrambling with digital encoding to produce high security over normal voice links

The Model DV-505 is a dynamically changing 5-band voice scrambler which provides a high level of voice privacy over telephone, single sideband, or VHF/UHF radio circuits. The DV-505 includes accurate digital timing circuitry to maintain synchronization over long distance, world-wide circuits, where transmission times as well as signal variations may be significant. For minimum size and maximum reliability, both digital and analog integrated circuits are used extensively.

The clear voice input is split into 5 frequency bands from 377 Hz to 2477 Hz, then rearranged (or scrambled) into 5 output bands, also from 377-2477 Hz. The rearrangement is accomplished by a heterodyne process which shifts and may or may not invert the frequency bands. Theoretically there are 3840 possible combinations. Most combinations offer little loss in intelligence (Example: inversion of the upper band only). Only the best 512 combinations are used, based on their unintelligibility.

Each 0.25 second, a new combination is selected automatically by the output of the random code generator. The code generator has over 2,000,000 possible user codes, selected by thumbwheel switches behind a locked front panel. In addition, the customer selects one of 16,000,000 code families by simple internal connections, thus customizing his units.

An internal crystal controlled clock within the DV-505 keeps the 0.25-second time frames in synchronization at the transmitting and receiving ends. Each time the conversation direction is reversed, a short digital burst signal is transmitted to synchronize the receiving unit. One-way conversations in excess of 20 minutes can be transmitted without need for rephasing. Interface with existing telephone and radio systems can be thru an acoustic coupler (optional) or direct connection to two-wire, or four-wire circuits.

The DV-505 is packaged in a portable metal carrying case approximately 9"x14"x16" (21x33x38 cm), and weighs approximately 35 pounds (16 kg). It operates from 115/230 VAC, 50-60 Hz, or optionally, from a 12 VDC source. The case contains the push-to-talk handset, and several operator controls.

DATOTEK INC, 8220 Westchester, Dallas, Texas 75225. Several excellent data protection systems for voice, Telex, and bit data type systems.

196

#007 LONG RANGE STAKEOUT TRANSMITTER

"TELEPHONE-STAKEOUT"

"NEW-IMPROVED"
500 MW OUTPUT

"ESPIONAGE" TRANSMITTING

"LONG-RANGE"

"ROOM-BUGGING"

"SECRET AGENT" INTELLIGENCE

"TELEPHONE-STAKEOUT"

SHOE HEEL TRANSMITTER

The transmitter is hidden in the heel of the right shoe. The antenna is crafted inside the sole. The heel is removable so that the battery can be changed and the transmitter tuned to another frequency if desired. Shoes can be worn without harm to the transmitter. Unit comes complete with pair of shoes and special receiver. Shoes available in black only.
SPECIFY SHOE SIZE WHEN ORDERING.
Cat. No. 118-575 . . . . $279.00

CIGARETTE LIGHTER TRANSMITTER

"COUNTER-SPY"

CRIMINAL RESEARCH PRODUCTS of Conshohocken, Pennsylvania specialize in police equipment. Notice how the "authority" slanted ads resemble your average, Madison Avenue type, washday ads. . .New Improved. . .Or how the "secret agent" role is subliminally played up. . .By the way, did you really think anyone made a shoe transmitter?

PS. They only sell to law enforcement bodies and will not even send you a catalog..........

SOUND SECURITY
Box 867
San Francisco, Cal 94101
CATALOG $1.00

Actual shape/size of a condenser microphone sold by Sound Security. Device has a BUILT IN FET transistor amplifier and operates on any voltage between 1-20 VDC. Very high sensitivity of about −54 at 6000 Hz makes this mic ideal for mini-transmitters, recording and other uses where a hearing sensitivity exceeding that of the human level is desirable. Price $20.00...............

WIRELESS
MINIATURE FM MICROPHONE

The unit is not much bigger than a matchbox and allows constant room monitoring for a period of about three months on only one battery.

The advantages of this unit are evident:

An extremely long time of operation without it being necessary to enter the room monitored to change batteries.

The pick-up sensitivity of the built-in capacitor microphone is twice as high as that of human hearing and conforms to studio quality.

With commercial transistor radios reception is on the VHF/FM band. The unit can be provided with a special transmission frequency range (see technical data) to achieve maximum security and elimination of unwanted monitoring; correspondingly tuned receivers are supplied by our company.

Technical Data:

Range: approx. 150 metres

Operating time: 2500 hours
amplifier (FET input stage)

High performance oscillator with three-stage low-noise A.F.

Operating voltage range: 0,9 to 2 V

Power consumption: with 1,5 V = 1 ma

Microphone: Elektred type capacitor microphone
transmitted frequency range 50 to 15 000 Hz

Flexible wire trailing antenna, plug-in type

Power supply: 1 battery Mallory ZM 9 C

All components are embedded in epoxy resin and silicone rubber to render them tropic and shock-proof

Housing: ABS, black, impact resistant

Weight: 80 g (incl. battery)

Dimensions: 58 x 38 x 18 mm

Carrier frequencies:

Standard type **TRM 100 A:** 85—110 MHz
(VHF/FM 3 m band) adjustable

XR 100

Unparelleled performance and battery life.
Professional quality. 6 Month guarantee. $295.00

SS also carries several types of Starlight night viewers, Mark II Voice Analyzer ($2495.00), several types of coutermeasure and detection gear.

SS is also reportedly marketing an ultrasonic jamming unit for tape recorders, bugs, and voice analyzers.

One of the most interesting suppliers operating today; SS stocks numerous lines of surveillance and anti-surveillance gear as well as several of their own designs. Some devices are not available elsewhere in the US, some are the better crop of other designers. A fun catalog......SS also preforms counter-surveillance work by appointment.

SOUND SECURITY

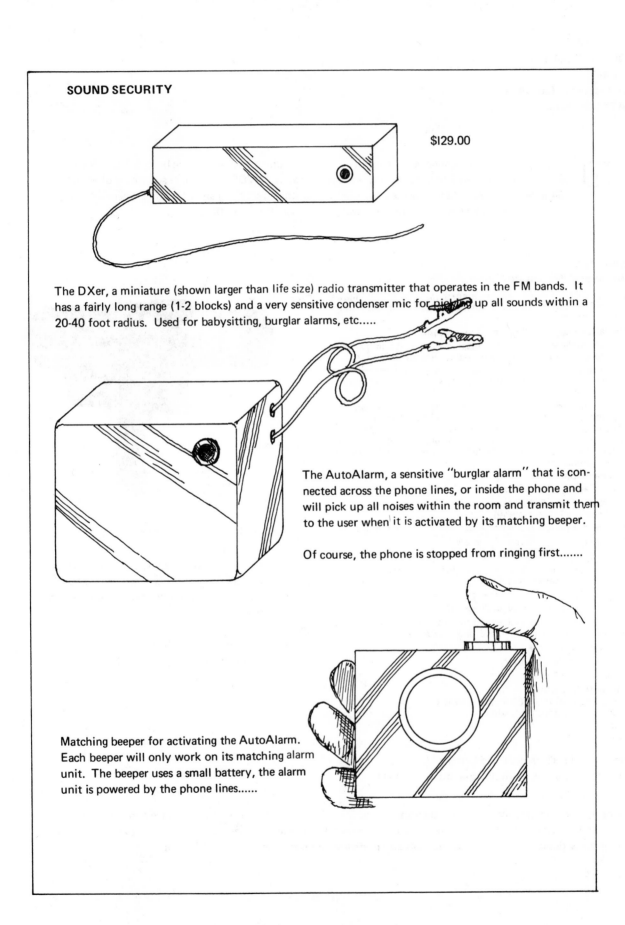

$129.00

The DXer, a miniature (shown larger than life size) radio transmitter that operates in the FM bands. It has a fairly long range (1-2 blocks) and a very sensitive condenser mic for picking up all sounds within a 20-40 foot radius. Used for babysitting, burglar alarms, etc.....

The AutoAlarm, a sensitive "burglar alarm" that is connected across the phone lines, or inside the phone and will pick up all noises within the room and transmit them to the user when it is activated by its matching beeper.

Of course, the phone is stopped from ringing first.......

Matching beeper for activating the AutoAlarm. Each beeper will only work on its matching alarm unit. The beeper uses a small battery, the alarm unit is powered by the phone lines......

WIRELESS FM MICROPHONE

This unit is an excellent example of the possibilities, qualities, performance and applicability of the equipment included in our supply programme. There is no comparable unit of this price class on the international market.

The optimal combination of most modern components and a powerful miniature capacitor microphone ensures a high transmitting power.

Even when placed in a wooden cabinet or a drawer the microphone will pick up whispered conversation up to a distance of 8 metres and transmits it with outstanding clearness.

An electronic polarity reversing device automatically ensures the proper polarity when fitting the batteries in the practical clips.

With commercial transistor radios reception is on the VHF/FM band. The unit can be provided with a special transmission frequency range (see technical data) to achieve maximum security and elimination of unwanted monitoring; correspondingly tuned receivers are supplied by our company.

Technical Data:

Range: 250 metres

Operating time: 60 hours full power with normal 9 V battery, declining after this
     180 hours full power with battery Mallory MN 1604, declining after this

High performance oscillator with three-stage low-noise A.F. amplifier (FET input stage)

Antenna output: 20 mW

Operating voltage range: 3 to 10 V

Power consumption: at 9 V = 3 ma

Microphone: Elektred capacitor microphone transmitted frequency range 50 to 15 000 Hz

Flexible wire trailing antenna, plug-in type

Power supply: 1 battery 9 V or 1 battery Mallory MN 1604

All components are embedded in epoxy resin and silicone rubber to render them tropic and shock-proof

Housing: ABS, black, impact resistant

Weight: 90 g (incl. battery)

Dimensions: 53 x 53 x 21 mm

ST-3 Sensatuner

The ST-3 Sensatuner, housed in a rugged, walnut-finish case, is an all solid-state, portable, tunable receiver designed for use with all EDCOR wireless microphones and other RF transmitters operating from 30-50 MHz. Audio outputs may be used with any high and low impedence sound system for amplification, and video, film or sound recording. FM and special noise-squelch circuitry eliminate static and background noise. Can be power line or battery operated.

List Price Each ST-3 286.00

TUNER (RECEIVER)

* PM-11 Lavalier Microphone

Easily clips on tie, dress or lapel. Unique crystal control system provides superb tone quality with no frequency drift. Electret microphone head has an omnidirectional pickup pattern. Transmitting frequencies to choose from: 30.84 MHz; 33.40 MHz; 35.02 MHz.

List Price Each   PM-11 186.00

XR I07
Professional quality
6 mo guarantee
$175

PR-1 Mini-Receiver

A compact, crystal controlled receiver designed to be worn on the body. Suitable for receiving transmissions from FM microphones or any FM transmitter operating in a frequency range of 30 to 50 MHz. Audio frequency range 50 to 12,000 Hz.

ST—3 Tuner $279.00
PR-I Set to choice of 5 freq $149.00
PM-I Transmitter $275.00

Other items including anti-surveillance gear in catalog.

PM-1 Lavalier Microphone

The combination hand-held/lavalier microphone provides broadcast quality, absolute stability and great versatility. The miniature, wireless, battery-operated mike fits comfortably in your hand. To convert in seconds: plug in the lavalier mike, clip it to tie, dress or lapel, and fasten the transmitter to your belt. Frequency Response: 50-14,000 Hz.

Dear old **AMC SALES, Dept BB, Downey, Cal 90241** has been advertising and selling a cheapo, "Micro Mini Wireless Mike" for a number of years. This little device is sold through ads in Playboy, True, and the like. It is a mere 1 7/8" x 1/2" x 5/8" and will "pickup and transmit most sounds without wires up to 450 feet through any FM radio".

It is, of course, used as a burglar alarm, wireless babysitter, intercom, music amplifier, etc, and sells for a mere $14.95 plus 50 cents postage and handling.

I have had occasion to test said device and discovered a number of useful things: A. It is a two transistor mini-oscillator. B. It will pick up most sounds in the vicinity, including human voices or animal guttural utterances, from about 6-10 feet away. C. Will transmiter the above named sounds to an FM radio (with its little antenna, not pictured in the ads nor mentioned in the size quotes) for a distance of 50-100 feet.

All in all, a real bargin for a mere $15.00, let me tell you......

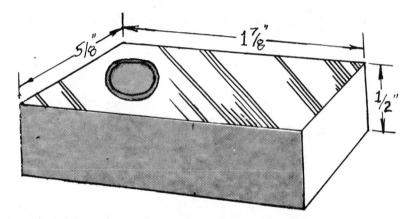

An automatic recorder actuator, whether it costs $175.00 from a fancy electronic device supplier, or whether you sprung $30 for it from Lafayette Electronics, does exactly the same thing; i.e., when attached to a phone, OR PHONE LINE (the radio parts/hobbyist shops seldom stress this fine point) and then to the remote jack of any tape recorder it senses the line condition and turns the recorder on when the phone is lifted from the cradle, records all the conversation, and then shuts the recorder down when the phone is replaced. One of the best places for this application is in the basement somewhere along the phone line before the surge protector......The recorder can then be hidden in some natural flora or fauna.....

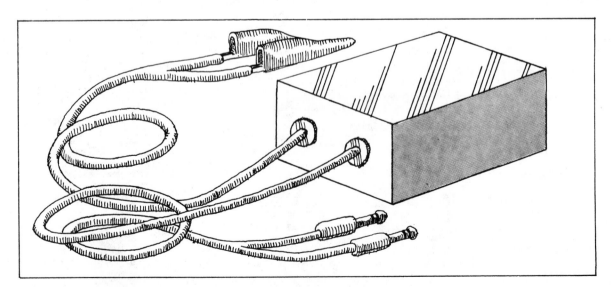

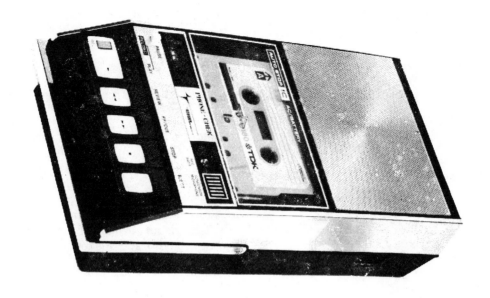

FEATURES

- **RECORDS 9 HOURS ON A CASSETTE, 4½ HOURS/SIDE.**
- **REWINDS 4½ HOURS IN LESS THAN 10 MINUTES.**
- **LONG TERM LOGGING FOR UNATTENDED SERVICE; VOICE & DATA.**
- **EASY-TO-USE — STANDARD CASSETTE OPERATION.**
- **BUILT-IN CONDENSER MICROPHONE.**
- **AUTOMATIC POWER CUT-OFF AT END OF TAPE.**
- **PUSH-BUTTON OR REMOTE CONTROL OPERATION.**
- **ONE CASSETTE SUPPLIED FOR 9 HOURS OPERATION.**
- **POWER SELECTABLE: 115VAC, 6VDC, FOUR C-BATTERIES**
- **OPTIONS:**
  AUTOMATIC TELEPHONE RECORDER.
  VOICE OPERATED SWITCH & MICROPHONE.
  EXTERNAL MIKE WITH REMOTE SWITCH.

ALRIGHT, here is the first J.C. Penney's of the electronics field.....one can purchase a radar sentry to warn when an agents car enters a field of dangerous enemy forces, several metal detectors, phone answering machines, Tele-Secretary, white noise phone-loaders (for hashing transmitters and infinity type bugs), a couple of cheap tape recorders (cassette) which have been slowed down to record up to 9 HOURS on a single cassette (for phone monitoring and such-cheap too; starting at $80) and even a VOX which starts any remote-start recorder at the sound of a voice and stops during silence, quite a bit of custom surveillance and counter gear available on special order.....................

The TSS-101-System offers proven protection from this common method of eavesdropping — the Telephone Compromise — by preventing the ever present telephone microphones from being able to receive usable room audio. This system magnetically induces an intense noise into the microphones which silently but effectively masks all room audio and makes it unusable to the eavesdropper.

$35.00

CCA-200/220
conference·call attachment

NOW YOU CAN
MAKE 3-WAY PHONE CALLS

Three people, at 3 different locations, can now speak to each other (or have a conference) simultaneously.

"ANSA-MAN"®

$84.95

the world's most economical
TELEPHONE ANSWERING MACHINE

warns of radar traffic zones . . . promotes safe driving

H. L. B. SECURITY ELECTRONICS, LTD.
211 EAST 43RD STREET, NEW YORK, NEW YORK 10017
(212) 986-1367

Security seems to maintain one of the most selective array of surveillance and anti-aurveillance goodies still available to you, me, or Joe Doe.

They are the only company that comes to mind who still sells the notorious infinity transmitter, or, excuse me, "TELE—EAR" Burglar Alarm......Right, see the idea is that you put the "device" on a phone, let's say, for the sake of conversation, your own phone, then you dial it up from any direct-dial phone in the world and use their little "beeper" to stop the target phone from ringing. Now the phone becomes a microphone allowing you to hear whatever is going on in the room.

Security has even gone the old infinity transmitter two better: they offer a device to monitor the room and amplify any sounds therein so you can "sleep peacefully, completely secure in the knowledge that you will be awakened by the slightest disturbance at the site being monitored." They also have designed their bug, er, burglar alarm into a phone wall box so you don't even have to take the telephone apart to install the device! Price is quite reasonable at $425 for the system.

They also stock a number of interesting devices: wearable transmitters (tuneable $295, crystal controlled $450), matching receivers at $195, 6 hour tape recorders for $250, or in a hidden briefcase arrangement for $395, a really nice little teeny stereo mini-cassette unit designed to be worn in various holsters in various parts of your body and pick up what your ears do (VOXed, of course) for a mere $600 (this is rumored to be the type the CIA uses).

They also offer an electronic tailing system, various telephone switchers which will lock your recorder into any line (in use) of a multi-line phone and start/stop the recorder with the conversation, and other interesting gear.

On the counter side they offer a couple of telephone defeat systems, a bug finder or two (field strength meters), and a large wiretap finder/defeat system which checks in at $2500.

Security is also flexible enough to talk about leasing their gear and offers custom design services for any little ideas you might have up your sleeve. .

NOW YOU CAN
CHECK YOUR PREMISES
ANYTIME...FROM ANYWHERE!

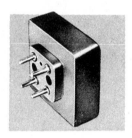

HERE'S HOW IT WORKS!

As you dial the last digit of your business telephone number, hold the REMOTE ACTIVATOR close to mouthpiece of telephone. A special frequency tone will instantly activate the **TELE-EAR** MONITOR at the site being called! The telephone will not ring, and any and all sounds at your business site will now be clearly heard on the telephone.

If you are calling from your home, simply turn on the **TELE-EAR** RECEIVER AMPLIFIER unit and hang up your telephone! You can now sleep peacefully . . . completely secure in the knowledge that you will be instantly awakened by the slightest disturbance at the site being monitored!

THE TELEPHONE NEVER RINGS!

YOU WON'T ALERT A BURGLAR BY A RINGING PHONE! The telephone in your office or business will not make the slightest sound! It will **sit** there just as innocently as ever . . . WHILE YOU SAFELY MONITOR THE PREMISES!

WARNING!
THE TELE-EAR IS NOT A "BUG"!

Because the very nature of this fantastic device makes it possible to monitor areas without observance, we must point out that federal law permits the use of the TELE-EAR ONLY as a burglar alarm.

It is illegal to use the **TELE-EAR** to surreptitiously monitor the conversations of parties that are unaware of its presence!

SECURITY ELECTRONICS

 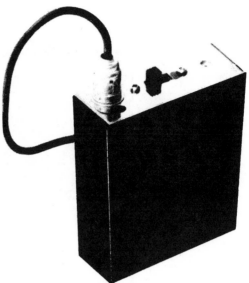

Keep your undercover agents under protective surveillance with Ultron X. It's microphone sensitivity is superior to the human ear, with a transmitting range of ¼ mile.

Consistently outperforms transmitters at twice the price, with a battery life of 100 hours continous use.

For complete privacy Ultron X is available at a frequency of 112 MC. For standard FM receivers, Ultron X is available at 87.5 MC. Self contained battery. One year warranty.

SECURITY ELECTRONICS

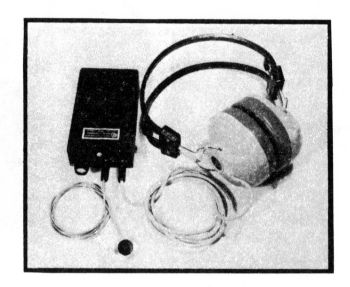

TRANSMITTER MODEL # 1000
AND CHARGER

RECEIVER # IR-1000

WJS offers a number of nifty items: first off, they have a "slim line, crystal controlled, FM, law enforcement transmitter," for a mere $500. This particular model has a number of noteworthy features; it puts out a full 1 watt (good for a fair distance, maybe a couple of miles under ideal circumstances), claims audio pickup from 30 feet and is rechargeable. The sacrifices made for the high output are size (almost 6 inches long) and operating time (three hours from each recharge). The matching receiver is $155.

They also make a cheap electronic tailing system; the transmitters only run $85 apiece, and the receiver, which clips under the dash and utilizes the vehicles own antenna, a mere $325. This is the single system type and does not have excellent direction finding capabilities, but does give a tone coupled range indication. Will get about 1½ miles. . .

They even offer a high gain "intelligence amplifier" which comes with a contact mic (no spike though...) and has tube and induction mics as extras.....Some de-bugging goodies also.

207

Transmitter Locator

TRACER Model WT #1
$385.00

TRACER ELECTRONICS
256 North Avenue
Palm Beach, Florida 33480

This unit transmits in the high VHF Band between 160-170 MHz. There is no danger of it being received by the subject's FM radio.

Also ideal for those "Just You and I" conversations, this truly concealable, --- World's Smallest Wearable Transmitter can be worn under just a sport shirt without being detectable. Can also be worn under an overcoat without loss of sensitivity.

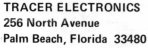

Auto Tailing System

Tracer offers two catalogs: one for you and me, and one for law enforcement bodies. Their commercial catalog lists a nice little "sub-miniature wearable transmitter" which operates in the VHF band for $385, a really nice electronic tailing system for about $800, and a few re-tagged Sony products.

They also offer two "bug finders", including one of the audio feedback ("Squealer") variety. All in all, fairly good stuff-fairly reasonable prices.

MIKE   ON-OFF   ANTENNA
JACKS   SWITCH   JACK

R.B. Clifton
11500 N.W. 7th Ave
Miami, Fla 33168

Clifton offers the usual "wearable" transmitter with ¼ mile range ($395), matching FM, VHF receiver ($170), along with a "Hound Dog" field strength meter-type bug detector ($100), and even an automatic oscillator for triggering infinity transmitters........

ONE HALF THE SIZE
OF A CIGARETTE!

29⁵⁰

WORLD'S SMALLEST TRANSMITTER! *

In-Store Cash Collection Case

The security cash collection case is designed
specifically for the collection and movement of cash or documents
inside premises, and in particular in retail stores. Important
features of the case include an ear-piercing 100 decibel audible
security alarm and an entirely new type of spring-loaded,
thief-proof opening.

Applications for the new case include collecting cash from
supermarket check-outs and cash registers in departmental
stores and in other types of retailing where cash needs to be
cleared from tills at frequent intervals.

Cal-Tronix is another mish-mash supplier; they carry much of the same gear that's kicking around as several other
suppliers in this section. Included are the VOX ($49.95), several slowed down cassette recorders that do upwards
of six hours on a cassette, "Tele-Ear", Tele-Secretary, De-Bug locators, and so on. One nice little money carrying
case that lets go with a cloud of staining orange dye/smoke and an alarm if snatched from the wrist of the holder.

Prices about average. Catalog costs $1.00.

*ed. note-bullshit......

FOR THE MAN OF ACTION............

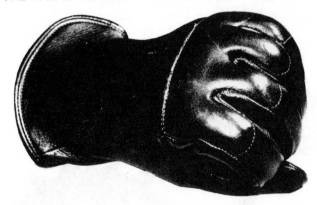

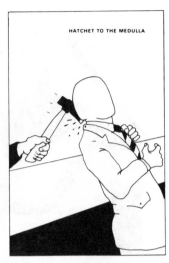

HATCHET TO THE MEDULLA

SAP GLOVES Wear Sap Gloves as standard equipment——better than a nightstick. They give weight to your authority; are instantly available in case of trouble and are a fine, unobvious defensive weapon. Damascus Sap Gloves are top quality and the very finest obtainable. The gloves are soft, pliable, longwearing leather. They are made by the finest craftsmen and look like dress gloves in every detail. To the casual observer these Sap Gloves resemble any other top grade black glove. The sap (6 ounces of powdered lead carefully built into each glove) is indistinguishable except to the initiated. Sap Gloves are in use in all parts of the U.S. They are rapidly becoming popular as standard equipment with officers in all departments of law enforcement and related fields: Patrolmen, Traffic Detail, Security Officers, Highway Patrol, Night Watchmen, Detectives, etc. The Sap Glove is especially useful in working with large or unruly crowds.

ORDER # PE 42

HOW TO KILL Inside expose of brutal techniques used by international killers. The object of this book is to instruct the reader in the technique of taking another human life, up close, and doing it well. Written for the benefit of military and government intelligence agencies, commando units and assassination squads. The ten revealing lessons cover it all! Everything from a hatchet job to silenced weapons. Over 50 photos and diagrams. 88 pages. A real eye—opener. NOT FOR THE SQUEAMISH! $5.95

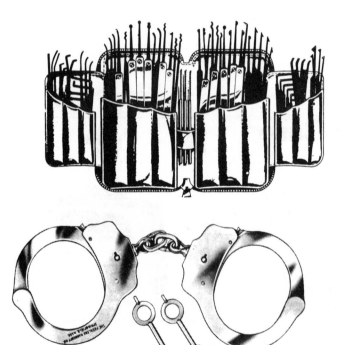

American Colonial Armament, 1 Riverside Rd, Riverside, Ill **60546**. Here we find an unusual breed of cat, ACA might better be termed Vigilante Armament.....Herein the "man of action" can buy such things as lead-loaded sap gloves (just like the police use), lock pick sets, including the Lock-Aid gun, rifle and pistol parts, bullet proof vests, saps, billy clubs, and a collection of books that ranges from ultra left wing kill 'em in the streets to straight Minuteman lierature dealing with silent killing methods, bombs, poisons, weapons of all sizes and shapes, etc.

Interesting stuff, just what the man of action needs; depending, of course, on your understanding of the term "action"...

Impressive special I.D. cards fit any professional badge case. On heavy card stock, each with badge insignia in background. Useful for positive identification . . . provides space for your photo and thumb print. Specify title or titles desired.
1504 SAME TITLES AS BUSINESS CARDS ABOVE ... **$2** EACH

650 - HEAVY DUTY HANDCUFFS — Professional flip-on wrist action cuffs lock instantly when applied to wrists. Sturdy, lifetime steel with polished nickel finish. A necessity for all law enforcement agents. Complete with two keys **$9.95**

International will send you a catalog of "confidential police and investigation equipment", which contains a few hokey commercial tape recorders and Kodak cameras, a couple of fingerprint powders and entire fingerprint kits, and then the hot ones: the Lock Aid lock pick gun (at a bit of a mark-up, I should add - $40) and a whole bunch of phony badges and ID cards which can be ordered ready-to-go, or can be "printed to your specifications".

Uh, huh...........

CARL CORDOVER & CO.

Solid State Modules - Semi-conductor Packs - Heat Sinks

SOLID STATE MODULES

COMMUNICATIONS MODULES

CW MONITOR. Monitor your "fist" as you transmit. Actuated by the RF energy surrounding your CW transmitter, this module produces ideal "monitoring volume level" code signals thru its internal audio oscillator each time you press your key. Operates from milliwatts to kilowatt transmitters. To operate—needs only: An 8-ohm PM speaker, and any 1½-volt battery. Size: 1½ x 1¼ x 1".
    Code CWM-1 ....$3.50

CODE OSCILLATOR. Provides clear tone ideal for learning Morse Code. To operate—needs only: A telegraph key, any PM speaker, and any 1½-volt battery. Size: 2 x 1¾ x ½".
    Code CPO-4 ....98¢

WIRELESS CODE OSCILLATOR. Broadcast code into any AM radio. Simplest and most convenient method of transmitting standard Morse code signals over short distances. To operate—needs only: A telegraph key, and a 9-volt transistor battery. Size: 1½ x 1¼ x 1".
    Code WC-5 ....$3.50

VHF POLICE AND FIRE CONVERTER. Permits reception of Police and Fire calls in the 30-50 MHz band on your standard broadcast band AM radio. To operate—needs only: A 9-volt transistor battery and about 30 feet of any kind of wire. Size: 1½ x 1¼ x 1".
    Code CM-P $5.00

INTERNATIONAL. Permits reception of world-wide short wave radio stations in the 25, 31 and 41 meter bands (7-12 MHz) on your standard broadcast band AM radio. To operate—needs only: A 9-volt transistor battery, and about 30 feet of any kind of wire. Size: 1½ x 1¼ x 1".
    Code CM-S $5.00

VHF AIRCRAFT CONVERTER. Permits reception of aircraft and control tower transmissions from 118 to 128 MHz on your standard broadcast band AM radio. To operate—needs only: A 9-volt transistor battery, and a few feet of wire (any kind) as an antenna. Size: 1½ x 1¼ x 1".
    Code CM-A $5.00

FM-VHF POLICE AND WEATHER CONVERTER. Permits reception of 150-164 MHz FM-VHF police, fire, emergency, marine and weather transmissions on a standard FM radio. To operate—needs only: A 9-volt transistor battery, a 5,000-ohm potentiometer and knob, and a few feet of wire (any kind). Size: 1½ x 1¼ x 1".
    Code CM-H $5.00

TV WIRELESS PHONO TRANSMITTER. Transmit music into your TV set over moderate distances within a home from the tone arm cartridge of a phonograph. To operate—needs only: One 100,000-ohm potentiometer (TVP-2 only) and a 9-volt transistor battery and battery clip. Size: 1½ x 1¼ x 1".
    Code TVP-1 For crystal or ceramic cartridge $5.00
    Code TVP-2 For magnetic cartridge $5.00

AMPLIFIER MODULES

BABY NURSE. An ultra-sensitive listening system which will amplify not only a baby's whimper, but can even report his normal movements and breathing in his crib. To operate—needs only: Two 8-ohm PM speakers, a 6-volt "lantern-type" battery, a 5,000-ohm volume control, and an SPST switch. Size: 1½ x 1¼ x 1".
    Code BN-9 ....$3.50

PHONOGRAPH AMPLIFIER. A modern, efficient phonograph amplifier that will drive any 8-ohm PM speaker at more than sufficient volume for average listening. To operate—needs only: A 1-megohm potentiometer, a 6-volt "lantern-type" battery and any 8-ohm PM speaker. Size: 1½ x 1¼ x 1".
    Code PH-7 ....$3.50

PUBLIC ADDRESS AMPLIFIER. A portable high gain PA system. To operate—needs only: A microphone (crystal, ceramic or dynamic), a 1-megohm volume control, an SPST switch, an 8-ohm PM speaker, and a 6-volt "lantern-type" battery. Size: 1½x1¼x1".
    Code PA-9 ....$3.50

PUBLIC ADDRESS AMPLIFIER (For Carbon Microphone). This module will drive any PM speaker with excellent speech intelligibility and good volume. To operate—needs only: Any PM speaker, a carbon microphone, and a 6-volt "lantern-type" battery. Size: 1" diameter x ½" high.
    Code PAA-2 ....$1.98

TV WIRELESS MICROPHONE TRANSMITTER. Transmit your voice into your television set over moderate distances within your home into channels 2, 3 or 4. To operate—needs only: A microphone, a 100,000-ohm potentiometer, and a 9-volt transistor battery and battery clip. Size: 1½ x 1¼ x 1".
    Code TVM-1 For high impedance microphone $5.00
    Code TVM-2 For low impedance microphone $5.00

FM WIRELESS BABY NURSE TRANSMITTER. This remote baby sitter will transmit from a monitoring speaker near baby's crib over moderate distances within a home into any FM radio. To operate—needs only: One PM speaker (any type), and one 1½-volt battery (any type). Size: 1" diameter x ½" high.
    Code FMB-2 ....$3.50

FM WIRELESS TELEPHONE TRANSMITTER. Permits group telephone listening by transmitting both sides of a telephone conversation over moderate distances within a home into any FM radio. To operate—needs only: One telephone "pick-up coil," and one 1½-volt battery (any type). Size: 1" diameter x ½" high.
    Code FMT-1 ....$3.50

AM WIRELESS TELEPHONE AMPLIFIER. Transmits both sides of a telephone conversation into any standard broadcast band radio. To operate—needs only: A telephone pick-up coil, and a 9-volt transistor battery. Size: 1½ x 1¼ x 1".
    Code WT-5 ....$3.50

FM WIRELESS MICROPHONE TRANSMITTER. Transmits your voice over moderate distances within a home into any FM radio. To operate—needs only: A microphone, and one 1½-volt battery (any type). Size: 1" diameter x ½" high.
    Code FMM-1 For high impedance microphone $3.50
    Code FMM-2 For low impedance microphone $3.50

AM WIRELESS MICROPHONE TRANSMITTER. Transmits your voice from high impedance microphone into any AM broadcast band radio. To operate—needs only: A high impedance microphone, and a 9-volt transistor battery. Size: 1½ x 1¼ x 1".
    Code WM-5 ....$3.50

FM WIRELESS PHONO TRANSMITTER. Transmits music over moderate distances within a home from the tone arm cartridge of a phonograph into any FM radio. To operate—needs only: One 500,000-ohm potentiometer (FMP-1 only) and one 1½-volt battery (any type). Size: 1" diameter x ½" high.
    Code FMP-1 For crystal or ceramic cartridge $3.50
    Code FMP-2 For magnetic cartridge $3.50

AM WIRELESS PHONO OSCILLATOR. This phono transmitter broadcasts music from the crystal or ceramic tone arm cartridge of a phonograph into any nearby AM broadcast band radio. To operate—needs only: A 1-megohm potentiometer, a 9-volt transistor battery, and a few feet of any kind of wire as an antenna. Size: 1½ x 1¼ x 1".
    Code WP-5 ....$3.50

TELEPHONE AMPLIFIER. Permits group telephone listening by direct amplification of both sides of a telephone conversation. To operate—needs only: A telephone pick-up coil, a 1-megohm volume control, an SPST switch, an 8-ohm PM speaker and a 6-volt "lantern-type" battery. Size: 1½ x 1¼ x 1".
    Code TA-9 ....$3.50

CB MICROPHONE PREAMP. This preamp more than doubles the sensitivity and output of your microphone to provide optimum CB modulation for more dependable communications. To operate—needs only: Any 1½-volt battery, a short length of shielded cable, a ½-megohm potentiometer and an SPST switch. Size: 1" diameter x ½" high.
    Code MP-7 ....$3.50

STEREO AMPLIFIER (For Crystal or Ceramic Stereo Cartridge). Good fidelity and channel separation, with adequate volume for average room level listening. To operate—needs only: Two 8-ohm PM speakers, two 1-megohm potentiometers, and a 6-volt "lantern-type" battery. Size: 1½ x 1¼ x 1".
    Code STX $5.00

Cordover & Co. is located at 3914 N. 29th Ave., Hollywood, Fla. 33020. They make many of the hobbyist type modules available in radio supply stores. The modules vary in effectiveness from so-so to sort of good, but they are all expendable due to their low cost.

See the construction section for a more complete run down and applications of these modules.

MISCELLANEOUS

KRYSTAL KITS, 2202 S.E. 14th, Bentonville, Ark. 72712—"Unusual" kits with the happy hobbyist in mind. Such devices as telephone scramblers, de-scramblers for police band receivers (to defeat the many police stations which are wising up to the amazing array of people purchasing "public service" band radios), and a series of phase locked loops and tight bandpass filters for infinity type transmitters or other tone controlled devices.....Very inexpensive, some plans available without buying the whole kits.

TOOLCO, 10961½ Rochester Ave., Los Angeles, Ca. 90024—Some surveillance plans, no kits. Two nice looking sub-mini mics (one dynamic $13, and one condenser $17).

WESTERN ELECTRONIC CONTROL, Box 1562, Riverside, Ca. 92502—Western representative for Communication Control Corporation.

SOUNDCRAFTSMEN, Box 2361, Santa Ana, Ca. 92707—Exotic playback equalizers for custom tailoring of sound, or filtering out unwanted portions (such as noise).

OLSON ELECTRONICS, 260 S. Forge St., Akron, Oh. 44327—General electronic supplies, "Tele-Secretary" auto recorder starter, direct coupled hi-gain amplifier for $10, 2 very small condenser mics ($24 and $60), some cheap module type stuff.

ALLIED ELECTRONICS, 1355 Sleepy Hollow Rd., Elgin, Ill. 60120—Various components, one wireless mic ($20), excellent test equipment for the general electronics trade.

LAFAYETTE ELECTRONICS, 111 Jericho Turnpike, Syosset, L.I., N.Y. 11791—General electronic supplies, musical contact mics, several inexpensive mini crystal and dynamic mics, several small amplifiers suitable for general surveillance amps including our recommendation, the dear old 99 E 90383, Miller coils and forms for construction of wireless mics, field strength meter, etc.

BA ELECTRONICS, 3199 Mercier, Kansas City, Mo. 64111—$30 Automatic recorder start (Tele-Secretary), some general test equipment and tools.

H. J. KNAPP CO., 3174 8th Ave., Largo, Fla. 33540—General electronic parts, some minor kits.

EDMUND SCIENTIFIC CO., Edscorp Bldg., Barrington, N.J. 08007—Edmund offers an array of scientific, near-scientific and outright games....some useful things including lasers, high gain parabolic mics, inexpensive wall metal detector, and a nice electronic stethoscope.

BUREAU OF SCIENTIFIC IDENTIFICATION, Box 1421, Burlingame, Ca. 94010—Also a distributor for CCC.

McGEE RADIO, 1901-07 McGee St., Kansas City, Mo.—General electronic gear, including several crystal controlled wireless mic systems that look exactly like the ones sold by several surveillance dealers at a considerable mark-up. . .

CIRCUITS

I WOULD LIKE TO AGAIN POINT OUT IT IS UNLAWFUL TO USE, SELL, TRANSPORT, OR EVEN HAVE DEVICES DESIGNED FOR ELECTRONIC SURVEILLANCE.

SOME OF THE FOLLOWING CIRCUITS HAVE LAWFUL USES, SOME ARE GIVEN FOR THE PURPOSE OF INFORMATION ONLY. IF ANY ARE USED FOR ILLEGAL SURVEILLANCE YOU COULD BE ARRESTED.

THE PUBLISHER AND AUTHOR OF THIS BOOK DO NOT ADVISE USE NOR CONSTRUCTION OF ANY OF THESE DEVICES AND TAKE NO RESPONSIBILITY FOR ANY ACTION RESULTING FROM USE, SALES, TRANSPORTATION, OR POSSESSION OF ANY DEVICE SHOWN HEREIN.

In fact, forget you ever heard of us..................

If you do decide to attempt construction of any device shown in this section, for legal purposes, use good general electronic practice when dealing with circuits operating in the MhZ range: keep all leads as short as possible, heat-sink all transistors and chips, observe all polarity markings, use components of at least 10% or better tolerance, and if at all possible, use printed circuit boards instead of breadboards........

If you are not familiar with electronic construction it would be a good idea to do a bit of reading on this subject before starting any such project, or, better yet, have someone who does understand the basics do the job for you.

All the devices in this section do work, some are copies of commercial devices, some have been designed by our engineering department. All components or their listed substitutes should be available from electronic parts supply houses, or from the general suppliers listed in our supplier section.

WIRELESS MICROPHONES

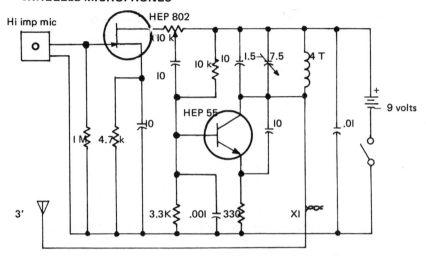

Wireless mic for commerical FM band. Tuning is accomplished by adjusting the variable cap. XI is made by twisting 2 inch lengths of small guage insulated wire together. Should give range of 2 blocks to ½ mile with good receiver. In any wireless mic a condenser mic can be substituted for the dynamic variety by simply adding a line to the power source as shown in the directions for the mic, this will give increased pick-up.

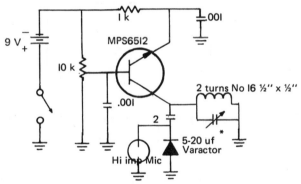

Ultra sub-mini transmitter uses modern circuit with a Poly Paks varactor to achieve FM modulation. Transmits about 300' in the commerical FM band directly from tank circuit. 3' antenna can be added to tank coil end for greater range. For super small power supply disassemble a 9 volt battery and use on bank of cells.

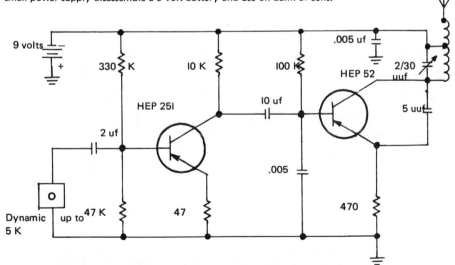

A simple, early circuit for a wireless mic. Use a 3/8" form for the coil and 18 enameled wire; wind seven turns, tap at number two. Frequency can be vaired by adding or subtracting from coil. The first transistor is an audio amp (any good audio type will suffice) and the second an rf oscillator (again, any like type will work).

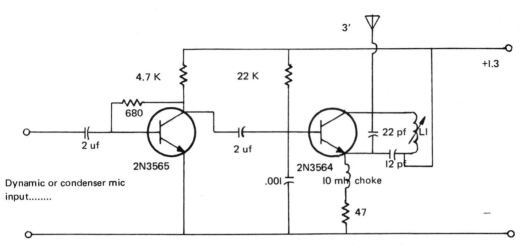

This is a circuit popularized in the late 60's (God bless 'em) as a "Micro-Mini 006 Transmitter". Many, many, such units were sold commerically. Entire unit can be built into a package not much bigger than a sugar cube including mercury battery. For commerical band use LI is 7 turns No. 22 enameled wire on Miller 4300-5 form.

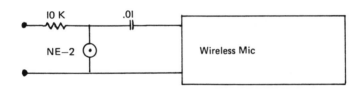

Almost any transmitter can be converted into a phone bug (parallel) by using this set-up instead of the microphone. This is connected across both phone lines.

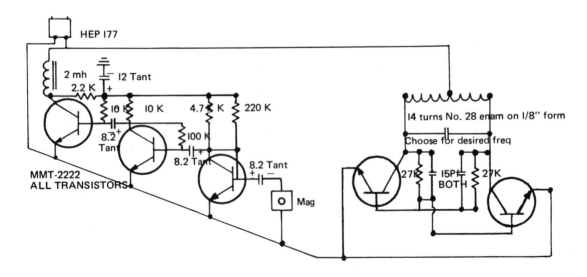

This is one example of a "drop in" mic; this entire unit can be constructed on a small circuit board and then mounted inside a standard microphone button in the mouthpiece of a telephone. The button must be taken apart by prying off or cutting both the metal rings (one of them is one the face, one on the rear of the button) holding the unit together. The carbon granules are thrown away and the magnetic mic used instead. The two leads from the HEP 177 are soldered onto the two contacts on the back of the mic. The unit is re-assembled and the rings soldered back into place.

217

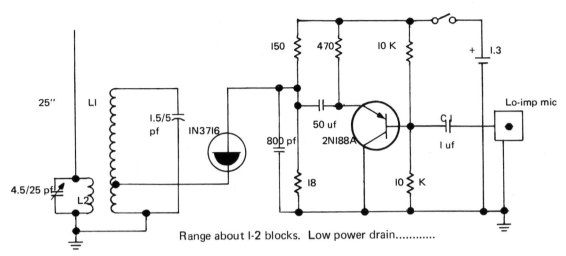

Range about I-2 blocks. Low power drain............

A unique circuit with a tunnel diode oscillating back to back with a transistor. This can be constructed in a very small space by using a I.3 volt mercury cell for power. LI is 6 turns No. I6 close-wound. Tap at I turn. L2 is 2 turns No. I6 wound I/8''. Use ceramic trimmer for L2 tank and electrolytic for CI.

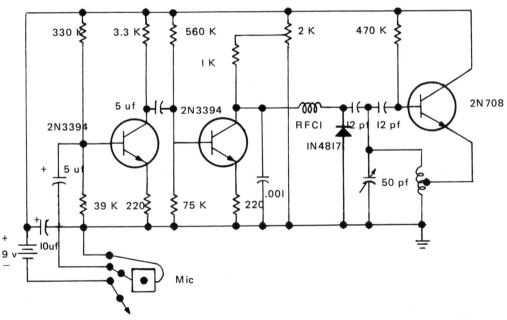

Diode modulates tuned circuit in commerical FM band. Coil is 4 turns No. I8, ¼'' wide, I'' long, tap 2 from ground.

TAILING TRANSMITTER SYSTEM

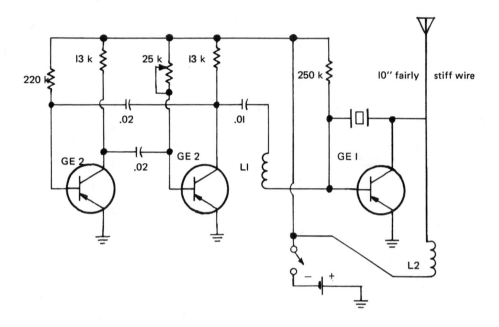

The transmitter (above) is concealed under the vehicle to be followed. It puts out a stream of beeps (adjusted by changing the 25 k pot) which are picked up by the receiver. Power is 3 volts, both coils are 1 mH rf chokes. Use any CB crystal (3rd overtone).

Receiver is tuned by adjusting the 36 pf cap until the beeps are heard. At this point turn the loop until maximum volume is heard in the earphones. At this point the transmitter is in a like plane with the loop. Drive a bit and re-fix (as transmitter can be in either direction from loop). Receiver power is also 3 volts.

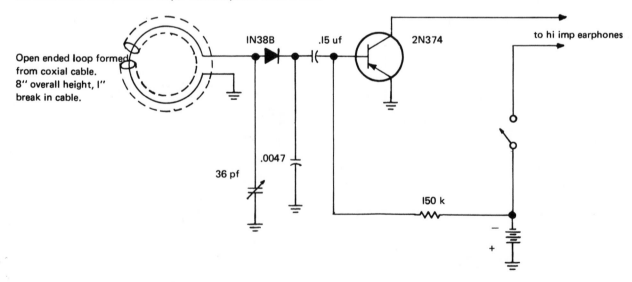

TELEPHONE TRANSMITTERS

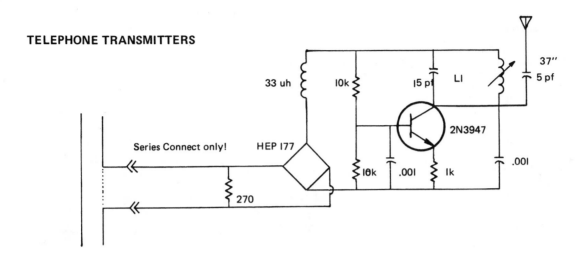

FM line transmitter. Transmits in the 40-50 MZ band when phone is in use. LI is 7 turns of No. 24 enameled wire on an adjustable form (such as a Miller). Cut one side of the phone line and attach as shown.

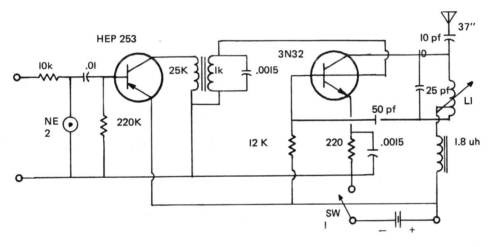

Parallel FM transmitter. Bare both wires of a phone line but DO NOT cut. Attatch transmitter across lines. Does not use any of the phones current. Sw I is any SPSW switch, LI is 5 t of 24 enameled wire on a 7/32" form, tapped I/1½ turns from the end. Battery is 6-9 volts.

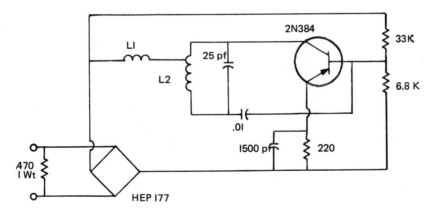

LI .5 mh, L2 10 turns No. 22 enameled wire on Miller form. Connect in series.

INFINITY TRANSMITTER

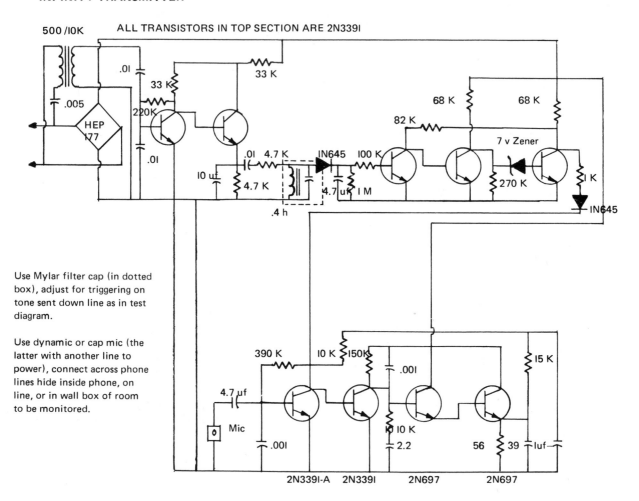

500 /10K   ALL TRANSISTORS IN TOP SECTION ARE 2N3391

Use Mylar filter cap (in dotted box), adjust for triggering on tone sent down line as in test diagram.

Use dynamic or cap mic (the latter with another line to power), connect across phone lines hide inside phone, on line, or in wall box of room to be monitored.

TONE GENERATOR FOR INFINITY TRANSMITTER (S).

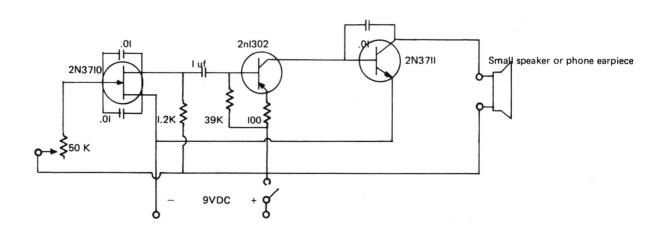

Small speaker or phone earpiece

221

EXPERIMENTIAL INFINITY TRANSMITTER

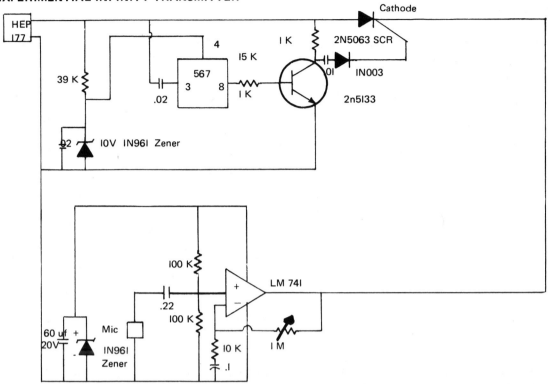

This experimential model utilizes a bare minimum of parts; the first IC is a Signetics NE 567 phase lock loop (tone decoder) this detects the tone sent down the line and turns on the SCR. It would be possible to employ touch tone type decoders that require two tones (applied at the same moment) to function, thus defeating the tone-sweep method of detection. The second IC functions as a high gain amplifier to transmit all room sounds down the wire, once activated by the 567. This unit should be set up and used in the same manner as a conventional unit.

Another VOX; hook up the relay to the remote start of a tape recorder and the input to the audio of a radio or mic/pre-amp—will start the recorder only when signal is present. Adjust * for correct relay operation, adjust .01 cap for delay-drop out time.

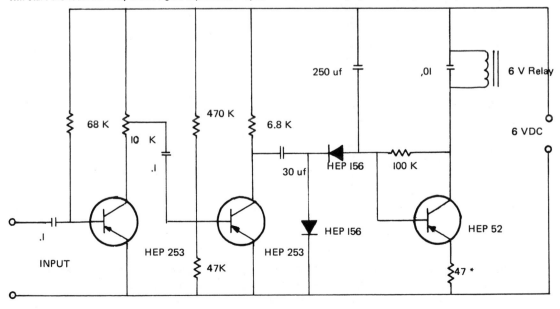

INFINITY TRANSMITTER TEST SET—UP

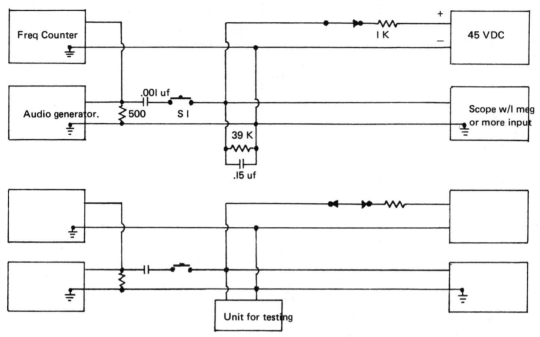

Connect circuit as shown in first figure and close S 2. Set scope to read AC and close S 1. Set signal generator to freq used to trigger unit (2800 Hz). Adjust signal generator to read 30 millivolts Peak to Peak at the scope. Remove the resistor and cap and connect the unit to be tested. Switch scope and look for 44 volts DC. Close S 1 for 1 second and look for +20 volts (3 or − 10 volts) at scope. Now switch scope back to AC and look for about 2 volts peak to peak when speaking into the mic on the unit from a normal distance. Waveform should not be distorted. Open S 2. Close S 2 and measure 44 volts DC.

If unit will not trigger at 2800 cycles trim the filter cap to resonate until it will trigger.

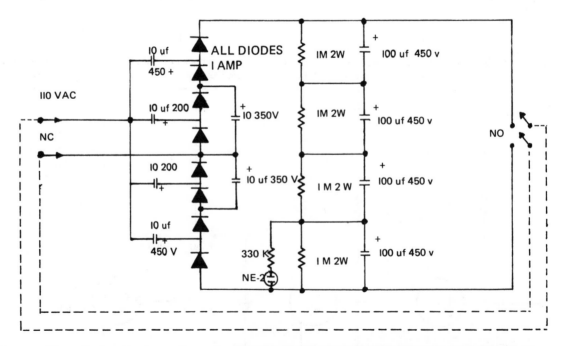

Use any silicon diodes. Hook up a phone line THAT HAS BEEN DISCONNECTED TO THE PHONE AS WELL AS TO THE WALL, OR SURGE PROTECTOR, OR BOX. Twist the opposite ends of the phone line together. Throw the switch; this disconnects the supply from the 110 AC and throws a VERY high voltage pulse down the phone line. This will burn any series bug, drop out relay, etc into a cinder. Repeat with ends untwisted. THIS COULD KILL, NEVER HANDLE THE OUTPUT!

CARRIER OPERATED SWITCH

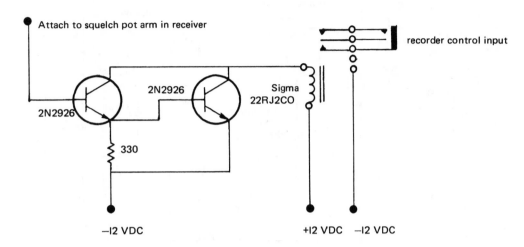

Attach to squelch pot arm in receiver

recorder control input

2N2926

2N2926

Sigma 22RJ2CO

330

−12 VDC

+12 VDC   −12 VDC

DROP OUT RELAY FOR TRANSMITTERS

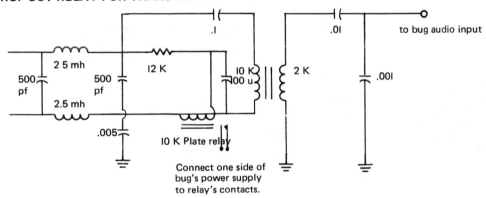

.1

.01

to bug audio input

2 5 mh

12 K

10 K
100 u

2 K

.001

500 pf

500 pf

2.5 mh

.005

10 K Plate relay

Connect one side of
bug's power supply
to relay's contacts.

Connected across a phone line this device will switch a bug on only when the phone is in use, saving batteries.

CHEAP DROP OUT RELAY

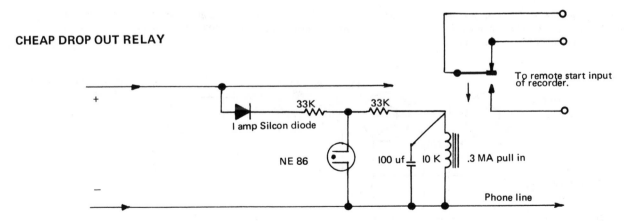

To remote start input
of recorder.

+

I amp Silcon diode

33K

33K

NE 86

100 uf   10 K

.3 MA pull in

−

Phone line

Hooked across the phone line this device will trun on a tape recorder or other device when the phone is lifted from the cradle. It
is cheap to make, so non-recovery is no big problem.

VOX

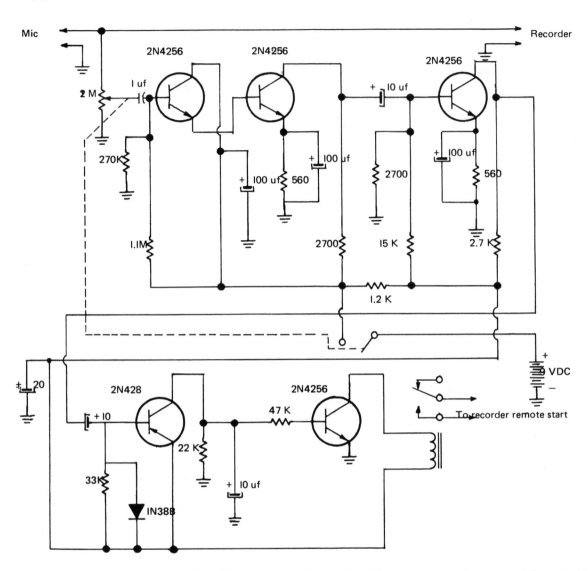

Hook up between mic and tape recorder; will start machine at first sound, hold on ½ second after last sound. Adjust sens with the 2 M pot. Use a 7 MA pull down relay, if a hefty relay is utilized (such as a Sigma IIF-I000-G/SIL) can be hooked directly across AC line of recorder rather than remote input.

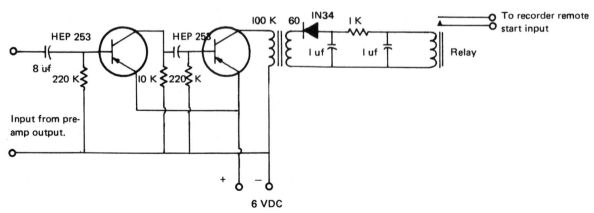

Signal controlled switch will start tape recorder only when a signal is present. Hooked up to receiver listening to phone bug, it will start the recorder only when phone is in use avoiding wasted tape.

ULTRASONIC JAMMER

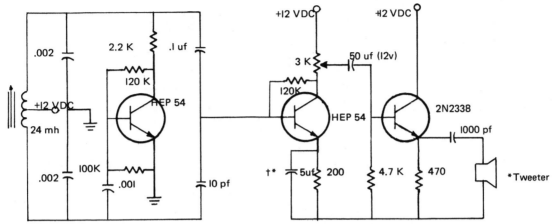

*Tweeter should be Mustang "Sphericon" or other capable of 40,000 hZ
†*May have to increase to prevent degen feedback.

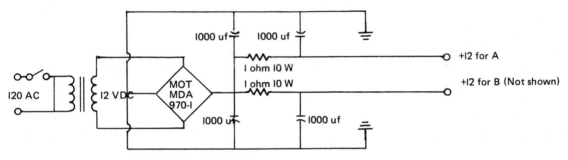

Two of the top units must be constructed; each is tuned by adjusting the chokes about 500-1000 cycles apart (this will be somewhere around 22,000 cycles—above human hearing). They use the common power supply, but should be electrostatically isolated from each other. The speakers must be seperated by several feet, or sonically seperated. The output is controlled by adjusting the 3 K pots. When adjusted correctly it will cause ALL (including telephone, hearing aid, tape recorder, bug, etc) microphones to squeal at the difference in thier frequencies. This will render useless all mics in the vincinity. Aim upward and let sound reflect from ceiling.

POWER SUPPLIES

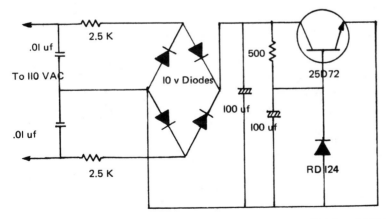

This supply can be connected across any 110 volt power line and will deliver 9 VDC for wireless mics. Ideal for constructing bugs in wall sockets, extension cords, etc.

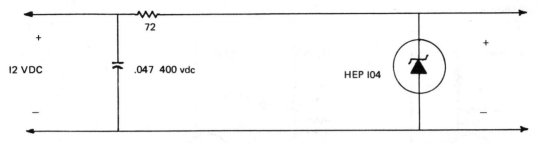

This supply will power any 9 volt bug from a 12 volt battery source; great for mounting a bug in a car.......

AUDIO COMPRESSOR

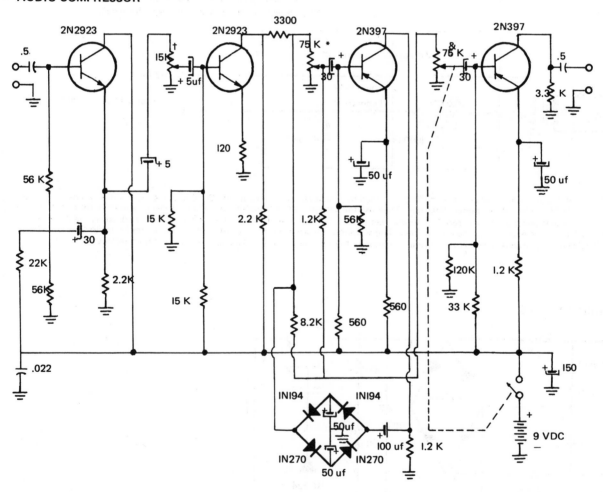

Connect between mic and recorder or transmitter; adjust † for correct level for softest noise in room, then fix * for loudest voice (bring it down to same level), now adjust & for proper recording level. Will now correct all levels to understandable recording level.

AMPLIFIERS

Low Noise Pre Amp

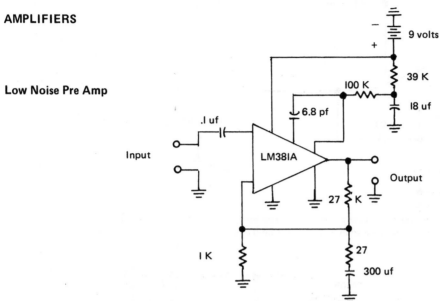

A very high gain (112 dB) low noise pre-amp for the voice bands (up to 10 KhZ). Input can be a mic, spike mic, etc. Output goes to earphones or into the Super Spy Amp described earlier.....

Wide Band High Gain Amp

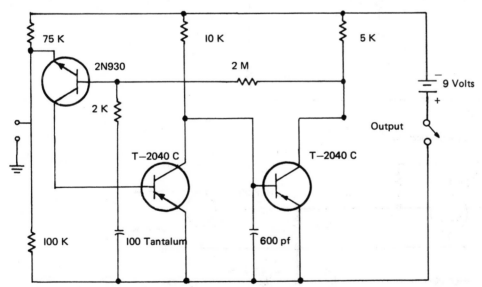

General amplifier with a high gain figure of about 60 dB from 2 cps to IM cps. Direct coupled design with feedback stabilization.

TELEPHONE PICK—UP AMPLIFIERS

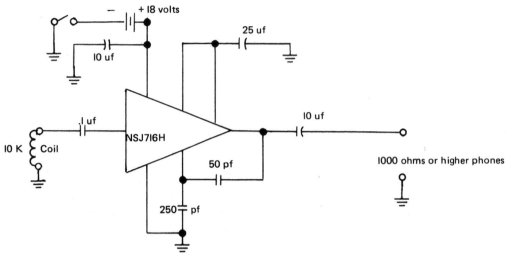

Uses pick-up coil to overhear, or record, both sides of phone conversation. Just bring coil near sidetone coil (in base) of phone of unused extension. May also work if phone lead in is wrapped around coil.

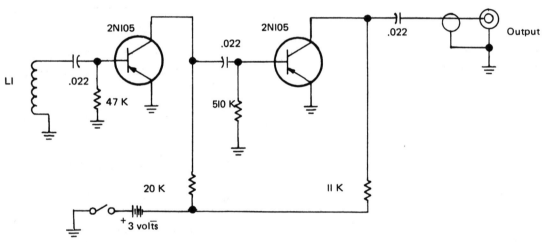

Another pick-up coil amp using a commerical coil.

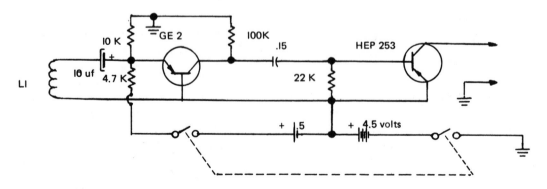

Commerical coil or 650 turns No. 30 enameled wire is used for LI. 10 feet of shielded cable can be run between coil and amp. Feed into earphones or general amp.

THE MIRACLE BUG.....

Slowly Buck Rodgers climbs down from his ship; after a quick glance, in which his razor honed mind takes in the whole scene, he is ready for action. The raiders seem to be holed up on the 3lst floor of the TransAmerica Pyramid. No doubt they are finalizing their plans for total conquest of the GOP at this very moment. How to overhear their wicked plans without tipping his hand?

Ah Ha! Buck slowly sets up a device which looks like a rifle designed for Mickey Rooney, aims it at the window in question through a telescopic sight, aims a seperate, larger telescope at the same window, turns everyone, eh, rather, everything, on....Suddenly every word comes through loud and clear! Just as he thought they are going to launch the dreaded germ-and-fag warfare plot against God-fearing Americans! Thank God he had the laser bug! Thank God this typewritter has a "!".!

Science fiction arranged by some doped out hippie writer? Well, old buddy, despite the fact that everyone from a highly respected newspaper columnist to the CIA denies every having heard of such an animal, it does indeed exist, and in fact is in use by the CIA and even a few top private operators. In fact, now just about anyone who has graduated from high school, made it halfway through a home correspondence course in basic electronics, and can read, can build such a device.....

The device in question is a laser which is aimed at a window UP TO ONE MILE AWAY directing a stream of coherent light against the window. Now a tiny bit of this light is reflected off the window and is changed (modulated) slightly by the movements of the window, which is, in turn, moved by any noise, i.e. conversation, in the room itself, or a Rod McCuen poem.

This tiny bit of reflected light is then picked up by a high powered telescope and fed into a receiver which translates it back into audio. You don't even have to gain access to the room; just park your van a block away, aim the gear, and you're in business. Every little word is brought to you without any real effort on your part.

Just picture the uses for this device, oh Lord won't you buy me a Mercedes Benz? Ever wanted to hear what goes on in that huge house on the hill, or in the penthouse of the Standard Oil building, or, or,....Shit!

The only real hang-up is that you would have a hard time convincing a judge it was an electronic babysitter....

The first plans we are showing you are one of the orginal laser bugging devices. It uses a photomultiplier tube in the receiver to decode the light. This device, as do most, uses pulse width modulation of the laser beam (the other variation is to use a steady stream and then beat the returning beam against a non-modulated beam to get the audio) by a power supply which triggers the laser with a high current pulse l0,000 times a second (modern units often use a much higher pulse rate).

The orginal unit does work, although it is a bit unwieldy. If you plan to use it remember a few things; using the laser listed is a good idea as it is infrared (so the beam cannot be seen) and fitted to the circuit. To aim the device it is wise to use a l00 watt light bulb in place of the laser (using 60 cycle AC), then adjust the receiving telescope for a best view of the light on the window. Place the photo tube on the eyepiece and adjust the receiver for the loudest 60 cycle signal. Now use the laser and again adjust the system for peak results by substituting an unfiltered 20 volt source on the 2N396l transistor (½ wave) and listening for the maximum 60 cycle signal. When adjusted repleace the power source with a filtered model.

Now, since the advent of this device several interesting factors have come into play....The most interesting is the appearance of laser communication systems on the market. These devices use a modulated laser beam for audio communication over a l0-20 mile range. The complete units start at $3000 and go quickly upward...HOWEVER, one company, American Laser Systems, l06 James Fowler Rd, Santa Barbara Airport, Goleta, Ca 930l7, sells the system in lower priced modules.

Their laser module sells for $300 for a l2 watt unit, and they offer a matching, avalanche photodetector in the same $300 range (these prices are not exact—they differ with size etc, write for a catalog). Now these basic building blocks

230

can be added to by using their audio demodulator ($135.00) and their pulsed supply (rigged to pulse without incoming audio), or by using the power supply shown.

These units come designed almost ready-to-go, and while not made for our uses, they should suffice nicely....One could build a complete laser bug for $1000—$1,500 (as opposed to $20,000 on the international underground market) with a minimum of work

In any system follow these general rules:

Use a telescopic rifle sight of at least 10X on the laser itself, (practice to see that it is aligned exactly with the projected beam).

Use a good quality astronomical telescope for the receiving end. This should be at LEAST a 4 inch, and hopefully a 8 or even a 12 inch model. This can be purchased from Edmund Scientific Co, Barrington, N.J. 08007 in completed, or in do-it-yourself forms.

Use the receiver telescope eyepiece for aiming the scope at exactly the same point on the window you have aimed the laser at (with the rifle scope). Then remove the eyepiece and substitute a PRECISE pinhole (also from Edmund) for the optical eyepiece to minimize distortion. The photomultiplier tube or avalanche diode is then mounted directly over this pinhole.

The angle between the sending and receiving units should be quite great.

Always try to pre-aim the units by using the system already described for the tube model, or by adding an audio source (as shown in the diagram) to the newer modules, and peaking the system up for maximum audio before attempting to eavesdrop.

Remember outside noises will also modulate the window. Loud traffic or a jackhammer will limit the system to a great degree.

There is no exact science to these devices; experiment around a bit and you should be able to rig up a unit equaling the CIA. Have fun, but be home by 11 pm.......

GENERAL LASER SET—UP

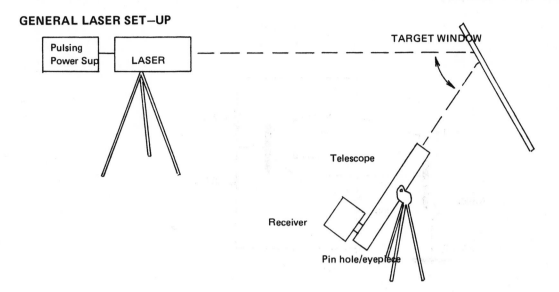

In any laser system several basic principles apply; the laser is pulsed by a triggered power supply so it emits short usuable bursts of light. These pulses are aimed at the target window where they are modulated slightly by the movement of the window (in turn modulated by room noise). A small portion are reflected outward, these are picked up by a powerful telescope and fed thru a precise pinhole into a receiver capable of detecting the variation in pulse width and converting it back into audio.

The angle between the two beams should be made as great as possible.

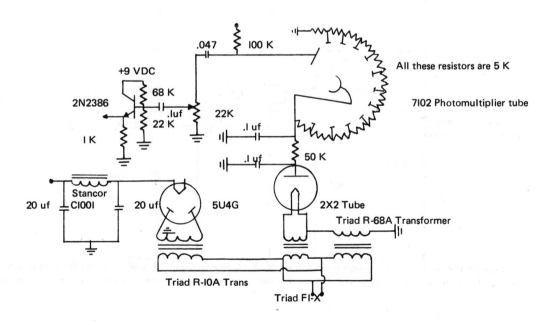

Orginal design for receiver. Photomultiplier tube sensitive to infrared light was utilized. This unit is coupled to the telescope thru a precise pin hole to minimize distortion. Tube (7102) is mounted directly on eyepiece.

LASER PULSED POWER SUPPLIES

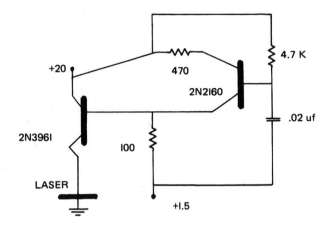

One of the orginal laser pulsing power supplies; use a VERY short lead from the transistor to the laser (less than one inch is nice..). This unit was designed around a general (in fact, General Electric) HIAl laser. This is an infrared laser which puts out around 14 watss when pulsed in this manner.

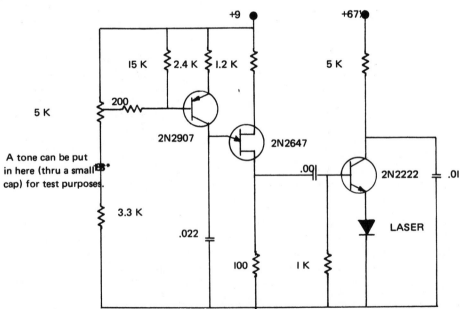

This is a modern plan for pulsing a laser such as those sold by American Laser. This will provide high current, ultra quick drive pulses to the laser. A signal generator can be hooked up at the point noted to provide a test tone for alignment.

Ga As LASER & DRIVER MODULE
WITH DRIVER CHARGING SUPPLY

FEATURES:

COMPLETE Ga As LASER TRANSMITTER

TEMPERATURE COMPENSATED

SMALL SIZE, CONVENIENT MOUNTING

LOW POWER CONSUMPTION

SINGLE SUPPLY OPERATION

INTERNALLY OR
EXTERNALLY CLOCKED

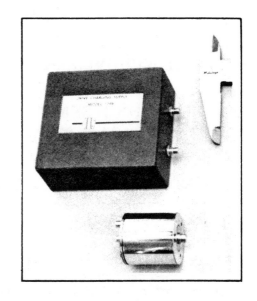

DESCRIPTION:

The Model 729A Gallium Arsenide Laser and Driver Module contains a 12 watt, 9 mil close confinement laser, the high speed, high current circuitry to drive it, and a built in wideband current probe for monitoring the drive current. Leave open when not in use otherwise use 50Ω coax terminated in 50Ω. The mating Model 729B Driver Charging Supply efficiently charges the energy storage capacitors in the driver and supplies the trigger for the driver.

The high efficiency Model 729B Driver Charging Supply charges the energy storage capacitors in the driver to the correct voltage so as to maintain constant peak output power from the laser as a function of temperature over the range from 0° F to 150° F (−18°C to 65°C).

The Model 729A Ga As Laser & Driver Module has been designed to fit and move for focusing purposes as a piston inside a cylinder assembly coaxial to the optical axis of the transmitter optics. The laser diode is on the mechanical axis of the module. The Model 729B Driver Charging Supply is embedded in a cast aluminum shielded housing intended for printed circuit mounting. The charging energy and the trigger are carried via miniature coaxial cables to the driver module.

The Model 729B Driver Charging Supply operates from a single 10 to 14 Volt D.C. supply and supplies all the voltages required by the 729A driver. Its quiescent power consumption is 60 mW or 5 mA from a 12V source. The driver produces a 40 A, 100 ns (10% current point) current pulse for each trigger applied to the input of the 729B Driver Charging Supply. The current drawn from a 12 V source at 25°C is only 12.7 μA per pulse per second.

The Model 729B Driver Charging Supply contains an internal clock which is continuously adjustable from 25 Hz to 10 KHz in two ranges. Connect Pins 2 and 3 for high frequency range and 2, 3 and 4 for low frequency range. For each pulse applied to the external trigger input of the 729B one pulse of light is emitted by the laser at repetition rates up to 10 KP/S. The input impedance is 100 KΩ. The trigger pulse must be between 7 and 14 volts and have a risetime of less than 100 ns. TTL input compatability is also offered as an option.

SILICON AVALANCHE PHOTODETECTOR RECEIVER & BIAS SUPPLY

FEATURES:

COMPLETE OPTICAL RECEIVER
HIGH S/N IMPROVEMENT FACTOR
LARGE GAIN BANDWIDTH PRODUCT
LOW NOISE, HIGH SENSITIVITY
SMALL SIZE & CONVENIENT MOUNTING
SINGLE SUPPLY, LOW POWER CONSUMPTION
EXTERNAL PHOTODETECTOR GAIN CONTROL

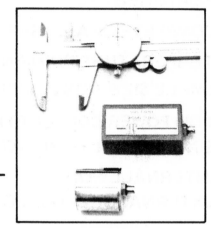

DESCRIPTION:

The Model 728A Photodetector and Preamplifier Module contains an .010 inch diameter, silicon avalanche photodetector and wideband low noise preamplifier. The mating Model 728C Bias Supply is a programmable voltage source for biasing the photodetector and regulating the power for the preamplifier. Together the 728A and 728C form a complete optical receiver.

In narrow field of view, low background, wide demodulation bandwidth applications, the 728A receiver produces a typical 100 to 1 increase in system signal to noise ratio over comparable Silicon PIN Photodetector receivers.

The optical receiver's demodulation bandwidth is 5 MHz, ideal for receiving pulses as narrow as 100 ns. The typical responsivity of the receiver is 2.4×10^6 V/W. Bandwidths up to 50 MHz can be specified with a corresponding change in responsivity. The low frequency cutoff is 200 Hz and may also be specified for higher frequencies.

The Noise Equivalent Power per $\sqrt{Hz}$ is typically .12 $\rho W/\sqrt{Hz}$ thus an optical signal of .58 nW produces a signal to noise ratio of 1 with a bandwidth of 5 MHz.

The 728C Bias Supply provides all the regulated voltages for the 728A Photodetector and Preamplifier Module and consumes only 7 mA. The Bias Supply was designed to operate from any dc voltage between 10 to 14V.

The external control terminal of the 728C Bias Supply can be used to maintain optimum gain or give 40 db of AGC range. $50\mu A$ of current sinking at the control terminal gives a 100:1 gain reduction. Feedback techniques acting on system noise can be used to maintain optimum detector gain as a function of increasing background irradiance.

The Model 728A Photodetector and Preamplifier Module is designed to fit and move as a piston in a cylinder assembly coaxial with the optical center line of the optics for purpose of focusing.

The Model 728C Bias Supply is embedded in a shielded aluminum housing and is intended for printed circuit mounting. The 728A and 728C are interconnected by a miniature four conductor shielded cable which carries the bias and power for both the detector and preamplifier as well as the bias control signal. The output signal from the preamplifier is carried via a miniature 50 Ω coax to the subsequent electronics such as the Model 728B Video Amplifier and Threshold Module.

.030 & .060 inch diameter photodetectors also available.

DETECTION GEAR

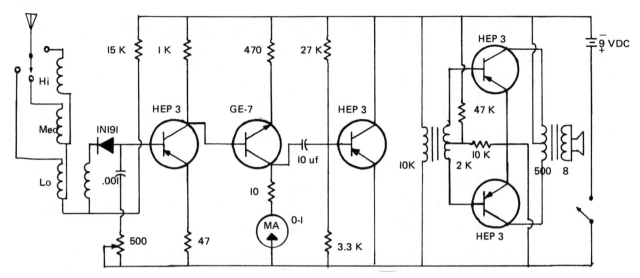

Transmitter locator with both amplified field strength meter and feedback detection. Wind or purchase coils for center of each band to be swept.

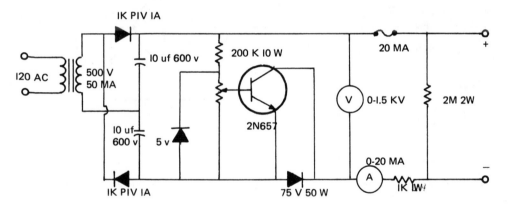

10 MA power supply for checking out telephones.

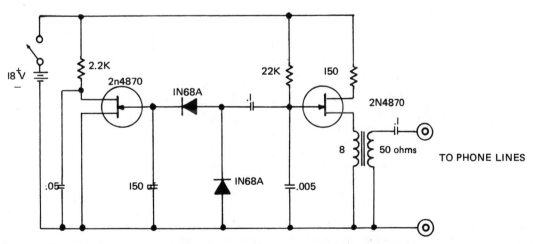

Connect to phone line; dial the number and close switch. Device will "sweep" through audio spectrum, if an infinity transmitter is in use the target phone will "answer" itself somewhere along the line.

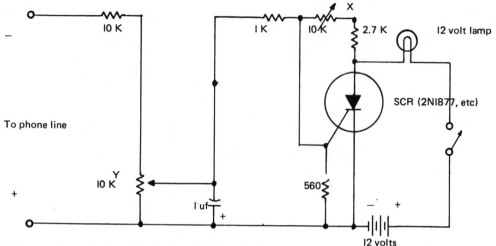

To phone line

Attach to phone pair after adjusting X for "ON" in SCR. Now adjust Y for "OFF" while connected. If the line is cut to install series bug or other tap, light will come on and remain on until you reset with switch.

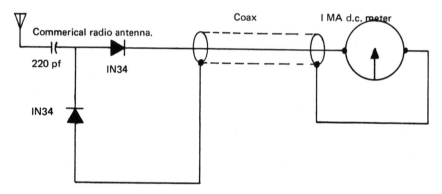

Ultra simple "locator" will show most hidden transmitters. Untuned circuit may also register local radio stations...Best used late at night to reduce number of outside influences.

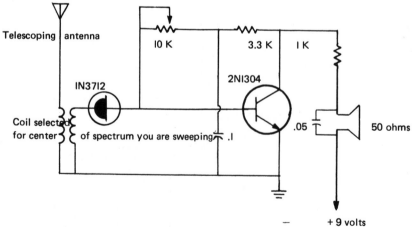

Sensitive tunnel diode creates a feedback type locator. When brought near the hidden transmitter a squeal will be heard. Coil (s) should be selected for mid-range of the bands you are searching.